Focused Observations

THIRD EDITION

▲▼▲▼▲

How to Observe Young Children for Assessment and Curriculum Planning

— ALSO FROM REDLEAF PRESS BY GAYE GRONLUND —

Saving Play: Addressing Standards through Play-Based Learning in Preschool and Kindergarten,
with Thomas Rendon

Focused Portfolios, 2nd edition: A Complete Assessment for the Young Child,
with Bev Engel

Individualized, Child-Focused Curriculum: A Differentiated Approach

Planning for Play, Observation, and Learning in Preschool and Kindergarten

Developmentally Appropriate Play: Guiding Young Children to a Higher Level

Make Early Learning Standards Come Alive, 2nd edition:
Connecting Your Practice and Curriculum to State Guidelines

Focused Observations

THIRD EDITION

How to Observe Young Children for
Assessment and Curriculum Planning

Gaye Gronlund and Marlyn James

Redleaf Press®
www.redleafpress.org
800-423-8309

Published by Redleaf Press
10 Yorkton Court
St. Paul, MN 55117
www.redleafpress.org

Portions of this edition were previously published as *Individualized Child-Focused Curriculum: A Differentiated Approach*

Excerpts from "Developmentally Appropriate Practice (DAP) Position Statement" copyright © 2020 NAEYC®. Reprinted with permission. Full text of this Position Statement is available at http://www.naeyc.org/resources /position-statements/dap/contents.

Third edition 2025
Cover design by Michelle Lee Lagerroos
Cover photograph by iStock.com/Fat Camera
Interior design by Wendy Holdman and typeset in Scala Pro and Myriad Pro
Printed in the United States of America
32 31 30 29 28 27 26 25   1 2 3 4 5 6 7 8

Library of Congress Cataloging-in-Publication Data

Names: Gronlund, Gaye, 1952- author. | James, Marlyn, author.
Title: Focused observations : how to observe young children for assessment and curriculum planning / by Gaye Gronlund and Marlyn James.
Description: Third edition. | St. Paul, MN : Redleaf Press, 2025. | Includes bibliographical references and index. | Summary: "Focused Observations, Third Edition, explains why observation is one of the best methods to get to know each child well, track progress, and plan individualized curriculum. It also provides tools and techniques to help you strengthen your observations, create portfolios with rich documentation, and support each child"— Provided by publisher.
Identifiers: LCCN 2024044181 (print) | LCCN 2024044182 (ebook) | ISBN 9781605548395 (paperback) | ISBN 9781605548401 (ebook)
Subjects: LCSH: Observation (Educational method) | Educational tests and measurements. | Early childhood education. | Curriculum planning.
Classification: LCC LB1027.28 .G76 2025 (print) | LCC LB1027.28 (ebook) | DDC 371.39--dc23/eng/20241024
LC record available at https://lccn.loc.gov/2024044181
LC ebook record available at https://lccn.loc.gov/2024044182

Printed on acid-free paper

Gaye: To Bruce, with all my love, and in memory
of my dear colleague and our close friend, Marlyn James

Marlyn: To my husband and life partner, Chuck,
for his ever-present support and encouragement. And in memory of my dad
for giving me the courage of my convictions and for always asking me "why?"

From both of us: To Betty Jones, Laila Aaen, and Louise Derman-Sparks.
You all inspired us to make the most of our Pacific Oaks experiences,
both as students and as faculty. Thank you for all of your contributions
to our thinking and understanding about early childhood practices.

Memorial to Marlyn James

▲▼▲▼▲

Marlyn James, my coauthor, collaborator, and dear friend passed away peacefully on June 25, 2016, from complications following brain surgery.

Marlyn was the chair of the Early Childhood Education Department at Flathead Community College in Kalispell, Montana. She was beloved by her students, inspiring them to continue working with children by implementing the best practices that she made so clear and understandable in her teachings, presentations, and writings.

She was nationally recognized as an author, presenter, and consultant working to make a difference in the lives of young children and the field of early childhood education. She and I presented at many National Association for the Education of Young Children (NAEYC) National Conferences and Professional Development Institutes as well as at various state conferences. We wrote three books together (all published by Redleaf Press):

- two editions of *Focused Observations: How to Observe Young Children for Assessment and Curriculum Planning*
- *Early Learning Standards and Staff Development: Best Practices in the Face of Change*

In addition, we produced a DVD and CD-ROM of video clips of young children in action so early childhood professionals could practice observation and documentation and further refine their skills.

Marlyn was an outdoors woman. She loved to hike. She loved flowers. She loved to pick the greens, herbs, and fresh vegetables from her gardens. She loved animals—her cats and dogs were family members too.

Marlyn was remarkably gifted as a friend. We will never forget her wicked eyes, her ready laugh, her what-you-see-is-what-you-get attitude, her listening ear, her wise counsel, her fierce commitment to being our friend, and the way she loved those of us lucky enough to have been in her circle. We are all better people because of her.

Marlyn was an incredibly loving woman. She spent her life caring for three boys, Patrick, Kevin, and Scott, shepherding them into manhood and ferociously loving her grandchildren, Kyle, Ian, and Emilee. She made the choice of a lifetime to end one marriage and follow her heart for love with Chuck, a tall young man who only wanted her. The two of them built a partnership based on the intimacy of souls and the courage to move to the mountains of Montana where they lived in a log house in the woods.

I miss my dear friend Marlyn terribly. The field of early childhood education lost one of its greatest champions. Hopefully, we all will try to live up to her legacy and continue to do what's right in the world, for young children, for our families, and for the planet.

With deep sadness,
Gaye Gronlund

Contents

▲▼▲▼▲

Acknowledgments

▲▽▲▽▲

Many thanks to the following people:

To the following teachers for sharing their comments:

Anton Wells, Preschool Teacher, Northwest Montana Head Start, Kalispell, Montana

April Garcia, Preschool Special Education Teacher, Las Cruces Schools, Las Cruces, New Mexico

Cathy Kelly, Intervention Specialist, Metropolitan School District at Willson School, Cleveland, Ohio

Danielle Vigh, Coteacher, Regular and Special Education Pre-Kindergarten, Cleveland Heights–University Heights, Ohio

Darlisa Davis, Preschool Teacher, Epworth Weekday Children's Ministries, Indianapolis, Indiana

Deanna Mackin, Professional Development Specialist, Montana Resource and Referral Network, Kalispell, Montana

Diana Lamb, former Teacher/Director at Little Lamb Nursery School, Lebanon, Indiana

Elizabeth Fallon, National Board Certified Preschool Special Education Teacher, Las Cruces Schools, Las Cruces, New Mexico

Jarrod Green, Assistant Director, Children's Community School, Philadelphia, Pennsylvania

Jodi Martinez, Even Start Teacher, Albuquerque Public Schools, Albuquerque, New Mexico

Johanna Schaub, Toddler Teacher, Epworth Weekday Children's Ministries, Indianapolis, Indiana

Jordan Foley, Teacher, Children's Community School, Philadelphia, Pennsylvania

Kelly Dorinsky, Kindergarten Teacher, Lakewood Catholic Academy, Lakewood, Ohio

Lillian Canos, Pre-K Teacher, Albuquerque Public Schools, Albuquerque, New Mexico

Mark Hopkins, Pre-K Teacher, Allemas Kids Campus, Solon, Ohio

Pam Berg, Preschool Teacher, Epworth Weekday Children's Ministries, Indianapolis, Indiana

Robin Jones, Preschool Teacher, Epworth Weekday Children's Ministries, Indianapolis, Indiana

Robin Sampaga, Kindergarten Teacher, Albuquerque Public Schools, Albuquerque, New Mexico

Rosemary Neely, Even Start Teacher, Albuquerque Public Schools, Albuquerque, New Mexico

Peggy Seaman, A Joyful Noise Family Child Care Home, Columbia Falls, Montana

Peggy Ward, Infant Teacher, Growing in God's Love, Whitefish, Montana

Valerie Black, Early Childhood Special Education Teacher, Four Rivers Special Education District, Jacksonville, Illinois

For the videotaping done in Albuquerque, New Mexico:

Anna Rodriguez, Emily Martinez, and the families at East San Jose Elementary Even Start Family Literacy Program

Crystal Sandoval, Director, the staff, and families at Noah's Ark Child Care

Elena Aguirre, Director, the staff, and families at University of New Mexico Children's Campus

Janet Rigo and the families at Rigo Family Child Care

Lillian Cano, Arla Jaramillo, and the families at Valley Vista Pre-K Program

Rosemary Neely, Maria Sanchez, and the families at Lavaland Elementary Even Start Family Literacy Program

Sue Gradisar and colleagues at Media-Designs, Inc.

All of the teachers and families of the New Mexico Office of Child Development Focused Portfolios Project

Students in the Early Childhood Education Program at Flathead Valley Community College, Kalispell, Montana

And to all our editors at Redleaf Press

Introduction

▲▼▲▼▲

Have you or your colleagues ever made a statement like this one? "I observe the children all day, but I don't have time to write down what I'm seeing. That takes me away from the kids. And they just need me too much."

Sound familiar? In our work as college instructors and consultants, we've heard variations on this comment many, many times. And we recognize how true it is! Your job is demanding and your time limited. If you are expected to observe and to document your observations, you can easily feel overwhelmed and frustrated.

That's why we wrote this book. We wanted to give practical explanations for how to observe children in order to assess their development and plan curriculum. We wanted to offer a comprehensive and user-friendly resource with realistic ideas for putting observation and documentation into practice. We wanted to offer lots of observation notes for you to review and suggestions for documentation strategies so you could get better at observing children and writing down what you see. We have also included links to video clips of children in action (available by scanning a QR code or entering the URL in your web browser) so you can practice observing and documenting. Our goal is to help early educators recognize the importance of observation and documentation and learn ways to fit both into a busy day with children.

The second edition of this book has continued to be useful to early childhood professionals, and this third edition will maintain much of the content of the earlier versions. In addition, it has been updated to reflect changes in the field of early childhood education as well as technological changes that can help educators continue to be more efficient as they document their observations.

Sadly, this third edition will not have new contributions from Marlyn James, as we lost her in 2016. Her spirit and incredible knowledge and understanding of best practices still permeate every page.

In this third edition, I have addressed some of the changes that have happened in the field of early childhood education since the publication of the second edition in 2013. I recognize that more attention is being paid to the early years. Many early educators feel that they are under greater pressure to be accountable for the learning of the children in their care. States across the nation have developed early learning guidelines, and many states support universal pre-K programs. The National Association for the Education of Young Children (NAEYC 2022) has published a fourth edition of *Developmentally Appropriate Practice in Early Childhood Programs: Serving Children from Birth through Age 8* with updated recommendations for more intentionality as teachers implement best practices.

We believe strongly that even with the calls for more accountability and intentionality, observational assessment is still the best assessment method for teachers of young children to use. Through observation and documentation, you can get to know each child well, track their progress, and plan individualized curriculum for them. There are many statements of support for observation and documentation in the new edition of *Developmentally Appropriate Practice* and other professional recommendations, but *how* teachers are asked to implement such assessment may vary. Throughout this book, we provide ways to use the observation and documentation processes so they inform your work to benefit children and their families. We explore rich and meaningful documentation that gives you an individualized picture of the unique aspects of each child. We guide you in sharing information with families in ways that help build partnerships to support children's further growth. We include comments from many teachers who are implementing observation and documentation in their programs—thus grounding our recommendations in the reality of classroom life. And we give attention to those of you who work with young children with disabilities.

From our experiences as teachers ourselves, as well as our work with early educators all over the country, we have learned that being a good observer and documenter makes working with children easier and more satisfying in the long run. When you observe children, you get to know them better. You can provide the right challenges and support; you can see trouble coming and head it off. It seems like more work—it *is* more work—but it will ultimately make your job easier.

We have included many ways for you to practice and refine your observation and documentation skills. You can try out various methods for documenting your observations. You can experiment with using what you learn about the children through observing them. And, through practice, you can figure out your own style of doing observation well. No two observers or documenters are the same. You each bring to the experience your personality, your educational and cultural background, and your life experiences.

In this book, we help you learn how to focus your observations. In addition, we share ways for you to systematically document or record what you learn about children through observation. In chapter 1, we address why it's important for teachers to observe children and what can be learned about them as they do so. In chapter 2, we look at the impact of early learning guidelines and calls for accountability on the observation and documentation processes. Chapter 3 focuses on how teachers do observation and documentation well, and chapter 4 offers time-saving strategies to fit these processes into busy classroom life. The next two chapters focus on the assessment process: using observation and documentation to assess each child's development (chapter 5), and sharing that assessment information (through portfolios, summary reports, and conferences) with families (chapter 6). Planning curriculum based on what is learned through observation and documentation is at the core of chapter 7, and chapter 8 shows how to build a case about each child. In chapter 9, we share suggestions for how to continue to grow as an observer and documenter. Throughout the book, we emphasize remembering to delight in children's development, celebrate their progress, and enjoy their very being.

All of the chapters include observation notes of children in action for you to review and learn more about children's development, see different ways of recording information, and draw conclusions about curricular strategies. We also share comments from early educators using observation and documentation. We hope that you will learn practical tips and helpful recommendations from their experiences.

Video clips accompany this book and can be accessed via QR codes or the URLs listed in appendix F. The book and the video clips are designed to go hand in hand. Each chapter concludes with identified video clips and suggested activities. Each chapter's suggested activities provide you the opportunity to practice observation in your own work or family setting. Applying what you read, trying it out for yourself, analyzing what worked and didn't work, and reflecting on what you learned through the observation experience can be done with the video clips or in your own life settings. It's the practice that is the most important!

There are three activities at the end of each chapter:

- Observation Practice
- Reflection
- Finding Your Observation Style

There are nineteen Observation Practice activities with video clips. The directions for viewing can be found at the end of each chapter and involve watching video clips with a specific focus in mind. These activities can be used by an individual or by groups in college course work, staff development sessions, in-service workshops, and staff meetings. We suggest that you read the chapter before viewing the video clips and doing the activities. In this way, you come to the video experience with basic knowledge and suggestions to apply to the viewing. For each observation practice we have identified a purpose, a video clip to observe, guiding questions to consider while watching the child and documenting what is seen, and a focus for group discussion. You can use each practice observation in many ways. Watching the same video clips more than once will increase your understanding of how much can be learned through observation and give you more in-depth knowledge of ways to interpret what is seen. You will see that you can easily watch video clips more than once. We also suggest that you practice observation and documentation in your own work and home settings. You can observe with the same purposes as those identified in the nineteen Observation Practice activities.

The Reflection activities are designed to help you think about the content of the chapter, analyzing and applying that content to your experiences with observation of children. You can answer the questions in written form, or you can use them for discussion starters with others.

Finding Your Observation Style activities are designed to be used in an ongoing journal format. We hope that by keeping a personal journal about your trials and errors with observation, you will discover your own strengths and weaknesses in observing children. We also hope that by the end of your experience with this book and the video clips, you will think differently about the comment we shared at the beginning of this introduction.

The next time you hear someone say, "I observe the children all day, but I don't have time to write down what I'm seeing. That takes me away from the kids. And they just need me too much," we hope you'll answer, "Yes, observation and documentation are hard work. But it's worth it! Now I make time for it because I see how much I learn about the children!"

CHAPTER 1

Why Observe Children?

▲▼▲▼▲

You observe children because you get to know them better and are more in tune with their needs and personalities. Knowing children better makes caring for them much easier. You are more able to head off trouble if you watch for the initial signals of an oncoming meltdown or a brewing confrontation between two children. You can observe and sense when you need to help a three-year-old who is getting frustrated putting together a difficult puzzle or a nine-month-old who has just started crawling and tends to get stuck when trying to get around objects in their way. You become aware of how a child copes with separation from family members and can be ready to help them. You learn how each child uniquely expresses their creativity and offer them materials to do so.

Your observations provide a fuller, richer picture of each child so your curriculum planning can address the specific capabilities of the children in your care. Through observation, the activities you plan will be more successful for you and the children. Because you will be aware of the children's strengths, weaknesses, interests, and passions, you will choose materials and projects that engage them for longer periods of time. Then you will be able to observe and document even more because children stay with the activity that much longer!

You observe children because that is the form of assessment recommended in the field of early childhood education. In position papers and books, the National Association for the Education of Young Children (NAEYC) recognizes the importance of authentic assessment and emphasizes observation for both assessment and curriculum planning. It gives this definition: "Authentic assessment: Age-appropriate approaches and culturally relevant assessment in a language the child understands—for infants, toddlers, preschoolers, and children in early grades, across developmental domains and curriculum areas" (NAEYC 2020, 35).

You observe children because your observations will make you a better teacher or a better care provider. Through observation, you are implementing best practices that demonstrate your professionalism and dedication to what is right for young children.

You naturally observe children anytime you care for them. If you are a parent caring for your baby, or an aunt or uncle taking care of a niece or nephew, you note what the baby's general mood is and make decisions based on what you see and hear. If the baby is smiling and cooing, you are likely to smile and coo back. You may feel reassured that you don't need to do anything else right then. If the baby is crying and fussy, you may try a variety of strategies to settle the baby down—including changing a diaper, offering a pacifier, picking the baby up and talking softly and gently to them, or heating up a bottle for a feeding. All of these actions are based on your observations of the child's signals and cues, their behavior, and their ways of communicating their needs.

You do the same when caring for preschool-aged children in your family. You listen to the children and watch their behavior carefully to determine how best to take care of the routines of the day, to help them learn and grow, and to help them gain self-control and develop independence. Through their observations, caring parents and relatives develop an intimacy with the children and a deep knowledge of their personalities, temperaments, and capabilities.

Whether you work with children in a child care setting, a family child care home, a preschool, or a special education program, you also naturally observe them. Observations help you to determine not only what needs the children have but also how you can be a more effective teacher for them. When new children begin in your program, you plan ways to get to know them. Observing new children in action with their family members, with the adults and children in your program, and by themselves helps you learn just who each child is and what they can do. If the child has identified disabilities, you observe to know more about their strengths as well as the areas that are difficult for them. Observations also guide you in determining the next steps to take with any child to support their growth and help them progress to their fullest potential.

Spontaneous or Planned Observation

Your observations can be spontaneous in nature. Sometimes you take in information as it happens and add it to your internal thinking about each child. In these instances, you are truly in the moment with the children and are enjoying the interactions to their fullest. You may document some of your spontaneous observations, writing them down when you can (in the moment or later in the day). Many teachers report that there is nothing as delightful as witnessing the sense of accomplishment when a child tries something new and, with bright eyes and a big grin, announces, "I did it!" Being there to smile with the child, to offer a hug, and to say, "Wow! You worked hard on that!" is very rewarding.

You can also plan for observation and documentation. To truly get to know all the children you teach and to be ready to figure out the best ways to help them, planned observations are necessary. Planned observations allow you to make sure no area of development or daily experience is missed. And documentation—writing down the observation—is essential if you want to remember clearly what each child can do and how each one responds to different situations. The documentation is an ongoing record to refer back to as you think about each child. And that documentation of your observations provides you with evidence to discuss with the child's family members or with other specialists if necessary. Documentation can also provide you with a means to explain what you are doing to help children learn and grow, so that families understand more about your curriculum. Parents tell us that when teachers share documented observations of their children at play, they understand more about the value of play and exploration. Teachers report that these parents then offer more support for what goes on in the program. Your observations open a window onto the world of their children that family members wouldn't otherwise see and invite them to share more fully in their children's experiences away from home.

Two Ways for You to Use Observation Information

You gain lots of information by observing children. There are two primary ways for you to use that information: for assessment and for curriculum planning. The two are intricately woven together. You observe children to learn more about who they are and document what they can do so you can more effectively plan activities, choose materials, offer adult guidance, and encourage peer interactions that support the children's growth and development. As you implement your plan for activities, materials, and interactions, you observe again to see how successfully your plan meets the children's needs. You assess that success and plan again! The process is ongoing.

Observing to Assess Children

Assessing children does not mean the same thing as testing children. Assessment involves gathering information about a child's capabilities and then evaluating that information. Gathering information may be done through observation and documentation. You may write down notes

Rosemary: Sharing my documentation with families helps them see their children as individuals—and that I see them that way as well. They feel I have taken the time to get to know their child and their family.

Lillian: Observing children is much more authentic than other types of evaluations. When you observe children, you are seeing their development in a natural and true setting. Through observations, a teacher can learn what children's needs are and what areas of development the teacher needs to focus on, and plan lessons around those needs.

about what you see children doing and hear them saying, and you may also collect work samples the children have made or photographs or videos of them playing or participating in various activities. You may also gather information through interviews with the child's family members. The information you gather provides you with evidence you can then evaluate. You evaluate the evidence to determine the children's skill levels, strengths, weaknesses, personality traits, and interests. Using a combination of the processes listed above helps you use your observations to determine teaching strategies and plan for learning experiences (Petitpas and Buchanan 2022).

Observing children for assessment purposes can be done in a spontaneous way or with careful planning for documentation. If you make informal, spontaneous observations for assessment, you must document them so the evidence is not only in your mind. Unless you write down the observations, there is no record for you or for others to follow that documents the child's changes over time, the child's progress, the child's struggles, the interventions teachers have attempted, and the results of those interventions. With no record of observations, bias and prejudice may go unrecognized and influence teachers' decisions about the child. Keeping the assessment process as only an internal one is not recommended.

Informal observation is more valuable for assessment when joined with more formal, planned, and documented observation. With written records of things witnessed, of what children said and did, you can build a case about each child. You can share this evidence with others, using it to support your conclusions about the child's development. Formal, planned, and documented observation ensures that no child is missed, no area of development is neglected, and appropriate next steps are planned.

When observing to assess a child's development, you can think in broad terms, trying to understand the child's cognitive stage of development or their general competencies in the social and emotional areas as they participate in deep, meaningful play experiences. Or you can observe for instances in which the child shows their skills and capabilities. These specific observations can then be tied to early learning guidelines or developmental checklists that include cognitive, physical, social, and emotional information for specific age groups. By turning to such sources to evaluate your observations, you are comparing the child's performance to reasonable expectations for children their age. Choosing reputable and respected sources for such information is a crucial part of the process. In chapter 2, we discuss ways to use early learning guidelines as you observe and document. And in chapter 5, we discuss in depth how to observe and document for assessment purposes using early learning guidelines, various developmental checklists, and other resources as references.

Robin S.: All of my teaching is based on observations. I differentiate my instruction, and this is done through observations. I learn the strengths of each child and build on those strengths through the strategies I choose to teach various skills.

Observing to Plan Curriculum

The purpose of observing and identifying children's developmental capabilities is not for accountability or reporting alone. It also helps you plan curriculum that meets the children's needs. Identifying each child's present performance gives you a place to start, a baseline. Then you take the all-important step of deciding which materials, activities, adult interactions, and peer involvement will be most effective in meeting a child's present level of performance and supporting their movement toward higher-level skills and capabilities.

Observing with curriculum in mind can be spontaneous and informal or more focused and planned. You may respond automatically to a child's request for a different material or immediately act upon your realization that more chairs are needed around the playdough table. You may lift an infant out of their seat as you notice their beginning agitation and carry them across the room so they can see what the other children are doing. These are all spontaneous curricular decisions. You are responding to something you have seen and are making changes in materials, environment, or interaction with the child.

> Teachers make in-the-moment decisions as they observe children at play to determine which strategy to use. Then, as they interact with the child or group of children, they continue to observe whether the strategy is successful or not. Again, this is at the heart of effective teaching. Skilled teachers pay close attention to what children are doing and saying and continually adjust their own actions accordingly. (Gronlund and Rendon 2017, 27)

Being more focused and planned often involves identifying areas of the classroom to observe more closely. You may see parts of the play area that are hardly used by the children, while other areas are overcrowded. Room rearrangement may be necessary to help with traffic flow. Or you may notice that the toddlers are especially fascinated with the fish in the aquarium this week. Figuring out ways to follow up on their interest will help you be responsive to the children and develop their engagement and understanding. Sometimes you may need to communicate with your colleagues to decide who will observe specific activities or watch for the children to demonstrate certain skills. For example, some teaching teams plan ahead to watch for children to demonstrate fine-motor skills by providing them with a variety of stringing beads and pegs and pegboards so the educators can collect information related to those skills.

Determining goals for the observation will help you collect information that can contribute to a later discussion with your teaching team or a change in curriculum plans. And documenting what you notice as you observe an activity or area will help you remember more clearly what was seen and make more effective decisions. In chapter 7, we offer more in-depth suggestions about using observation and documentation for curriculum planning.

If a child has identified disabilities, you will use your observations to help you adapt activities so the child can be successful. You will pay attention to the identified individualized family service plan (IFSP) or individualized education program (IEP) goals and document ways the child is working toward those goals. While observation and documentation cannot be used to diagnose a child's disability or determine placement, they can be used to improve teaching strategies and implement individualized curriculum, even when no disability or condition has been diagnosed.

What Can You Learn by Observing Children?

Whether you are observing children and documenting for assessment or curriculum planning purposes, you will learn more about the children in your program. Observation and documentation give a thorough, well-rounded picture of what is important to know about children. You learn about all these facets of the whole child:

- their developmental capabilities in all areas: social, emotional, physical, and cognitive
- their personalities
- their ways of coping with difficult situations and solving problems
- reasons for their behavior
- their deep interests and passions
- the information and knowledge they are constructing
- their expression of their cultural backgrounds

On the following pages are several observation notes that illustrate each of the above possibilities of what can be learned about children. We recognize that most of the time you will learn about *many* aspects of a child's development as you observe. A child might be showing you what they're interested in as well as how they cope with a difficult situation. In the observation notes that follow, we are more focused in our examples. After each note, we show how you can use the information gained from that observation to assess the child's development and to plan curriculum accordingly.

Pam: This was my sixth year of teaching preschool, and I feel like I know my kids so much better than I ever have before because I'm watching them more closely. I'm paying attention to the little things they're doing.

Learning about Children's Developmental Capabilities

Observing a child's participation in daily routines, play, and activities is a way to collect facts about their developmental capabilities. Think about all of the developmental areas that are possible to observe during a daily routine such as snack. The potential for seeing development in action is limitless. Practice by analyzing the following observation note about Angel. This observation took place over just four or five minutes. As you read the note, write down the areas of development—cognitive, physical, social, and emotional—covered by this observation.

Angel (four years, ten months)

At snack Angel saves a chair and calls to his friend Luis, "You sit here next to me!" He takes three crackers, counting out, "One, two, three," as he puts them on his napkin. He uses a knife to spread peanut butter across each one. He calls out, "More juice, please!" In conversation with his friends he says, "At our farm we have chickens and goats. And the goats are very loud. I have to cover my ears because they are so loud." Angel covers his ears with two napkins, and his friend Luis does the same, but Luis uses his crackers. Both boys laugh.

We identified the following capabilities that Angel is demonstrating and organized them into the major areas, or domains, of child development. We encourage you to consider others as well. Do you notice that every major area was exhibited in this short observation?

- **Cognitive development:** counting to three with one-to-one correspondence, figuring out to cover his ears with his napkin, using language to ask for more and to express his life experiences
- **Physical development:** sitting on a chair at a table, spreading peanut butter with a knife
- **Social development:** asking his friend to sit with him
- **Emotional development:** talking with and enjoying his friend

Using information for assessment Assessing Angel's capabilities means relating his actions to what you know about children his age. Turning to early learning guidelines, developmental checklists, or other sources of information, you could determine that Angel is functioning right at age level in his social interactions with his friend, his use of language to express himself, and his ability to use his fine-motor skills to spread with a knife. You may note that counting to three with one-to-one correspondence is at the level of a younger child. Developmental checklists indicate that an almost-five-year-old should be counting a higher quantity of objects.

Using information for planning You may decide that in the areas of social, language, and physical capabilities all that you and your colleagues need to do is to support Angel. In the cognitive area as demonstrated by his counting, you may decide to do some specific counting activities to see if Angel can indeed count higher quantities of objects and maintain the one-to-one correspondence. You may offer him many opportunities to play with and count manipulatives, to count the children in the room, and to count as he jumps on a trampoline or swings on a swing outside.

Learning about Children's Personalities

When observing children, you can see their personalities in action and identify ways each child functions in the world. Using this information helps you support each child's integration into the community of your classroom. Read the following observation note about Kassandra and write down what you are learning about her personality.

Peggy W.: By observing the children, I can learn about their temperaments and personal preferences. As I observe, I watch for what the child is able to do, how the child does it, and to what extent of excitement, pleasure, curiosity, or calmness the child does it in. This gives me a good picture of who the child is and what he or she enjoys.

> **Kassandra** (three years, eleven months)
>
> Kassandra has been absent for a few days, and when she comes into the classroom, she goes up to her teacher and says, "Hello! I'm back! Did you miss me?" The teacher replies, "Yes, I did! And I'm so happy to see you back and feeling better." Kassandra then goes up to one of her peers and says, "Hello. See, I'm back, and I'm not crying. Let's go play!"

Using information for assessment You can see that Kassandra has a positive sense of self. The egocentricity (or self-centered nature) of an almost-four-year-old is evident, as is her confidence in her teacher's and friend's concern for her. She uses language to express herself well. You could refer to developmental checklists to help you recognize that the skills she demonstrates in this observation are at her age level.

Using information for planning If you have a history with Kassandra, you would know that she has had problems in the past with feeling sad and crying when she arrived at your program, especially after being absent for a few days. Here you can recognize that she is adjusting to being back in the

Why Observe Children? ◄ 9

classroom with smiles and no tears. Giving her a hug or patting her on the back and telling her how you are noticing her growth and self-confidence may encourage her to continue to separate from her family members more easily. You can tell her mother at pickup time what happened in the morning so she can also celebrate Kassandra's progress in separating with no tears. If Kassandra does have a hard day again in the future, you can remind her of this day and her success or invite her to draw or paint how she is feeling to help her express herself in other ways.

Learning about How Children Cope with Difficult Situations

When you care for children, you see the ways they cope with the ins and outs of difficult times throughout the day. Getting along in a group setting is hard work for them and involves developing problem-solving skills. Read the following observation note about Corlyn, and write down the strategies she uses to find comfort when she is upset.

> ## Corlyn (one year, three months)
> When Corlyn rubs her eyes and starts to cry after eating lunch, she walks to her cubby and reaches for her diaper bag. She looks in the side pocket for her pacifier. She takes it out and sticks it in her mouth. Then she finds her blanket on her cot and goes to sleep.

Using information for assessment Corlyn independently seeks out her pacifier to comfort herself. She knows where it's located and shows initiative to get it. Referring to developmental checklists shows that she has excellent skills for her age level.

Using information for planning Anticipating Corlyn's difficult time after lunch and having her pacifier or a stuffed animal nearby may prevent her initial crying. Supporting her when she does get her own pacifier with positive words and a quick hug may help her settle down into naptime with adult comfort as well.

Insight into Children's Behavior

Observation can provide insight into children's behavior, whether positive or negative. Many children, like Ansen in the following observation note, are trying hard to learn appropriate ways to get their needs met. But often they become frustrated and communicate through hitting or other physical means and need an adult's help to negotiate with other children. Read the following observation note about Ansen and write down what you are learning about his behavior.

> ## Ansen (four years, ten months)
>
> Ansen is playing on the hanging bars. A child is hanging upside down. Ansen asks, "When will you be done? I have been waiting a long time." The child does not respond. Ansen waits a few more minutes and then raises his fist. A teacher walks over and asks why he has a fist. Ansen replies, "I want a turn, and Kristen won't get down. She stuck her tongue out at me." "Is there a better way to get a turn?" asks the teacher. Ansen says, "I used my words, and she won't listen. She wants it all to herself." The teacher asks the child to listen to Ansen. Ansen says, "I want a turn when you're done. I won't hit you. But you listen." The teacher talks to both children, and they continue playing on the bars.

Using information for assessment Ansen does not quite have the self-control to stop himself from raising a fist at another child when frustrated. Yet he does use words to express his feelings and is successful in resolving the problem once an adult helps him talk with the other child. According to developmental checklists, resolving such disagreements with adult help is common for children his age.

Using information for planning Ansen will likely still need adults nearby and ready to step in to prevent him from harming other children and to help him work out disagreements more appropriately. You and your colleagues might decide to have someone always keeping an eye on him to be ready to provide that support. When he does resolve disagreements peacefully, acknowledge his use of words and perhaps give him pats on the back or high fives to reward his hard work.

Learning about Children's Deep Interests and Passions

Observation helps you see what children's interests are. Noting which areas of the classroom they spend time in or which materials they choose to use again and again gives you insight into their strengths and favorites. Paying attention to the topics they talk about or incorporate into their play can help you plan curriculum that is more motivating to them because it is based on their interests. Read the following observation note about Darius and Justin. Notice how they show their interest in cooking, then write down follow-up activities you would plan for these boys both indoors and outdoors to continue to build on that interest.

> **Elizabeth:** Through observation I learn about children's strengths and needs, likes and dislikes, what's important to them, and how they think. I also gain an initial assessment of each child's abilities.

Darius (four years, five months),
Justin (four years, eight months)

Darius and Justin go to play in the sandbox after a cooking project. Darius says to Justin, "Let's make what Antonio's mom makes. Pass the sugar. That's one cup of teaspoon. We crack the eggs. We need milk, cinnamon, need teaspoon salt." He uses a shovel to add sand to the measuring cup. He takes the cup and pours it into the bowl. He takes a spoon and adds more sand, then moves the spoon around in the bowl. He pours it onto a plate and tells Justin, "Okay. Take it to the oven."

Using information for assessment Both boys are playing out cooking steps that they experienced in classroom cooking activities. Such representation of real objects with sand shows their abstract thinking and ability to pretend, all important cognitive capabilities for children their age.

Using information for planning Inviting Darius and Justin to help prepare snack foods, to write out simple recipes, to plan future cooking activities, and to use measuring cups and spoons in sand and water outdoors would all be ways of using this observation for curriculum planning purposes.

Learning about the Information and Knowledge Children Are Constructing

Through their play and use of materials, children often show you what information and knowledge they are figuring out and what skills they are working on. Read the following note about Fernando and identify what knowledge and skills he is showing in this observation.

Fernando (three years, seven months)

While drawing at the art table, Fernando uses many colors of markers. When he finishes, I ask him to tell me about his picture. He points to the large yellow circle and says it is a big animal. Then he says, "This is purple, and this is red." Fernando then gets a purple marker and draws the letter *F* in the left-hand corner. He says, "*F* for Fernando."

Using information for assessment Fernando is showing his beginning literacy and fine-motor skills as he draws a circle and a letter *F*, all advanced skills for his age according to developmental checklists. He also is showing his growing vocabulary and understanding of concepts by identifying colors.

Using information for planning Fernando may enjoy working with a name card so he can see the other letters in his name and attempt to represent them. To help him continue to develop the muscles in his hand for writing, you could provide him with opportunities to work with playdough, string beads, build with small connecting blocks, and draw and write with a variety of writing tools. Offering him opportunities to match and label colored objects will help build his vocabulary of color words.

Learning about Children's Expression of Their Cultural Backgrounds

Children's cultural backgrounds show through in their play and the ways the children function in everyday routines. For example, sometimes teachers' assumptions about how a child should go about eating or toileting are different from a family's assumptions. Whether this difference is due to culture, socioeconomic class, or another factor, to serve the child well, teachers have to understand the difference. Read this note about Yuta and note the difference between the early educators' assumptions and the child's and family's expectations.

Yuta (one year, eight months)

Every day Yuta sits in his chair waiting to be fed. He does not eat the food that is placed on his tray. He eats when we feed him.

Using information for assessment and planning In this case, the teachers involved decided that they needed more information in order to understand Yuta's behavior around eating. Here is what the teacher says about what this team did:

> After talking with the family, we learned that it was typical for Japanese families to feed their children for a long time, not stopping completely until the child starts grade school. We had to deal with our assumptions and accept that this was a part of this family's culture. We now feed Yuta each day.

Observation can provide you with a wealth of information about children. You decide how best to use that information to be a better teacher, to understand a child's behavior more fully, and to communicate with others about what you are learning.

Finding Your Observation Style

Implementing observation is a process that may look different from one teacher to another, from one care setting to another. Finding your unique style of watching children in action—figuring out when to document your observations, how to file and organize those records, and how to evaluate them and present them to families—is an important part of developing your own professionalism. Throughout this book you are offered many ideas, tips, and strategies based on early childhood professionals' experiences with observation. Use these ideas to help you find your unique observation style and make it successful for you in your work with young children and families.

· · · · · · ·

In the next chapter, we explore ways to use observation with early learning guidelines. Recommendations for integrating the two will show that teachers can be focused on supporting children's growth and development while they pay attention to the expectations in such state documents.

· · · · · · ·

Observation Practice #1:
What Can You Learn by Observing a Child?

Purpose: To identify what can be learned by observing a child for a brief period of time.

What to Do: Watch Video Clip #1 (scan the QR code or go to www.vimeo .com/1022181405). As you watch this very brief clip, consider what you are learning about this four-and-one-half-year-old girl. Since the video clip is so brief, we suggest that you watch it more than once to make sure you capture as many details as possible in your observation.

Guiding Questions: After viewing, generate a list of the child's capabilities, skills, social interactions, personality traits, and behaviors that you observed her demonstrating. In addition, consider these questions:

- Were you surprised at how much you learned in a short observation?
- If you had a history with this child, do you think that you would have seen things differently? In what ways?
- What curriculum plans might you make based on what you learned?

Be prepared to share with others the list you made about the girl as well as your thoughts about the questions above.

Observation Practice #2:
What Can You Learn by Observing a Child?

Purpose: To identify what can be learned by observing a child engaged in a longer play experience.

What to Do: Watch Video Clip #2 (scan the QR code or go to www.vimeo .com/1022181412) of a two-year-old boy, a three-and-one-half-year-old girl, and a teacher engaged in dramatic play. Focus on the two-year-old boy.

Guiding Questions: After viewing, generate a list of the capabilities, skills, social interactions, personality traits, and behaviors that you observed him demonstrating. In addition, consider these questions:

- Were you surprised at how much you learned in a longer observation?
- If you had a history with either of these children, do you think that you would have seen things differently? In what ways?
- What curriculum plans might you make based on what you learned?

Be prepared to share with others the list you made about this boy as well as your thoughts about the questions above.

Reflection

Purpose: To reflect on how observation affects adults' relationships with children.

What to Do: Think about a time in your life when you learned something special about a child. Then discuss or write about these questions:

- What factors were present that allowed you to learn about this child?
- Did observing the child contribute to your learning about them? In what situations did you observe this child?
- How did the relationship change as you got to know the child better?
- Did learning about the child help you to understand the child's motivations?

Finding Your Observation Style

Purpose: To discover what you already know about observation and documentation and what you want to learn more about.

What to Do: Begin an ongoing journal in which you record your answers to questions posed throughout this book. Here are some questions to get you started. Spend a few minutes jotting down your responses to them.

- What do you already know about observation and documentation? Do you observe children in your work and life? What do you think you learn by observing children?
- What are some reasons to observe children and document what they are doing and saying?
- What are some questions you have about observation and documentation? What do you want to learn more about?
- Why is documentation an important part of the observation process?

How Do Observation and Documentation Work with Early Learning Guidelines and Calls for Accountability?

▲▼▲▼▲

The field of early childhood care and education continues to change. The importance of the early years in shaping children's futures is increasingly recognized by both policy makers and the public. Researchers continue to investigate children's brain development and learning capabilities, showing that in their early years children develop skills and concepts that will serve them throughout their lives. We also know that adults can influence young children's learning and development (NAEYC 2020).

Another change is the development of guidelines for children from infancy through the preschool years. (We use the word *guidelines* here as we are seeing more states move to this term—instead of the word *standards*—when revising their documents.) At the national level, the Head Start Early Learning Outcomes Framework was updated in 2015 and, in 2020, released as the *ELOF2GO* mobile app. At the state level, as of 2019 all fifty states and the District of Columbia had developed early learning guidelines (National Center on Early Childhood Quality Assurance 2019).

These documents give educators a clear set of criteria for the typical development of children at different age ranges. In Gronlund's (2014) second edition of *Make Early Learning Standards Come Alive: Connecting Your Practice and Curriculum to State Guidelines*, many state guidelines are reviewed. And we, as authors, were also integrally involved in writing guidelines for the states of New Mexico, Illinois, and Montana. Across the country, we see the early learning guidelines for each state as a set of *reasonable expectations* that are:

- appropriate for the ages for which they were written,
- based on the best child development knowledge, and
- endorsed by the most recent recommendations regarding developmentally appropriate practices.

We do not see "push-down" expectations, such as the language of kindergarten or first-grade standards used to describe expectations for three- or four-year-olds. Rather, we see expectations that were written by early childhood professionals in each state who understand age-appropriate expectations and have extensive child development knowledge. This is good news!

In *Saving Play: Addressing Standards through Play-Based Learning in Preschool and Kindergarten*, Gronlund and Rendon (2017) give the following explanation of the importance of standards:

> Standards can provide the foundation for high-quality preschool and kindergarten education. Sometimes called guidelines, standards guide curriculum, instruction, and assessment. They express what adults want for children. They embody core values to ensure that society progresses and improves. They are a set of goals, perhaps even dreams, for what children will know and achieve. Like blueprints in architecture, standards are the blueprints in education. They are detailed drawings, sketches, or outlines. They describe expectations for children's learning at different ages that will help them survive and thrive into adulthood. (37)

Because of this recognition of the learning and growth in the early years and widespread development of early learning guidelines, leaders in the field of early childhood education have become more focused on accountability. Teachers of young children are asked to demonstrate how they are ensuring that each child will meet the guidelines and reach their potential. Policy makers and funders ask for data about children's accomplishments and connect those data to the quality of an early childhood program. They want to see statistical results. They ask: "How are taxpayer monies being spent in a way that is benefiting young children right away and raising their educational achievement over time?"

We are concerned, however, when we see policy makers, administrators, and early educators misuse their state's early learning guidelines. In our experience, it's the *implementation* of guidelines that can be troublesome, rather than the guidelines themselves. Many teachers report feeling pressured and unsure of how best to continue teaching and assessing in ways that are just right for children. Accountability in and of itself is a good thing. There is nothing wrong with a desire to implement high-quality education and care services for young children. Early educators *should* know if programs are making a difference in the lives of the children who attend. Often, however, the wrong methods are used to determine how children are learning and growing and, therefore, to rate the quality of a program. Sometimes children are given brief, on-demand assessments or mini-tests that capture only what they do at one point in time. Curricular practices change in order to "teach to the test" so time for play and exploration is devalued and teacher-led activities dominate.

Observation and Early Learning Guidelines *Can* Work Together

We believe strongly that when teachers observe children's performance and collect documentation over time, they will gather much better data to demonstrate quality programming and track children's learning and progress. Yet some calls for accountability seem not to value the wealth of knowledge that can be gained through observation and documentation. As demonstrated in chapter 1, early educators can learn much by observing children. And, as this chapter illustrates, it's possible to observe and document while also implementing guidelines and being accountable for quality results. To do this, you need a systematized process of daily observation and documentation as children play, explore, and participate in daily routines. In this approach, you are making sure that accountability to standards is done in a way that is beneficial to children.

> **Lillian:** What I think of when observing preschoolers is what stage of development the child is in and what is typical for this age group. I also try to consider each child's background and previous experiences and try to think of ways I can scaffold each child's learning.

Appropriate Assessment and Curriculum Related to Guidelines

We have seen programs where teachers do formal assessment in a naturalistic way, observing children in the flow of activities and routines throughout the day and documenting what they see them do and hear them say. The information they gather builds over time so teachers get a true and reliable picture of each child's development. What we wrote in *Early Learning Standards and Staff Development* is still true:

> We strongly believe that standards can be incorporated into programs without giving up the most enjoyable parts about working with young children, such as spontaneity, discovering each child's emerging skills and interests, and the opportunity to develop our own unique skills and interests. (Gronlund and James 2008, 13)

And there is a strong foundation of support for observational assessment related to learning goals in the position statement on developmentally appropriate practices adopted in 2020 by the National Association for the Education of Young Children (NAEYC). This document contains many key recommendations for appropriate assessment and curriculum related to guidelines.

> **B. Assessment focuses on children's progress toward developmental and educational goals....**
>
> **C. A system is in place to collect, make sense of, and use observations, documentation, and assessment information to guide what goes on in the early learning setting.** Educators use this information in planning curriculum and learning experiences and in the moment-to-moment interactions with children—that is, educators continually engage in assessment for the purpose of improving teaching and learning....
>
> **F. Decisions that have a major impact on children** . . . should be based on multiple sources of relevant information, including that obtained from observations of and interactions with children by educators, family members, and specialists as needed. (NAEYC 2020, 20)

Your observations cannot be random in nature—they must be systematic and well-planned and contain several key components. Your observations must be:

- ongoing and embedded in everyday activities and routines;
- criterion based (you observe for identified guidelines);
- documented and recorded (as close to the time it occurs as possible);
- objective and descriptive (not interpretive, evaluative, or judgmental); and
- used to determine what skills are emerging and what has been learned to improve teaching and to support the child's progress.

The observation and documentation are not random but rather are intentional, thoughtful, and ongoing. You should watch for, and document, what children are doing and saying throughout the time they are with you. Watch children at play. Watch children while diapering them or taking them to the bathroom. Watch children during meals and snacktimes. Watch children outdoors and in large- and small-group experiences. Formally plan for documentation of your observations so you can collect evidence of what you have observed. Then you can review, reflect on, evaluate, and share the observations with others.

This is all part of being an intentional teacher. You are connecting well-defined criteria, or goals, to your practice. As Ann S. Epstein (2014) explains in *The Intentional Teacher: Choosing the Best Strategies for Young Children's Learning*:

> An "intentional" teacher aims at clearly defined learning objectives for children, employs instructional strategies likely to help children achieve the objectives, and continually assesses progress and adjusts the strategies based on the assessment. (5)

The criteria or goals are your state's early learning guidelines. Children are not compared to one another, but rather are assessed in comparison to the reasonable expectations for their age group identified in the guidelines. In implementing observational assessment, writing down observations as close as possible to the time of the events provides more reliable information. Writing factually and objectively gives the evidence you will need to draw conclusions about how each child is doing and what progress has been made.

Observational assessment needs to be integrated with curriculum planning. Therefore, early learning guidelines are an important part of curriculum planning as well. As you watch children and document the things they do related to early learning guidelines, you gain a clearer picture of what each child can do and how to plan the next steps for each one. Often the guidelines are written in a continuum format so teachers can see how the next level of expectations in a domain unfolds. This allows you to easily refer to the guidelines to plan activities that will meet each child where they are performing and think about ways to support continued development and learning in that area.

Early learning guidelines provide you with a strong foundation on which to base your curriculum and a focus for your observations of the children in action. The guidelines have been researched and developed so teachers across each state can have a common understanding of expectations for children's performance. You do not need to guess what a two-year-old should be doing in the fine-motor domain or what a four-year-old should be doing related to alphabetic awareness. Instead, you can refer to your state's guidelines and find performance indicators that describe what children do at different ages in a variety of domains. In this way, the field of early childhood education is becoming more professional. Teachers and care providers are not making up their own developmental checklists. Instead, by using state guidelines, you are raising the quality of your program because you have well-accepted criteria on which to base your assessment conclusions and curriculum planning. You can communicate clearly with

Peggy W.: I focus on what each child is able to do and to what extent he or she can do it, rather than on what the child should be doing at that age. By focusing on where the child is now, I can create an environment that will encourage natural growth in his or her development.

families about children's progress and determine more easily when you need to raise a concern about a child's developmental capabilities in an area. And you can refer to the guidelines to determine when to make referrals to specialists, who, when necessary, can determine a child's special needs and plan programming appropriate for that child.

Connecting Observation and Documentation to Guidelines

In most state guidelines for infants and toddlers, the titles of the domains and descriptive language of the guidelines are different from those used in the preschool documents. And that's appropriate. Infants and toddlers grow and learn in different ways than children in the preschool years. Take, for example, the guidelines in the cognitive domain for infants and toddlers. They are especially different from those of preschoolers:

- Infants' and toddlers' receptive language blossoms before their expressive language. They listen and learn as others talk and sing with them. Then they try to communicate their needs and wants and learn more words and word combinations. Their language development is the basis for their later literacy skills—the greater their vocabulary (both receptive and expressive), the better readers they will become.
- Infants and toddlers are beginning to learn how the world works. They explore what happens when they reach for something or swat at it. They experiment with what happens when they shake the rattle or push the button on the toy.
- Infants and toddlers develop understanding of concepts such as cause and effect and object permanence.
- Infants and toddlers begin to develop awareness of language when listening to books and looking at the pictures with their caregivers.

In preschool guidelines, the cognitive domain is often divided into the content areas of language and literacy, mathematics, and science. In addition, many states include the area of social studies with indicators that describe how children are learning to get along in a classroom community, gaining an understanding of family and neighborhood, and learning the basics of democratic citizenship (as in taking turns and voting to make group decisions). Another area that is included in many state documents (for infants, toddlers, and preschoolers) is called "approaches to learning." These include developing persistence, focused attention, curiosity, initiative, and problem-solving skills. A direct connection has been determined between children's approaches to learning and later academic success.

Read the anecdote about Angel again and see how the description of his actions fits within early learning guidelines.

Angel (four years, ten months)

At snack Angel saves a chair and calls to his friend Luis, "You sit here next to me!" He takes three crackers, counting out, "One, two, three," as he puts them on his napkin. He uses a knife to spread peanut butter across each one. He calls out, "More juice, please!" In conversation with his friends he says, "At our farm we have chickens and goats. And the goats are very loud. I have to cover my ears because they are so loud." Angel covers his ears with two napkins, and his friend Luis does the same, but Luis uses his crackers. Both boys laugh.

The following is a list of Angel's capabilities that we identified and organized into the major areas, or domains, as specified in the *New Mexico Early Learning Guidelines: Birth through Kindergarten* (New Mexico Kids 2014), which can be found at www.newmexicokids.org. Within the domains, performance indicators describe specific ways preschool children are developing in that domain. Here are the indicators that Angel is demonstrating in each of the domains identified:

- literacy: listens with understanding to directions and conversations; converses effectively in his home language (62)
- numeracy: uses numbers and counting as means for solving problems and determining quantity (63)
- fine-motor development: coordinates eye-hand movements (61)
- self, family, and community: expresses cultural influences from home, neighborhood, and community; plays and interacts with various children sharing experiences and ideas (65)
- approaches to learning: develops increasing independence during activities, routines, and play (66)

As you can see, five domains and seven indicators can be related to this observation of Angel as he participated in snacktime, a daily occurrence in his preschool program. His teachers did not have to plan for a special activity tied to the guidelines, nor did they have to pull Angel aside and do an on-demand assessment with him to see how he performed related to the indicators in the list above. They were able to observe him in the flow of the day and document what they saw to gain more information about how he is growing and learning. They can continue to observe and document as he

Rosemary: The documentation often helps me think about what is an appropriate activity for individual children. Do I change the activity to make it multidimensional, to allow for differentiation? Do all of the children need to participate in this activity? Does the activity contribute to a child's learning? What guideline or goal does it meet for that child?

participates in play experiences, large- and small-group activities, and other daily routines, such as outdoor play, transitions, hand washing, toileting, arrival, and departure, to build a comprehensive picture about Angel that relates his growth and development to the guidelines. In this way, his teachers are meeting requirements for accountability and continuing to do what is best for young children.

In chapter 5, there are several observation notes that illustrate the ways children demonstrate early learning guidelines from different states. Reading them will give you an opportunity to learn more about how to assess guidelines through observation and documentation. You will notice that many guidelines can be seen in each observation, just as in the observation about Angel. And in appendix A, there are many more anecdotes for you to read, review, and relate to your state's guidelines.

• • • • • • •

We see calls for accountability and implementation of early learning guidelines as good things if they focus on benefiting children. When observational assessment and integration of curriculum planning based on reasonable, age-appropriate expectations are the basis for high-quality programming, children do benefit indeed! Throughout this book, we show you ways to use observation and documentation to the fullest so you know each child well and are doing what is best for each one. In the next chapter, we focus on how to do both observation and documentation well.

• • • • • • •

Observation Practice #3:
Relating Infant/Toddler Guidelines to Observation and Documentation

Purpose: To see the connection between what toddlers do and say and early learning guidelines.

What to Do: Watch Video Clip #3 (scan the QR code or go to www.vimeo .com/1022181431) of young toddlers playing in the sand with their teacher.

Guiding Questions: After viewing, use your state's infant/toddler guidelines (you should be able to access them easily online) to find specific indicators that match what you observed the children doing and saying. Do not hesitate to look in multiple domains or areas of development. In addition, consider these questions:

- Were you able to relate what you observed back to the infant/ toddler guidelines?
- Could you relate your documentation across multiple domains or areas of development? What domains were you able to identify?

Be prepared to share with others the list of infant/toddler guidelines that you identified and your thoughts about the questions above.

Observation Practice #4:
Relating Preschool Early Learning Guidelines to Observation and Documentation

Purpose: To see the connection between what preschoolers do and say and early learning guidelines.

What to Do: Watch Video Clip #4 (scan the QR code or go to www.vimeo .com/1022181458) of a preschooler reading a familiar story. He reads in Spanish. English subtitles are provided for you if you are not a Spanish speaker.

Guiding Questions: After viewing, use your state's preschool early learning guidelines (you should be able to access them easily online) and find specific indicators that match what you observed the child doing and saying. Do not hesitate to look in multiple domains or areas of development. In addition, consider these questions:

- Were you able to relate what you observed back to the preschool early learning guidelines?
- Could you relate your documentation across multiple domains or areas of development? What domains were you able to identify?

Be prepared to share with others the list of preschool guidelines that you identified and your thoughts about the questions above.

Review of Documentation:
Tying Guidelines to Observation Notes

Purpose: To practice identifying guidelines in documenting children's actions.

What to Do: Refer to your state's infant/toddler and preschool early learning guidelines (you should be able to access them easily online) as you review the anecdotes in appendix A. Determine which indicators from multiple domains can be seen for each of the anecdotes describing a child's actions.

Reflection

Purpose: To reflect on the ways that guidelines can be seen as children go about daily activities in your program.

What to Do: Think about your daily schedule with the children with whom you work. Consider the following activities that happen every day in your program, and identify some guidelines that could be addressed at that time:

> arrival
>
> indoor playtime
>
> snack
>
> diapering or toileting
>
> outdoors
>
> nap
>
> departure

Finding Your Observation Style

Purpose: To learn to pay attention to all domains or areas of development.

What to Do: Respond to these questions in your journal:

- Do you tend to find that your observations fit in one domain or area of development more than another? Why do you think that happens?
- How will you familiarize yourself with all of the domains or areas of development in your state's guidelines?
- What will your strategies be to make sure your observation and documentation are reflective of all domains or areas of development for each child?

CHAPTER 3

How Do You Do Observation and Documentation Well?

▲▼▲▼▲

When you start out observing and documenting children's actions, you may feel overwhelmed by the amount of information you can potentially gather as you observe. You may struggle to determine where to focus your attention and what or how much to document. You may miss getting documentation about some of the children. Some children may demand your attention and are easy to focus on, while others seem to slip under the radar. Or you may find that there are areas of development or certain areas of the classroom that you tend to pay attention to more than others. It's likely that you may try a number of documentation strategies looking for the right ways to capture what you are seeing children do.

Becoming a skillful observer takes time, practice, and a commitment to the process of regular observation. It is just like anything else in life that you want to do well. When you are learning to ride a bike, you try again and again until you are able to ride with ease. You may not feel very confident at first. But eventually you are on your own, riding down the street thinking, "I can do this! It's not so hard after all." The next step is refining your newfound abilities with a bike. You learn how to use the brakes and the handlebars effectively. Pretty soon you are zooming down the road, the wind blowing in your hair. You are not giving much thought to the individual steps involved in bike riding. You've put the whole process together through practice. Learning to do observation well uses the same process. Every time you try, the process becomes a little easier and more satisfying. As Hilary Seitz explains,

> Learning to really see each individual child—their abilities, their strengths, and their possibilities—is an art. Documenting this and making thinking, learning, and development visible help early childhood educators understand the child better and help

others value the child's capabilities. Documentation takes practice, collaboration, and support. It also takes an internal motivation to truly understand children. (Seitz 2023a, 7)

It is important to give yourself the time to practice observation. You need to honor your own learning style and think about ways to create the time to practice and learn. That might mean just stepping back for a few minutes each day and watching a child or two as they engage in play or participate in daily routines in your program. You may want to work out times with your coworkers every day for each of you to practice watching various activities and then discuss what you noticed at the end of the day. It will be exciting and rewarding for you to see your own growth and progress as you take the time to observe children more closely, not focusing on what the next activity will be, but rather giving all of your attention to them to see how they are thinking, problem solving, socializing, and exploring the world of your classroom.

You cannot possibly document everything that you have seen the children do in a day. Documenting your observations involves some decision-making on your part. First, choose a focus for the observations that you will document. You and your colleagues may want to divide up where in the classroom or which children you each will observe and document to help make the best use of your time. Throughout this book are numerous tips and strategies to help you figure out the best ways to document observations when you are in the midst of running a busy classroom. In this chapter, we provide ways to do observation well and document your observations so they are factual, descriptive, and informative. With practice, you can learn to do observation well by doing the following:

- choosing a focus for your observations
- using all of your senses to observe
- becoming open and ready for children

And with practice you can learn to do documentation well by doing the following:

- thinking of observation and documentation as research
- practicing different kinds of documentation strategies
- giving yourself time to reflect on your observations and documentation
- becoming aware of your own biases
- documenting factually
- interpreting children's actions
- working hard not to miss any children as you observe and document

Diana: I think part of it is not to be overwhelmed by it all at first. If you just are overwhelmed, like you can't do the whole thing, take bits and pieces of it and start. You don't have to do it all at the beginning.

In this chapter, we go through each of these to help you increase your capabilities as an observer and documenter of children in action.

Focusing Observations

We recognize that observing children can be overwhelming. As you watch children, you see and hear so many things. Figuring out ways to focus your observations will lessen the amount of information coming in and help you determine where to turn your attention. Sometimes your focus will be more general in nature and, at other times, more specific. Here are some specific things you might choose to focus on:

- one moment with one particular child
- a group of children
- specific daily routines, activities, or areas of the classroom
- skills, early learning guidelines, domains, or areas of development (such as fine-motor skills or early literacy understanding)
- challenges a child is having

Allowing yourself the freedom to move back and forth among the ways to focus will help you juggle the demands of the classroom and still be a competent observer. We recognize that you will more than likely focus in all of these ways but not necessarily at the same time.

Observing with All of Your Senses

Being a good observer involves using your eyes to scan the room, taking in the big picture of what all of the children are doing, as well as focusing on and really watching closely what individual children are doing. But seeing cannot stand alone in observing the intricacies of each child's performance. Every day, in addition to your sense of sight, you use your senses of hearing, touch, and smell and even your heart to help you know what's happening with each child. Think of a time when you were with a child or a group of children and you had to look away for a minute. Perhaps you had to turn your back to take some materials off a shelf. Would you say that you were still observing the children? Of course you were! That's because you were listening.

Taking in information by listening is a critical part of the observation process. Hearing a baby's cries or coos and responding appropriately helps the baby learn to trust their caregivers and know that they will be well taken care of. Listening to a child's story of their visit to Grandma's house validates their experience and encourages their communication with others. Listening to a child's wheezing cough raises concerns about their health

Robin J.: The reality in this field is that we don't get paid a lot of money. And we don't have a lot of time to do observation and documentation as well as they need to be done. And so, if you can view it almost as a labor of love and just shift your attitude to know why you're doing this . . . it will help you become a better teacher. Keeping my attitude focused and being able to force myself to do these observations in a more focused way helps me to pick up where I drop the ball sometimes. My class is more well rounded.

and might lead to calling their family so they can take them to the clinic. Listening to an infant's calm breathing assures you that naptime is going smoothly. Sometimes even knowing when things have gotten too quiet in one part of the classroom is a form of observation and may cause you to check out what might be going on with the children there.

Sense of touch is an important part of the observation process as well. Early childhood teachers often touch children as a way of building relationships with them. Babies are held so the caregiver can be within the child's range of vision and provide the stimulation and nurturing that are so important. Toddlers explore their independence and return to the safe haven of their favorite teacher's loving arms. For toddlers and preschoolers, a pat on the back, a handshake, a high five, and a hug are ways to say "Hello," to recognize a job well done, or to comfort a hurt feeling or an injury. Inviting children to sit on your lap is often part of reading stories during a small- or large-group time. Your lap can provide a sense of security for a child who is missing Mom or Dad, or help a child who does not have control of their own body to settle down and participate more appropriately in the activity.

Sensitive care providers recognize that each child has their own comfort levels with touch. Some children welcome affection and often initiate it themselves. Others have a stronger sense of personal space and bristle or withdraw from too invasive a gesture from an adult. This can be especially true in the early days of a relationship, but some children are less open to touch in general. There are also cultural differences regarding physical interaction among people. For example, in some cultures adults carry the children longer into their preschool years than in others. The accepted distance between two people when talking also varies from culture to culture. Some people are comfortable being very close when communicating, while others prefer more distance. Becoming aware of the cultural preferences of the children and families in your program will help you interpret more accurately what you observe through physical contact and touch.

An alert teacher can watch carefully for the signals a child is sending through the child's response to touch. You can also read the child's body language through your own sense of touch. Is the baby you are holding squirming and agitated? Or are they nestled against you, relaxed and restful? Is the child sitting on your lap rigid and stiff when hugged? Do they hug back or withdraw slightly? Paying attention to physical cues is an important part of observation.

Sense of smell is also useful in observing children. For babies and toddlers especially and sometimes for preschoolers as well, your sense of smell is important regarding changing diapers or handling toileting accidents. Concerns about children's hygiene can be identified through sense of smell. Making referrals to administrators and outside agencies when children are unkempt and not bathed may be the start of some helpful intervention for a family. And identifying health concerns for children often begins with smells. When a child arrives at school with a stuffed-up nose, breathing through their mouth, you may note the smell of their breath and recognize that an infection may be developing in their throat. Alerting a family member that medical attention is needed is an important part of communication about a child's care.

Finally, dedicated teachers observe with their hearts. As you get to know the children and you build a strong relationship based on your observations and interactions with each child, you can "see" with your heart when something is not right for a child. You may find yourself saying something like, "She just wasn't herself today." Then you can ask the parents if anything is going on in the child's life that might be affecting her mood or behavior. Being sensitive to your gut feelings is a way of listening to your heart as you try to do what's best for each child.

Becoming Open and Ready for Children

You will become a better observer when you allow yourself to be in the moment with children, to be open and ready to what they have to show you. It's likely that you sincerely enjoy children and have chosen this field because of that enjoyment. Sitting on the floor with an infant and playing peekaboo can be fun as the child squeals with delight when you reveal yourself behind your hands. Singing and dancing with toddlers can bring out the child in you. And seeing the light bulb turn on as a preschooler masters a new concept or skill is truly rewarding. You are a partner in helping each child along the journey of life and in establishing who the child will become. As Deb Curtis and Margie Carter (2011, 87) write in the second edition of *Reflecting Children's Lives: A Handbook for Planning Your Child-Centered Curriculum*, "If you can come to the powerful realization that children have the capacity and desire for deep connections, then you will support and coach them to grow into their best selves."

How do you become open and ready to be in the moment with children? One way is to tame the voice in your head that is running through the list of your duties. Taking a deep breath, sitting with the children, and listening to them lets you see more clearly what they are doing and what is important to them. Letting their energy and personalities flow over you, remembering to smile and laugh with them, and pausing to reflect on what you are seeing are ways to become more aware. Not being so concerned about the next activity but rather focusing on the present one will help you see things more clearly. Recognizing that you cannot observe everything in one day

April: Observing children is one of the most important jobs I do every day. As children play around the classroom, I learn about their thoughts and views of the world around them. I learn what they are interested in learning and how they see themselves in their family and classroom environment. This helps me to be respectful of their views and beliefs. Observing them and finding out their individual interests helps me to plan and scaffold from what they already know and develop projects that inspire learning.

and that you can document only so much relieves the pressure of documentation and accountability, allowing you to watch and enjoy.

Being open and ready involves remembering to observe children to see what they *can* do rather than what they *cannot*. Even with greater calls for accountability and the implementation of early learning guidelines, your focus should still be on what children *can* and *are* doing, on where they are successful and competent both independently and with help. Red flags may still go up in your mind as you see a child struggle with a particular task. However, observing and documenting exactly what the child does will help you reach an informed decision, supported by the evidence of your observation notes. You will know what the child's strengths are and where extra support and intervention may be needed.

For example, five-year-old Grant was born a typically developing child, but a slowly progressing neurological disease is causing him to lose his hearing and his mobility. He can't walk, but he can crawl along the floor, pulling his body with his arms. Grant's teacher, Cami, does not observe Grant for the purpose of identifying everything he *cannot* do. Instead, she carefully documents what he can do, what he is capable of. She and her colleagues choose to focus on Grant's crawling abilities and set up obstacle courses of soft cushions in the classroom for Grant to maneuver around. They place him at the top of the slide in the gym and carefully support him as he crawls to the sliding board and slides down. They make sure he can participate in activities in ways the other five-year-olds do by placing him in a standing device that supports his limbs and back. One of his favorite activities is to stand at the sensory table. The smile on Grant's face is contagious! His caregivers recognize and support his capabilities and are open and ready for him to show them just what he can do.

Natacha Ndabahagamye Jones, Amber T. Fowler, and Jennifer Keys Adair (2023) call this "keen observing," observing through curious eyes rather than evaluatory ones:

> We are *keen observers* when we observe children's capabilities, interests, and relationships as well as where they spend time, what materials animate them, and what kinds of contributions they enjoy making to the classroom community. . . . We can focus on young children as human beings with interests, desires, struggles, and cultural values. (22)

Grant's teachers were most certainly engaged in keen observing.

Thinking of Observation and Documentation as Research

Like scientists, teachers conduct research. Every day they study the children in their care. Children are the focus. Here are some ways teachers learn more about the children:

- They observe them in multiple experiences.
- They think about and analyze what they see them do and hear them say.
- They form hypotheses and test those hypotheses by offering children different materials, experiences, and levels of support.
- They experiment with different teaching strategies and evaluate the results.
- They draw conclusions, make adaptations, implement new processes within different parameters, and observe the results.
- They reflect, question, ponder, and wonder.

Notice that observation is essential in the research process as well as the teaching process. As teachers spend time with the children in their care, they are continually learning about them. As Deb Curtis and Margie Carter (2011, 103) have written,

> Learning to be an observer, gathering data about who the children are—their interests, questions, strengths, and challenges—constitutes the starting point for building a child-centered curriculum. Observation is a critical tool for ongoing assessment, planning, and responses to children.

Here is one teacher's description of her experience with observation:

When I was teaching children, I felt like I was running a video camera in my head all day long. And at the end of the day, that video camera was full of scenes that I had observed, interactions that had occurred, and my impressions about the children. As I wound down after the children left for the day, I "replayed" that internal tape and reviewed in my mind what stood out, considered what I wanted to remember, and wondered about where to go next with specific children. Sometimes this carried over into conversations with colleagues or into later reflection as I went about my daily life at home. Occasionally these thoughts would even find their way into my dreams that night!

But at times the video in my head was overwhelming. I had taken in so much information about the children that I had trouble sorting through it. Just relying on my memory and my own internal "video recording" was not always sufficient to help me be the best teacher that I could be.

That's where documentation is helpful. Writing down what you have observed as close as possible to the time of the observation is one way to make sure nothing is lost or forgotten. Taking photographs of children in action can jog your memory at a later time. Recording videos or audio with various devices can also be helpful. And collecting samples of children's creations or work (such as writing samples, drawings, or paintings) can also help you get to know each child better.

Documentation is an essential part of the observation process. We recognize that writing down your observations can feel overwhelming. However, so much can be learned about children through observing them. Accepting the importance of observation *and* documentation and figuring out ways to do them better will enhance the enjoyment you experience with the children.

Documentation of a good observation is not necessarily very long. It is factual and descriptive and provides details about what a child can do. It is focused and clear and provides information specific to the child and who they are.

When observing children, you are collecting information about them just as a scientific researcher does about their topic. If you rely only on your memory, you may miss important information about the child. Therefore, to be a careful researcher, you must document some of your observations. Documentation becomes the evidence that shows what you have learned about the child's strengths, weaknesses, interests, and capabilities. You are collecting documentation to answer the following questions:

- Who is this child?
- How is this child showing me skills, understandings, and capabilities (which can be related back to early learning guidelines)?
- What are this child's special needs, life experiences, and family and cultural influences?

Documenting observations related to these questions can be done in several ways: written notes that describe what the child does and says (as we've shown in the previous chapters) or quick memory joggers for you to enhance at a later time. At times you may use a checklist format on which to record very brief bits of information. It's important to know when to use each format so that the information you are documenting is indeed contributing to the research you are doing about each child. In the next chapter, we show several different formats for documenting your observations and give guidelines for when to use them most effectively.

As you observe and document, you can add to the research you are doing by interacting with the children to learn more about their thinking and understanding. Engage in a babbling conversation with an infant and observe the way they respond. When conversing with older toddlers and preschool-age children, ask open-ended questions or make open-ended comments to encourage them to share more about their thinking and reveal more of their internal worlds.

Open-ended questions or comments do not have one right answer. Instead, the question invites responses that can go in a variety of directions. For example, "What do you know about that?" "Why do you think so?" and "What might happen next?" are open-ended questions. In contrast, closed questions have one correct response. Questions such as "What color is this?" "How many do you have?" and "Where does this puzzle piece go?" are closed questions. Closed questions do not give the questioner any insight into the child's way of thinking or feeling at that particular time. Some children, if they do not know the answer, shut down completely and refuse to answer any more questions. Learning to use open-ended questions and comments will help you gain more information about each child and elicit more revealing information from children. When you observe a child, it is perfectly appropriate to ask open-ended questions and include them and the child's responses as part of the documentation notes. The following are anecdotes that include the teacher's questioning. Read them and decide if you have more insight into the child's thinking and problem solving because of the questions the teacher asked.

Louisa (five years)

After I read a book to the class about sadness and laughter, I ask the children, "What did that book make you think about? How did it make you feel?" Louisa raises her hand and says, "When you're feeling sad, don't feel bad, because it's inside you."

Kazyan (four years, eight months)

Kazyan goes into the science area and takes out eyedroppers and three cups. He sits down at the table and sticks the eyedropper into the water and takes it out. There is no water in the eyedropper. He sticks it back into the water and, once again, no water. "Miss Nita, how does this work?" he asks. I ask, "Well, what could you do to make it work?" He says, "I need to get the water in here." I say, "That's right, Kazyan. How can you do that?" "I don't know how to get it in there. You need to show me." I take the dropper and say, "Look at the dropper, Kazyan. What do you see?" Kazyan says, "I see this black thing and the thing where the water needs to go." "That's right." I then ask him, "How does that black thing feel?" Kazyan says, "It's squishy." "So what do you think you should do with the squishy black thing?" Kazyan takes the dropper, holds it on the black, squishy end, and presses his fingers together. "I need to squeeze it together." He places the eyedropper in the water, squeezes, and after a few tries fills the dropper with water again and again. With a big smile, he announces, "I did it!"

Sometimes offering open-ended questions or comments allows children to solve disagreements on their own. Here are two examples in which the teacher's comments do that.

Yasmina (four years, two months)

Yasmina is sitting in the quiet area when Jacob comes and sits beside her. He takes a book away from her. Yasmina says, "Hey, I was looking at that first!" Jacob says, "Me too!" Yasmina says, "Teacher, Jacob is taking the book." I say, "What are some things you could do?" Yasmina tells Jacob, "Jacob, sit by me and we can read it together." She places part of it on her lap and the other half on Jacob's. She says, "See, I can share."

Max (five years, seven months)

Max and his buddies are riding the scooters on the bike path. They leave and go to play with the wagon and mud. Max returns five minutes later, and Claudia is on the scooter he was using. Max grabs the handles of the scooter and says, "Hey, I was using that. That's my scooter." Claudia does not get off the scooter and says, "Well, you left and were doing something else." Max holds on tight and repeats, "It's my turn. I was using it." This standoff continues until Max calls my name and says, "Tracy, I was using this scooter." I approach them and say, "It looks like you both want the same scooter. I wonder what you could do so both of you are happy." Max replies, "We could take turns, and I'm first." "How many times would you like to go around?" I ask. "Five," says Max. "Two," says Claudia. "Five," says Max. "Three," says Claudia. "Five," says Max. "Six," says Claudia. "Five," says Max. "Okay, five," says Claudia. Claudia gets off and lets Max get on the scooter. After five times around, he gives the scooter to her.

Sometimes, reflecting back to the child in an open and ready manner provides them with an opportunity to surprise you with their thinking and problem solving, as in this example.

Ayiana (five years, two months)

Today in circle time all the children are gathering around a song poster on the wall to take turns identifying the letters of the alphabet. Everyone is sitting on their knees. They are in three rows. Some of them can't see the song on the wall because the person in front of them is taller than they are. Ayiana says, "I know what to do." I ask her, "What would you do?" She gets up and begins moving the taller kids to the back row. Then Ayiana has the rest of the kids stand up so she can see "who is the shortest." She picks out the "short" kids and puts them in front. "Now everyone can see," Ayiana says with a smile. And they can!

Practicing Different Documentation Strategies

Everyone has a different organizational style, a different way of writing, and a different approach to documentation. Trying out and practicing various kinds of documentation strategies is as important as practicing observation of children in action. You may find that one method works better for you, while another is more suited to your colleague's style. You may prefer to jot down brief notes that you reflect on and enhance at a later time in the day. Your teaching partner may be better at getting information down right in the moment with a child. In the next chapter, we introduce several different recording methods and give guidance about how and when to use each one most effectively. We encourage you to try them out, discuss with your colleagues how each method works for each of you, and continue to refine your documentation skills.

Giving Yourself Time to Reflect on Your Observations and Documentation

You need time for reviewing your documentation to consider each child's accomplishments and needs and to plan effectively for the next steps to support continued growth and development. Making a commitment to reflect on your observations and giving yourself the gift of time to review your notes will help make your observations useful in your work with the children. You may see patterns in children's behavior. You may suddenly notice that many children have trouble with a certain transition in your day or a certain area of the room. Or you might see that a given child always does better in the afternoon after nap.

Not all reflection has to occur in a quiet, after-hours setting. You may set aside time to reflect on the children by yourself, or you may engage in a conversation with your colleagues. There are many opportunities for reflection:

- spontaneously at the time of the observation
- continually, throughout the day, as you observe the child in other activities and routines and piece together a whole picture
- in daily personal reflection in a planned quiet time
- in daily or weekly group discussions with colleagues
- in ongoing review (perhaps weekly) as you organize and file your documentation
- in a planned reflection to look over the documentation you have completed after several weeks of observing a child

The most important question to consider when reflecting about your observations is: What have I learned about this child? You can go on to ask more detailed questions:

- What are this child's interests? What really excites them?
- What are this child's personality traits? Just who are they?
- What are this child's accomplishments, and where have they made progress?
- In what particular areas does this child experience challenge or difficulty?
- What have my colleagues and I done with this child that has worked well?
- What has not worked well with this child?
- What changes should we consider?
- What goals should we set?

Taking the time to consider these questions for each child and making plans accordingly will help you be much more in tune with the children. Your job will be easier because you will read the children's signals more clearly, anticipating trouble and heading it off, building on the successes that have gone before, and helping each child continue to experience even more success. And sometimes reflection time is the only time you have to record your observations. In the next chapter, we discuss using this time for documentation more fully.

Becoming Aware of Your Own Biases

Observing children in action is a human endeavor, not a mechanical one. Therefore, total objectivity is not possible. As an early educator watching children at work or at play, you are influenced by your own life experiences, your understanding of child development, your attitudes about yourself and others, and your inherent biases and prejudices. Each person looks at the world through a unique lens. Therefore, each educator looks at children through their own unique lens as well.

For example, each educator looks at children's behavior differently. When two or more teachers observe the same child, each will use their own viewpoint, or lens. Deb Curtis and Margie Carter describe two contrasting views: one negative and one competent. The teacher viewing the child in a negative light sees that the child is lacking self-control and acting inappropriately. The teacher viewing the child as competent sees a child striving to learn how to get along in the world, trying to understand the societal cues that

Darlisa: As I organized my observation notes, the thing that was really amazing, humbling, and surprising to me was that I saw the children much differently than I did when observing in the classroom. Sitting back, reflecting, and reading really helped me. I felt like the Grinch whose heart started growing.

adults are giving, and doing their best to apply them. These two viewpoints affect what each teacher sees. Here is how Curtis and Carter (2011, 85) present a child's same behavior from these two points of view.

Negative View	Competent View
The child has no idea of what is safe.	The child is an energetic explorer, a tireless experimenter, and a dedicated scientist.
The child lacks patience.	The child is eager to learn from every experience and interaction he has.
The child cannot keep his hands off of things.	The child is figuring out how to control his behavior and look after himself, others, and the world around him.
The child has temper tantrums.	The child is moving from dependence to independence.

Reflective teachers are aware of the lenses through which they are looking at behavior. They try to understand the underlying causes of a child's behavior. They consider the child's perspective and analyze the situation from different angles so they can prevent outbursts in the future and help the child most effectively in the long term. As Louise Derman-Sparks and Julie Olsen Edwards (2010, 1) write in *Anti-Bias Education for Young Children and Ourselves*, "When educators treat children as if they are strong, intelligent, and kind, children are far more likely to behave in strong, intelligent, kind ways. They are more likely to learn and thrive and succeed."

Lack of experience with cultures other than your own or misunderstandings of others' values can also influence the way you interpret what a child is doing. To be a truly effective observer, you must continually develop your own awareness of your cultural experience and the experiences of the children and families with whom you work. Such self-scrutiny is an ongoing process that takes maturity, thought, reflection, and openness to new ideas. Your goal is for your documented observations to represent the child's actual performance and not be skewed by hidden bias in any way.

Sometimes conflicts arise due to differences or misunderstandings between teachers' cultural backgrounds and those of the families and children with whom they work. Differences in views on issues such as feeding and sleeping, attachment and separation, play, exploration, and socialization can all become sources of miscommunication. Misunderstandings about cultural practices can lead to incorrect assumptions about a child's behavior. No one belief system is right or wrong. Educating yourself by talking with children's families about their traditions and approaches to child rearing will help broaden your understanding of children's actions. This is identified in the latest version of *Developmentally Appropriate*

Practice in Early Childhood Programs as an essential step in providing a supportive environment for all children and their families: "Closely consulting with families is vital to bridging potential cultural disconnects" (NAEYC 2022, 56). As you develop your own awareness of how your experience with different cultures affects your perceptions, you will grow as an observer and be able to see what children do through a clearer lens.

The Head Start Early Childhood Learning and Knowledge Center (2024) points out the importance of recognizing both cultural disconnects and personality traits:

- Every person comes from a culture, and every family's culture is unique. Culture—attitudes, beliefs, expectations about people and events—shapes us as humans and as early childhood professionals. For example, some cultures consider it respectful to look someone in the eye when speaking or being spoken to. Other cultures consider it respectful to look down when someone is speaking. A home visitor whose culture values looking someone in the eye when speaking may think that a child or family member whose culture values eyes down when someone speaks is ignoring her or being disrespectful.

- Traits such as temperament (e.g., being cautious, outgoing, or sensitive; having a need for order), personal interests and preferences, and feelings (e.g., what makes us feel excited, apprehensive, uncomfortable) also affect how adults see and relate to children. These traits may help them feel closer to children with similar traits. They may pay more attention to children with similar traits and observe them more frequently than other children. These traits may also drive adults away from children whose traits are different. Staff may pay them less attention or interpret their behaviors more negatively. For example, a teacher who has a high tolerance for bright lights, environmental noise, and a lot of "stuff" on shelves and walls may have a hard time figuring out that an infant who cries frequently may be overstimulated by those same things.

Being aware of the potential biases that can result from both cultural influences and personality traits is an important task in developing your own observation style.

In the activity for Finding Your Observation Style at the end of this chapter (see page 50), there are several self-awareness exercises from Derman-Sparks and Edwards (2010). Going through these exercises by yourself or with a trusted friend or group of colleagues will help you think carefully about the lens through which you are observing children.

Identifying the possible ways your lens is cracked or foggy and not giving a true picture of the child will make your observations far more reliable and informative. You will come to understand not only who you are but also the wonderful richness and diversity of the children and families you serve.

Documenting Factually

To do observation and documentation well, it is critical that the written observations are factual. They need to be descriptive notes rather than interpretive, judgmental ones. Since each person sees a situation or a child through the filters of their own unique experience, writing down observations as objectively and factually as possible helps eliminate inherent bias. Objectivity means seeing and recording what is actually taking place, trying not to be influenced by value judgments or biases, and not recording interpretations of the behaviors being observed. It means separating out the pieces, factually describing what you see, and then going back at a later time to interpret the facts that have been written down. Easy to say, not so easy to do—especially with children whom you work with often and know well. However, the more you observe children, the better you will write objectively.

Here is a subjective, interpretive anecdote. Notice how judgment and evaluation give it a more negative tone.

> ## Joshua (four years, three months)
>
> Joshua was very bad today at circle time. He never listens or sits still. He always wiggles and disturbs his neighbor, and I had to sit with him and hold him.

Certain words stand out in this description of Joshua at circle time: *bad, never, always, disturbs.* The problem with these words is the variety of ways they can be perceived by different people. One adult might define *bad* as hitting another child or kicking a chair, while another might define *bad* as not listening to the teacher or talking out of turn. The words *always* and *never* are not good descriptive words to use. They are too broad for describing this one incident with Joshua. The word *disturbs* can also have multiple meanings that lead the reader to question exactly what Joshua did that disturbed his neighbors. Was he leaning against them? Whispering in their ears? Pinching, hitting, or kicking? Asking them questions? And finally, in this anecdote the tone of the last phrase, "I had to sit with him and hold him," reflects a negative attitude on the part of the observer, as if this teacher resents having to intervene in this manner to help Joshua be successful at circle time.

It is easy to see that this observation record is interpretive and judgmental. There is, however, a way to describe Joshua's behavior at circle time so the anecdote is factual and descriptive. This gives anyone who reads it the information that tells exactly what Joshua did and said. Based on that information, then, readers can make their own judgments and determine what the next steps would be for Joshua. Analyze the following rewritten anecdote about Joshua to see how interpretation is replaced by description.

> ## Joshua (four years, three months)
>
> Joshua sits still for approximately one minute at a time and then gets up and stands or walks away. Each time, I bring him back to the circle and sit him back down. When sitting, he pokes the child next to him and talks to him. I sit next to Joshua and ask him if he will sit on my lap. He agrees. He leans against my chest, sucks his thumb, and listens to the story for five minutes.

In this factual description, you can see that Joshua has trouble sitting still and participating in group time until he is placed in an adult's lap. Then he settles down. Therefore, any curriculum planning for him at group times should include the opportunity for him to sit with an adult so he is more likely to participate successfully.

Following is a chart from the book *Focused Portfolios: A Complete Assessment for the Young Child*, 2nd edition (Gronlund and Engel 2019, 72). Look over the words and phrases in the left-hand column and notice how many of those you see in the first observation about Joshua, as well as in the subjective anecdotes that follow. Then, when reading the factual and descriptive anecdotes on later pages, refer back to this chart to see how the words and phrases change from evaluative and interpretive to factual and descriptive, as in the right-hand column of the chart. You will also find the chart in appendix B and linked on the Focused Observations product page at www.redleafpress.org.

Words and Phrases to Avoid	Words and Phrases to Use
The child loves . . .	He often chooses . . .
The child likes . . .	I saw him . . .
He enjoys . . .	I heard her say . . .
She spends a long time at . . .	He spends five minutes doing . . .
It seems like . . .	She said . . .
It appears . . .	Almost every day, he . . .
I thought . . .	Once or twice a month, she . . .
I felt . . .	Each time, he . . .
I wonder . . .	She consistently . . .
He does . . . very well . . .	We observed a pattern of . . .
She is bad at . . .	
This is difficult for . . .	

Analyze the rest of these anecdotes for the words and phrases they contain that are not factual and descriptive.

Jennifer (six months)

Jennifer is a very fussy baby. She cries when her mom leaves. She demands a lot of adult attention. She has trouble settling down unless she has her pacifier or is being held. She startles easily and gets upset when the toddlers come near her.

Carrie (three years, two months)

Carrie runs outside to the bikes at riding time because she wants to have first choice of the bikes. She always wants the red bike and forgets the rule of walking outside to the bike area.

> ### Nico (two years, six months)
>
> During art time today, Nico really enjoys painting a picture. He uses up a lot of paint—green, blue, brown, and red. His picture is very interesting. It looks like he painted some people and a house. Nico paints almost every day, and it seems to be his favorite activity.

Here is an example of an observation note that is written with no opinion or judgment included, only a description of what the child did and said. Note that quoting a child is a form of factually describing what occurred.

> ### Lupita (two years, five months)
>
> At lunch Lupita sees Lorrain put chile on her burrito. Lupita says, "Mama chile." Lorrain asks her if her mom eats chiles, and Lupita says, "Sí." When she wants more food, she says, "Más [more]," and when we ask her to say "por favor [please]," she does so. Later she watches Jason eat. She points to him and says, "Mira [Look], Jason!"

Johanna: I found it very freeing to be able to just write what they are doing. I enjoyed that. It freed me from having to evaluate it while I was observing. I could just write what they did.

Diana: One of the challenges is being able to write it the right, correct way.

The reader of this anecdote has a good sense of how Lupita uses language at lunchtime. The context of the situation is described, as well as the teachers' interaction with Lupita. There is no evaluation of Lupita's language skills. Instead, there is reporting of her words and phrases. Here are two other factual and descriptive anecdotes to consider.

> ### Naomi (seven months)
>
> Naomi is lying on a blanket on the floor with the jungle gym hanging over her. After a couple of minutes, she starts to cry. Her mom is in the room fixing a bottle for her. Mom says, "I hear you, sweetie. I'll be right there." Naomi places both hands together in a fist and places it over her mouth. She starts to move her fist back and forth and babbles, "Ba, ba, ba, ba." This continues for a few minutes until Mom picks her up and feeds her the bottle.

> ## Garrett (five years, one month)
>
> Garrett asks me to read *The Very Hungry Caterpillar*. When it says, "That night he had a stomachache," Garrett says, "Well, he ate all of the food in the world." I read the part where he built a small house, and Garrett says, "It's a cocoon." I reply, "Yes, Garrett, it's a cocoon." After the book is finished, Garrett says, "One time at my grandma's house, I saw a cocoon. But the next night, it did not turn into a butterfly. It stayed a cocoon."

Interpreting Children's Actions

You may be wondering where judgment, evaluation, and interpretation fit into the observation process. The problem with interpretation is that there may be several possible ways to look at a child's actions. You want to be sure you have enough evidence to support any conclusions you are making about a child. Read the following description of Elijah in the block area.

> ## Elijah (three years, nine months)
>
> Elijah is in the block area. He has several animals in his hand. Several other children are in this area with him. He runs around in circles with the animals, and another child chases him. He laughs and screams, "You can't catch me."

When reading this anecdote, you can draw many different conclusions about Elijah's actions even though you don't know him. You may decide that he is out of control and desperately needs adult intervention to help him settle down. Or you may think that he is running off extra energy. You may determine that he is a threat to other children in the area or that he is only expressing the joy and exuberance of a young child.

The facts on hand from this one observation are not enough to know which conclusion is the correct one. Therefore, if you move too quickly to a judgment about Elijah's behavior, you may very well be mistaken. Instead, the only way to be sure of your interpretation is to observe Elijah many more times in a variety of situations to see how he handles his energy and exuberance. Then the record of his actions will provide a growing collection of evidence about Elijah. From that record, you will be able to determine how best to help and support him in the classroom.

The process of writing down your thoughts, ideas, and interpretations needs to be kept separate to ensure objectivity. Some teachers use a format for documentation that includes both the factual description and their interpretation. They divide their paper into two columns, one for writing down the actions of the child, the other for writing the possibilities for interpreting those actions. We have designed a form for you to use to record factual observations and possible interpretations. You can copy the form from appendix B in the book or print it out from the Focused Observations product page at www.redleafpress.org. Often teachers follow those possible interpretations with a question mark because they recognize that they do not really know exactly why the child is doing what they are doing. This helps them to remember that their interpretations need to be continually readjusted as more situations are observed.

The following chart shows the Elijah observation recorded in this way:

Facts	Possible Interpretations
Elijah is in the block area. He has several animals in his hand. Several other children are in this area with him. He runs around in circles with the animals, and another child chases him. He laughs and screams, "You can't catch me."	Is he out of control and desperately needing adult intervention to help him settle down? Is he running off extra energy that day? Is he that energetic every day? Is he a threat to other children in the area? Is he merely expressing his joy and exuberance?

The next step in this process is using the information, both fact and interpretation, to plan intervention strategies that will ensure success for the child and maximize his potential to develop and learn. As multiple observations are recorded factually and descriptively, you can review them, thinking about the evidence they present. For Elijah, multiple observations may show a pattern emerging that he is a very expressive child, showing his joy in just being alive. Then his teachers might choose to sit back and laugh with him, give him hugs, and join him in his positive approach to his days at preschool. On the other hand, multiple observations may show that he is often out of control. In that case, his teachers will provide him with adult guidance and protect other children. Steps would be planned to help him throughout every day so he works toward developing self-control through using facial expressions or words to express his feelings, stomping his feet when angry, going to a teacher for help, and so on. In chapter 6 we explore in-depth curricular planning based on observational documentation.

Not Missing Any Children

You must commit to attempt to observe and collect documentation for each child. This does not mean that you document everything you see children doing. Instead, you identify the important things in specific areas of development that give a well-rounded and complete picture of who each child is, what they are capable of, what they are working on, and what you are doing to help them be successful. As you attempt to run a busy classroom and provide loving care for a group of children, you may find yourself paying attention to some children more than others. Some children demand your attention. They may act out or need help with their own self-control. Having an adult nearby who helps them to learn to express their feelings appropriately and not hurt other children is essential. Other children demand attention by looking to you for love and affection, for praise and validation. These are the children who continually bring drawings or paintings to you, who say things like, "Look what I did, Teacher!" or "I love you." They are asking for positive attention. The observational records of children who demand negative or positive attention are often filled with notes. Teachers generally report that they do not have difficulty remembering to document these children's accomplishments.

There is also often a group of children who can be identified as "invisible" when it comes to their observation records. These are the children who do not ask for a lot of attention. In fact, often these are children who are comfortable going about their days in the early childhood classroom quite independently and successfully. Because these children are not requiring an adult's intervention very often, teachers report that this is the group about whom they tend to have less documentation. These children are easier to miss. It's easy to say, "Oh, I'll remember that later," and then forget to write it down. When observation is the source of information for assessment purposes, for accountability purposes, and for reflection and planning purposes, no child can be missed.

• • • • • • •

Teachers and care providers observe children all the time but do not necessarily document everything they see and hear. They have to figure out what is most important to document as they act as researchers learning more about each child. It's important to work at improving observation skills, becoming more open and ready to learn about each child. Then, figuring out the best ways to document what is observed takes time and practice. You *can* learn to do observation and documentation well.

• • • • • • •

Observation Practice #5:
Factual versus Interpretive Anecdotes

Purpose: To learn to document what is actually seen and record what is taking place rather than writing anecdotes that are influenced by value judgments and interpretation.

What to Do: Watch Video Clip #5 (scan the QR code or go to www.vimeo .com/1022181480) of preschool girls and their teacher involved in dramatic play. Take notes about what you observe. As you write, think about the difference between factual and interpretive anecdotes. One of the girls is a Spanish speaker. English subtitles are provided.

Guiding Questions: After viewing, look over your notes. Decide which comments are factual and which are interpretive, referring back to the chart of words and phrases to use and to avoid on page 44 (you will also find the chart in appendix B and on the Focused Observations product page at www.redleafpress.org). Were you surprised by what you discovered about your use of words? Be prepared to discuss your own thinking about factual and interpretive words and phrases with others.

Observation Practice #6:
Considering the Lenses through Which We View Children

Purpose: To learn another way to distinguish between fact and interpretation when writing anecdotes.

What to Do: Before you view Video Clip #6 (scan the QR code or go to www .vimeo.com/1022181502), consider the lenses that we shared for a negative versus a competent view of a child on page 40. As you do your observation, think in terms of these two lenses and take notes that would reflect each one.

Guiding Questions: After viewing the video clip, consider how your observations were different depending on the lens through which you were looking. Did you find that it was easier to view the child's actions through one lens or the other? Be prepared to discuss with others why you think that might be so.

Observation Practice #7: Using the Facts/Interpretation Form

Purpose: To learn another way to distinguish between fact and interpretation when writing anecdotes.

What to Do: For this observation, you will watch Video Clip #7 (which is a repeat of #2) (scan the QR code or go to www.vimeo.com/1022181531). Before viewing, be prepared to use the Facts/Interpretation Form to record your observation (you can copy the form from appendix B in the book or print it out from the Focused Observations product page at www .redleafpress.org). You may focus on one of the children or attempt to document what you see each of them doing. As you document, edit your notes to separate your factual description of what they are doing from your interpretation of their actions.

Guiding Questions: Consider how you separated the facts from your interpretations. Did the use of the form help you in this process? Why or why not? Be prepared to discuss with others.

Reflection

Purpose: To reflect on ways to do observation and documentation well.

What to Do: Consider the following questions:

- What steps will you take to give yourself time to practice observing and documenting?
- In what ways are you open and ready to observe what children can do?
- How will you plan for reflection times about your observations and documentation?
- Identify a time when your own opinions or biases influenced your thinking about a child.

Finding Your Observation Style

Purpose: To identify the characteristics of your personal observation style and help you strategize to make your observations more objective.

What to Do: Review the chart "Words and Phrases to Avoid/Words and Phrases to Use" on page 44.

1. Identify some of the phrases you tend to use and write them in your journal.
2. Think of ways you can move toward more objective documentation. What steps will you take to work on this part of documentation? Write a list of steps in your journal.
3. Think of the way you view children's meltdowns, inappropriate behaviors, or trying times. Are you viewing the child through the lens of a "naughty" child or a competent child? Analyze a recent time when you had to help a child who was behaving poorly and consider through which lens you observed the child's behavior and responded to help them.
4. Write out your answers and thoughts for the following self-awareness exercises or discuss them with a trusted friend or group of colleagues to help you think carefully about the lens through which you are observing children.
   - What is your social identity—your gender, race, ethnicity, economic class, family structure, sexual orientation, and abilities/disabilities? Think back on a time when you did *not* belong or when a door was closed based on your identity. How did you feel?
   - What memories do you have of what your family taught you about various kinds of diversity among people? Was their behavior consistent with what they said?
   - What do you remember from childhood about how you made sense out of human differences? What confused you?
   - In what ways do you agree or disagree with your parents' views about race, ethnicity, gender, and physical abilities? If you disagree, how did you develop your own ideas? Who were significant influences on you? What do you plan to teach your own children?

(Derman-Sparks and Edwards 2010)

CHAPTER 4

How Do You Fit in Observation and Documentation?

▲▼▲▼▲

You may be wondering how you are going to manage to observe children, document your observations, and still interact fully with the children. You do so by figuring out the best times to observe and by trying different recording methods. There is no one right time or perfect method. To effectively document what you see children doing, you will need to try out several formats, thinking about the purpose of your observation, the amount of time you have, and the interruptions you might experience. You will also need to think about your own personal writing style. Finding the right format will reduce the stress of combining observation and documentation. But it takes time to figure it out. The perfect format for you might be completely different from that of your colleague in the room next door. Part of being successful at this process is to experiment then reflect on and learn what works best for you.

When teachers describe having issues with time related to observation, they are really describing issues with documentation. Here are some of the most significant questions teachers often ask about observation and documentation:

- How can I truly be present with children and still write down all of my observations? If I write while I'm with them, I feel it takes me away from interacting with them.
- Sometimes I get interrupted and don't get back to the documentation in a timely manner, and then I forget what I was trying to document. When is it best to write the documentation?
- What does a good written observation look like? How much should I write?
- How many observations should I document and about what? What are my goals in collecting written documentation of my observations about each child?

To be truly present with children is the all-encompassing, most essential task of teachers of young children. You cannot possibly be a good observer if you are not fully in the moment with the children in your care. And they will not demonstrate as much of what they are able to do if they do not trust that you are interested, listening, and willing to pay attention and engage with them. Teachers who observe and document do not have to withdraw from the group and sit in a corner writing observation notes. Observation and documentation should not take away from good teaching!

When to Observe and Document

So when is it best to document observations? The most successful teachers pick and choose different documentation strategies and formats and use them at different times of the day. Such teachers are always ready to put down their pen and paper and engage fully with the children. If they have a variety of strategies in mind and use them consistently, they create documentation of their observations that helps them know children better and plan appropriately for them throughout the day.

You will discover what works best for you as you experiment with different times to fit in observation and documentation. We recommend that you try documenting your observations at the following times:

- in the moment with the child
- as soon as possible after the event
- when you can step out of the action to observe
- in reflection

In the Moment with the Child

You have most likely experienced the thrill of seeing a child accomplish something and wanting to remember and document the activity. What you observed might fit into developmental criteria or match the language of your state's early learning guidelines. It might be reflective of the child's achieving a certain milestone. Or you might be seeing the child do something for the first time. You recognize that what you are seeing is important and should be written down as quickly as possible. So you grab your clipboard, notepad, or electronic device and you record your observation right then.

The advantage of being able to observe and document what you are seeing right away is that you are capturing the authentic, spontaneous actions of children. Because you are recording so close to the event, it is easier for you to remember details and direct quotes of the child's language.

Pam: I used the back of a paper bag in the room to write observations on because I couldn't find any paper. But they had this great conversation going, and I was actually going to be able to write everything down. I found a paper bag and a pencil, and I'm writing on the back of a paper bag!

Peggy W.: I am constantly observing—that is why I keep a few index cards in my pocket so that I can write notes on them. When I see something begin to unfold and want to gain more written information, I grab a spiral notebook and begin to take more detailed notes.

To do this, you must have documentation tools handy. Many teachers carry pads of sticky notes and a pen in their pockets. Sometimes teachers have written down the moments they observe on scraps of paper with crayons or anything that was close by and could be used. If time doesn't allow you to record the full observation, short notes written in the moment can still capture the basics of what the child did and serve as a "memory jogger" later. When you're ready, you can use this note to remind yourself so you can fill in the missing details. And any of these methods can be used on an electronic device.

As Soon as Possible after the Event

Another time for documentation is as soon as possible after the event. Sometimes you are just too busy with the children and cannot document an observation as it is occurring. You might be busy cleaning up after snack when you observe a child across the room doing something you want to document. Your job is to finish cleaning up rather than worry about finding a way to document your observation. So you observe the child while you wash up, trying hard to focus on the details you want to remember, and then document what you have seen as soon as possible after the fact. The advantage of this type of documentation is that you are able to observe and still complete the tasks of running a classroom.

But there are also some disadvantages to waiting to document until after the event.

- **You may forget important details.** The longer you wait to document something, the more likely you are to forget parts of the activity or behavior that was observed. The sooner you write it down, the more likely you are to remember it accurately.
- **It's hard to document complete language samples a while after you heard them.** Remembering after the fact every word that a child said is close to impossible. The best you can do is to get the gist of what was said, hopefully with a few direct quotes included.
- **It's harder to be objective and descriptive in the anecdote.** The more time that passes between the initial actions of the child and the documentation of those actions, the more you may tend to write down interpretations of what happened instead of simply a factual description. Internally editing yourself as you write down observations after the event will help you keep the anecdote objective.

Again, a memory jogger may be helpful. Some teachers find they can fit in a quick moment to snap a photograph of the child in action. The photo,

Valerie: I generally document directly following the activity. I utilize the clipboard (each child has one designated for his or her data collection) if the activity we are doing involves working on one of the children's goals or objectives.

Jodi: As the children are playing, if I see a child demonstrating something new, or a skill that I have no documentation for, I will jot it down as quickly as possible. Sometimes I must rely on my memory and write what I saw after the children have left. Taking pictures and documenting what was seen later is another method I've used.

then, serves to jog their memory when they find time to record more of a description of what the child was doing. A child's work sample (such as a painting, art creation, or writing sample) can also be a memory jogger. As you put the painting, creation, or writing sample in the child's cubby or display it on a bulletin board, you can write a more extensive description of what the child did and said as they worked on it.

When You Can Step Out of the Action

For those of you teaching in teams, another way to observe and document is to step out of the daily action for a while. This is a wonderful way to learn about children because your only responsibilities are listening, watching, and writing. You and your colleagues must decide who will step out of the action, when that will fit into the day, and who will supervise the children. This takes coordination, communication, and planning. For example, during a story-reading time with the large group, one teacher may read the story and attempt to maintain the interest and engagement of all the children. The other teacher may then sit near the story area and take notes during the reading activity. They are always ready to step back into the action if something happens—if a child's safety is of concern or if their colleague needs help with a child's behavior. Then the observation and documentation stop, and they interact with the children as needed.

Stepping out of the action may also happen spontaneously. There will be occasional moments when the children are all busily engaged. You look around the room and realize that none of the children needs your intervention or assistance. This is the time to take a few minutes to sit and write what you are seeing them do. You might observe a specific child you have been wondering about or a group of children involved in an activity. Again, you are always ready to step back into the action if the children need you. Realistically, the older the children in the class, the more likely you'll have time to step out of the action. When caring for infants and toddlers, stepping out of the action may happen infrequently. Infant and toddler teachers almost always need to be available to the young ones in their care. The growing independence of preschoolers may allow for more times when watching children in this manner is possible.

The advantage of observing and documenting out of the action is that you can concentrate more fully on what you are observing and documenting. You may be able to write a very detailed description or include language samples with direct quotes from a child. Many different recording methods can be effective because you can look across the classroom for a longer period of time, following one specific child's choices and time engagements or tracking several children at a time. The disadvantage is

Deanna: I found my documentation style through much trial and error. What works for one person may be different than what works for another. What I found easiest was to create an envelope for each child with their name and photo on the front. On index cards, I write a description of what the child did and/or said, related content areas, the date, and if there is a photo or work sample to refer back to. Then I put the finished note in the child's envelope.

the planning and coordination with colleagues involved and the interruptions that can occur when you need to step back in and assist the children.

But you never want to use observation and documentation as a reason *not* to interact with children. Your job is to relate to children, be interested in what they are doing, and talk with them as they play or go about daily routines. Stepping out of the action to observe and document should only occur in brief segments of time so you can continue to be fully engaged as a facilitator and a caring adult with the children.

In Reflection

Reflection is another option for recording observations. Sitting down at naptime or at the end of the day and reflecting back on what you have seen may be the only realistic way to document what has happened with the children in your care. This is especially true if you spend your days as the only adult with a group of children. Regardless of whether you work alone, to use reflection time most effectively, you can jog your memory with a variety of cues: photographs, brief notes, conversations with colleagues, and work samples.

During your time with the children, you might have time only to document their actions with photographs but not to sit and write down what you have observed. Or you might have jotted down very brief notes or used a check sheet to help remind you of what you want to remember about the children that day. (A little later in this chapter, we'll show examples of recording sheets for quick documentation.) Then you can use those photos, brief notes, and recording sheets at naptime, the end of the day, or even at the end of the week to help you remember what went on. If you use a digital camera or take photos with an electronic device, you can look over the photos at the end of the day or week. Saving children's drawings, paintings, writing samples, or other creations (or taking a photograph of them) may also help you remember the details of the observation.

When you schedule reflection time, those of you working in teaching teams will find that talking with your colleagues helps everyone's memory. Scheduling a debriefing time of just five minutes each day can help your team get more documentation done. We call this meeting time "Take Five" and urge you to make it a regular aspect of your work with your colleagues. Figure out a time when you can take five minutes to sit and talk together. Consider what documentation you might want to get done at that time. The conversation is brief. The focus is on the question "What happened today that we don't want to forget?" As you determine the answer to that question, you can assign the writing tasks among the group to divide up the workload of documentation.

Elizabeth: Realistically, I fit in documentation between my a.m. and p.m. classes, after the children leave, in the evening when I'm at home, or in the morning before children arrive.

Deanna: I always found my coworkers to be an asset when it came to reviewing and discussing everyone's observations. This helped us get an even better understanding of where our infants and toddlers were at and what steps we needed to take to ensure each child had the opportunity to gain new skills. We would discuss ways we could help a child during caregiving routines, materials we wanted to include in the environment, or questions we could ask a family to help us better care for their child.

Cathy: I write observations of the children on sticky notes. And sometimes my teaching assistant contributes. We later discuss the child's strengths and next steps for our IEPs [individualized education programs]. This way we can really get at who each child is—their growth, how their strengths evolve, and where they are in their development in different domains.

If you work in a program where all children depart at the same time, you may schedule this time after the children leave. Before you clean the room or set up for the next session, take five minutes for discussion. If you work in a program where shifts of caregivers overlap, we encourage you to find a way to take five minutes for some debriefing and discussion about what was observed and what documentation should be completed. We know this is challenging, and yet we hear from teachers how valuable it is. The following is a documentation of a Take Five discussion among a team of caregivers, Mariah and Jason, who care for mobile infants.

Mariah noticed that all of the mobile infants in their room were sleeping (not always a common occurrence) and decided to take advantage of the moment to meet with Jason for five minutes to reflect on what they had observed so far that day and complete some documentation. The two sat in rocking chairs with the children's file folders divided on their laps. Mariah asked, "What have we seen today that we don't want to forget?" Jason answered, "It looks like Kyle is just about ready to walk. He's cruising, holding on to shelves, starting to let go, and balancing briefly. I think he may take steps on his own any day." Mariah agreed that this was an important observation, so Jason wrote a brief note about Kyle's balance and their plan to continue to observe him and build on the observation as Kyle developed the capability to walk. Mariah said, "And, I noticed Keisha playing with the shape sorter. She continued to problem solve, turning shapes and trying to fit them until they went in. I'll write about that." Just then, a child began to stir, and they ended their conversation.

This same kind of discussion could happen at the end of the week, especially if your teaching team has a dedicated planning time. Before you begin planning for the next week, ask yourselves, "What happened this week that we don't want to forget?" and again divide up the writing task so important information is documented. For both Take Five and planning sessions, it helps to have a list of the children's names so no one is overlooked. And it can be helpful to have your early learning guidelines, curricular objectives, or assessment tool handy as well. In this way, you and your colleagues will be focused on what you need to be documenting for accountability purposes.

Taking a few minutes at home is another way to use reflection as a means of recalling the activities of the day. Early childhood professionals often find that they think about the children in their care even after

Jarrod: When we take the time to reflect and discuss individual children, I find it really helpful in making specific plans.

leaving the workday. Taking a moment to write down those thoughts adds to the collection of observation information you are putting together for each child.

The advantage of documenting in reflection is that it fits into the context of a busy and active day with children. Reflective anecdotes tend to be more of a summary in nature. And this can be an advantage: When looking back, you have the whole picture in mind. You can think through the events of the day and place the child's actions in context. The written observation can cover several times of the day and note any patterns in the child's behavior and interactions. Noting how the child has gone about a task in the past as compared to that day helps document the progress the child is making.

The downside is that it is difficult to remember an event after a long day. And if you wait until the end of the week, recalling exactly what happened is very hard. Details become cloudy, and objectivity is always a concern. The more you can use various cues to jog your memory, the more successful this type of documentation can be.

Where to Document Observations

There are many different materials and some time-saving formats and technologies available to use when documenting your observations. Sometimes it's most important to have paper and a pen in your pocket or nearby to quickly write down what you are seeing. Sticky-note pads, index cards, notebooks, and clipboards can all be easily transported around the classroom and used to write down anecdotal information. Small square sticky pads easily fit in pockets. The lined five-by-seven-inch size allows for more room to include child quotes and detailed observation notes. Other providers use small spiral-bound notebooks of index cards. The cards are perforated for easy removal to place in a child's file at a later time. These kinds of notebooks are also small enough to carry (with a pen) around the classroom. Electronic devices like cell phones (if allowed) and tablets can also be useful for entering brief notes and observations, as well as for snapping photos or recording videos.

Small spiral-bound notebooks with lined paper can also be used. Some teachers prefer a three-ring binder with lined or unlined paper. Three-ring binders are larger and must be carried around the classroom if they are to be handy for quick documentation. To avoid this, place more than one binder with the same setup in various spots throughout the room so they are easily available when needed. Many teachers divide the binder(s) into sections for each child. They may also prepare the papers for each child ahead of time so specific areas for observation are identified.

Lillian: I carry a binder as well as my camera with me so that when anything I want to document happens, I have pen and paper ready and can snap a quick photograph. Documentation can happen at any time. I especially enjoy documenting children's conversations during their play.

Jodi: I have struggled with different documentation strategies. I have used sticky notes and jotted things down. I have also tried a clipboard with each child's name on it to assure that I have documentation on each child. I also take photographs of children's work.

It's important to try out different documentation strategies and figure out not only what works best for your personal style but also which strategies are more successful in various situations in your time with the children. We recommend you try memory joggers, along with the several observation formats below.

Memory Joggers

Memory joggers can be brief notes, photographs, or children's work samples that you capture on the run as you interact with the children. They are a way for you to create a very short documentation that will jog your memory when you go back and fill in the details later. While you are engaged with the children, you can write very short notes on sticky notes, index cards, small pads, adhesive labels, or electronic devices. Some teachers use clipboards with notebook paper to write down brief comments. To be more focused on specific children, some teachers place sheets of blank address-size labels on a clipboard and print the children's names on them. The labels used for documentation are removed and placed in those children's folders. The next day, the teacher can be sure to observe the children whose labels remain on the clipboard.

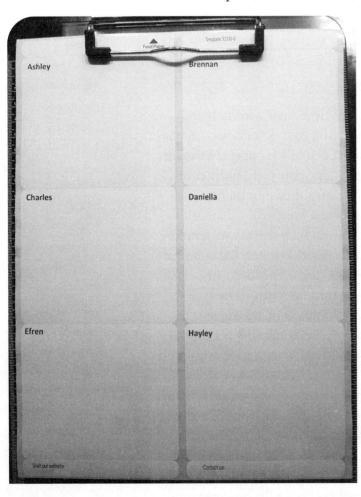

You then fill out the details of the observation at a later time—whether that is at naptime, during specials, at the end of the day, or during your weekly planning meeting.

Following are some examples of brief notes teachers wrote in the moment with the children followed by more detailed notes completed when the teachers were able to reflect and jog their memories.

Initial observation: Dylan and Malik—lining up bears, counting 1–10, singing "Ants Go Marching"

Details added at end of day: Today Dylan was lining up the bears. "I'm lining up the army," he said. As he lined them up, he sang "The Ants Go Marching" (which we learned last week). As he sang, he added bears. He counted correctly with one-to-one correspondence from one to ten but did not maintain one-to-one beyond ten. Malik approached and asked if he could play. Dylan said, "Sure. Do you want to sing?" They continued singing the song as they added bears.

Initial observation: Alissa—alphabet puzzle

Details added at end of day: Today Alissa went to the puzzle shelf and pulled out the ABC puzzle and dumped out all of the letters on the table. I observed as she placed each letter in its place, saying the letter, looking at the picture on the letter piece, and saying the word for that picture (each begins with that letter). She worked at this for approximately ten minutes and then called me over to show me what she had done. "I know all my ABCs!" she said.

You can also take photos or collect work samples while engaged with the children and use them as memory joggers. At a later time, you review the photo or work sample and write a description of what the child did and said related to that experience (again, you can do this at naptime, during specials, at the end of the day, or during your weekly planning meeting). Here are some examples.

Description written at a later time: Samir played with our collection of plastic animals and sorted the ones that live in the ocean by placing them in our "ocean" (a bowl of water). When he finished, he counted how many he had in the water. "I have fifteen!" He did indeed have fifteen sea creatures in his ocean.

Description written at a later time: Today Darla drew a picture of a person and brought it to me. I asked her to indicate the various parts of the face and body using sign language, but she did not respond. She did point to the marks at the top of the page and signed, "My name."

Observation Formats

We have designed several observation formats that allow you to quickly note information about children. You can find blank copies of these formats in appendix B or on the Focused Observations product page at www.redleafpress.org.

Depending on the situation, you can use one of the following:

- Observation Record with Common Preschool Domains
- Observation Record with Open Domains
- Quick Check Recording Sheet
- Brief Notes Recording Sheet
- Small-Group Observation Form

For each of these formats, you will review the recording sheet after the event and use it to write a fuller description of what the child did and said related to that experience (again, you can do this at naptime, during specials, at the end of the day, or during your weekly planning meeting).

Observation Records The Observation Record with Common Preschool Domains identifies domains usually found in most preschool guidelines or assessment tools. Another Observation Record is provided with no identified domains. This format allows you to fill in the domains that are most appropriate for your program. You may look to your state's infant/toddler or preschool guidelines or assessment tools to identify the domains that you will focus on as you record what each child is doing. You can also use this second format if you teach in a special education setting. You can record observations related to the IFSP or IEP goals for children with identified disabilities.

Quick Check Recording Sheet Instead of labels, clipboards can also hold a piece of paper with a class list or a Quick Check Recording Sheet with all of the children's names on it. Recording in this way is quick and easy, especially when working with a small group of children. You can jot down information about more than one child at a time and still be interacting with them, guiding the activity at hand.

For some observations, making check marks or very brief notes is appropriate. For others, this format will not work. The Quick Check Recording Sheet can be used when only very brief notation is needed. Some guidelines or indicators lend themselves more to this kind of documentation, and some do not. Most gross-motor skills can be notated in this brief manner, as can many fine-motor ones. However, a child's developing receptive and expressive language would not lend itself to this kind of documentation, nor would their developing social-emotional capabilities or cognitive problem solving. It's important to consider matching this recording format to appropriate indicators. In chapter 6, we examine this matching process in more detail as we contrast it with more informative portfolio documentation.

Look at the first column of the completed Quick Check Recording Sheet that follows. The teacher was observing children's skills with scissors. For those children who cut with ease, the teacher made a check mark. For those children who did not, she left the space blank. You can decide what kind of mark you want to make (such as an X or a no) to help keep the information clear for future reference.

The second column of the completed sheet shows another way to record brief notes in this format. The focus of the observation was counting objects with one-to-one correspondence. In this case, the answers were recorded with

Quick Check Recording Sheet

Children's Names	Date and Activity cutting with scissors 9/14	Date and Activity counts with 1-to-1 corr. 9/20	Date and Activity	Date and Activity
Ashley	✔	5		
Brian		3		
Cameron				
David	✔	20		
Ebony		6		

the number to which each child counted with one-to-one correspondence (for one child it was only three, while for another it was twenty).

Teachers with whom we have worked report that looking at their required expectations and determining which can be documented in this way is very helpful. They are able to do this documentation quickly and give more attention to observations that require descriptive notes. And they say that the quick check format allows them to see trends across their whole group of students and plan curriculum accordingly.

Brief Notes Recording Sheet Sometimes you want to include more information while still keeping your notes very short. The Brief Notes Recording Sheet puts the full list of children you are observing in front of you and lets you write down more than just a check mark or a yes or no.

This form might be used when you are sitting with children and helping them listen to your colleague read a story. You might note next to each child's name who was responding to the story by asking questions or making related comments. Or if you are working with a small group of children to create patterns with colored beads, you would have more room to write down the information about each child's pattern on the Brief Notes Recording Sheet.

Small-Group Observation Form For small-group times with children, you may also want to use a format designed by April Garcia, a teacher in Las Cruces, New Mexico. As you can see, this form can be used to record observations for up to twelve children at a time as you work with them on a specific activity and/or goal.

• • •

The benefit of using any of these recording sheets is that you see exactly who has been observed and who has been missed. This system ensures that no child is neglected when you are doing your observations. Again, clipboards with these forms must be carried around the classroom so they are handy for quick documentation. As with three-ring binders, one solution is to have multiple clipboards with the same setup so they can be placed in various spots throughout the room to be easily available when needed.

File folders are also easily transported around the classroom. You can use a file folder that contains sticky notes or index cards on which to write. On the following page are two easy-to-make designs for file folder documentation.

A File Folder with Sticky Notes

1. Open a file folder and lay it flat.

2. Using a ruler and marker, divide the folder into boxes, one for each child. (A letter-size file folder can be divided into twenty-four approximately three-by-three-inch boxes. If you are responsible for fewer than twenty-four children or want more space and larger notes, make the boxes larger.)

3. Label the boxes with each of the children's names.

4. Place sticky notes into these boxes as observations are written on them. Be sure to record the child's name on the sticky note so you can continue to easily find the child's square.

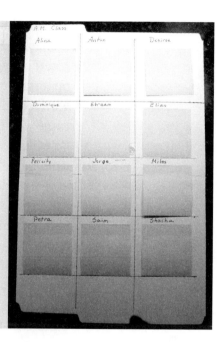

Folder with Index Cards

1. Open a file folder and lay it flat.

2. Using clear tape, layer the index cards from bottom to top so that only the bottom inch or so of the card is visible. Up to fifteen index cards can fit on each side of the file folder.

3. On that bottom inch of each card, write a child's name, one for each child.

4. Write observations for a child on their card, flipping up the other cards as necessary to access the card you need to write on. When a card is full, it can easily be removed and replaced with another.

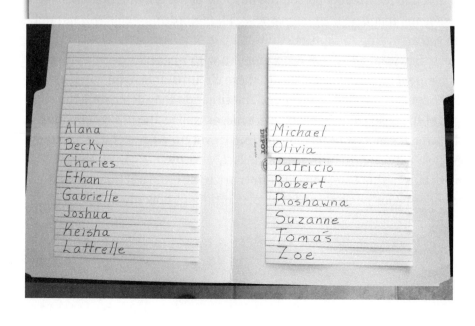

In addition to good old-fashioned pen and paper, technology is readily available for teachers to use for observation and documentation. Digitally recording young children's actions and emerging language provides the opportunity to document a lot of information at one time. The problem with recording is that you must review the video or audio recording, determine which portions are significant, and decide how best to use them. So when using these technologies, you must include reflection and review time, as well as make a plan for writing down the information recorded.

Early educators can work with the observations within the device's applications, download the files to their computer, or text or email them to the child's family members. In this way, families can see their child in action at the program. The immediacy and ease of technology can be very enticing. And, if used well, such programs can be wonderful tools. However, there are cautions related to using this technology. Sometimes the many applications can distract educators from focusing on interactions with the children—the most important part of the job.

As teachers try out these different documentation strategies and begin the daily practice of a Take Five reflection meeting, they will want to consider which methods worked best in which situations. Each teacher needs to figure out the ways they can be most successful at documenting the observations they want to remember—that involves trial and error to determine what's best for each individual. Teachers may learn that their colleagues prefer different methods than they do—that's not a problem as long as everyone is committed to collecting documentation that will help them know children better.

How Much to Record

How much to record depends on the purpose of the documentation as well as the format that best fits that purpose. The recording sheets will not work when you are trying to capture children's use of language or are describing how they went about solving a problem with materials or resolving a disagreement with another child. In these circumstances you will need to document with more description. The situation may determine the length of the description. If you have time, as well as the luxury of being undisturbed, you may be able to document everything the child says and does. If you are documenting after the fact, your memory may not recall every detail. In this case, you can summarize the child's actions in your description. Your personal style can also influence how much you write or document. Some teachers prefer to use complete sentences and tell a story. Others tend to be list makers who highlight the important things they saw in bulleted points on the page.

In this section we describe three formats for observation:

- running records
- summaries
- lists

Running Records

This form of documentation is helpful but not always easily implemented because of the need for few distractions. Therefore, we do not recommend you use it very often. To do a running record well, you step out of the action and remain undisturbed so you can capture on paper everything you are seeing the child do and hearing them say. To do this, you will need to coordinate with your colleagues to make sure the children are well supervised while you observe. A clipboard and notepaper or a handheld electronic device, if you prefer typing, is helpful for this kind of documentation, because you will write more than with some of the other formats. This kind of observation requires writing or typing fast! You may need to develop a shorthand or series of abbreviations for yourself. You can also dictate a running record into your electronic device (but will have to listen to it at a later time to remind yourself of what you observed). Many teachers identify children in running records by using the first letter of their first names. A running record requires intense focus. Setting a time limit and staying true to it makes this task more manageable. Fifteen minutes may be about the maximum amount of time to allot so you are not exhausted trying to watch and write for a longer period. Here are two examples of running records.

Priscylla (two years, four months)

P. is sitting on the floor with the shape sorter. P. picks up the square shape with her right hand and pushes it into the square opening. P. picks up the circle shape with her right hand and pushes it into the container. She picks up the triangle shape and pushes it into the triangle-shaped hole. This took place over a two-minute period.

Skye (four years, four months)

S. goes to art area, gets brown construction paper. Folds it with both hands. Then with right hand cuts blue papers in small rectangle shapes. Puts shapes in folded brown paper. Brings them to me and says, "Here's a book with blue Band-Aids." Goes back and folds a light purple paper. Reopens it and closes it several times. Makes a cut on one side and says, "That airplane doesn't work." Gets a dark purple paper, folds it, and makes several cuts in it. Brings me both papers and says, "This airplane doesn't work, and here's another kind of airplane." Goes back to the table, cuts some newspaper, and says, "Bigger Band-Aids." Gets four pieces of paper and cuts out a shape that she drew. Cuts all four pieces, comes to me and says, "Here's some bigger Band-Aids, and I cut this out." Puts them on the table with the book and airplanes. Goes back, gets another purple paper, a pencil, crayon, glue, and buttons. Turns the glue upside down and then back right side up. Using both hands, squeezes the bottle and turns the lid. Pounds the bottle on the table. Looks at the bottle, pokes the tip with her finger. Twists the top again then squeezes the glue onto the newspaper that is on the table. Then glues buttons on the purple paper and draws her "heart helicopter." After she tells me about her picture, she says, "I'm done. Now I'll clean up." This was over a fifteen-minute period.

Summaries

Running records tend to be long, especially if they take place across a fairly extended period of time, as with the anecdote about Skye. A less time-consuming way to write about a child's extensive involvement is to summarize what they do and say. The summative anecdote is still factual and descriptive in nature, but it does not include every single detail of the child's actions and words. Instead, it gives the highlights. The previous observation about Skye is very long and detailed. Here are four sentences that summarize Skye's actions and words. Read through them and see if you still get the same information and understanding of Skye and her capabilities.

> **Skye** (four years, four months)
>
> Skye goes to the art area and stays for over fifteen minutes folding and cutting papers, using her right hand to cut. She puts the shapes in the folded paper and tells me, "Here's a book with blue Band-Aids." She glues buttons on a paper, squeezing and pounding to get the glue out. She tells me her picture is a "heart helicopter," then says, "I'm done. Now I'll clean up."

This summary is much shorter. Unimportant details such as the colors of the paper, the exact steps she took to fold and cut each set of papers, and the sequence she followed to unclog the glue bottle are deleted. Those deletions are a judgment call on the part of the writer. If you were Skye's teacher and you thought her patience and multiple attempts with the glue bottle were an important indicator of how she goes about solving a problem without exhibiting frustration, you might choose to include that information.

Summaries do involve some judgment in what is included and what is not. However, they provide a more efficient way of recording what children are doing and can be focused to help provide information about specific areas of development. They are also helpful for looking at a child's actions across time. The following summary gives information about how Adam routinely comforts himself. This note is a compilation of several observations across time. Evaluation and interpretation are still not included; only factual description is written. Yet the reader has a clear picture of how Adam handles himself when upset or sad.

> **Adam** (twelve months)
>
> Adam comforts himself by sucking on his finger and also by drinking his bottle. I have observed him comfort himself both ways on multiple occasions.

Lists

Some teachers find that writing lists or bulleted points fits their own personal style of thinking more closely than writing out full sentences or telling more of a story in the anecdote. As shown in the following examples, lists can be especially good for recording a child's spoken words or tracking a sequence of activities in which the child engages. As long as a reader can look at the list and figure out exactly what the child was doing, this type of anecdote can be another effective way to get information down quickly.

> **David** (one year, ten months)
>
> Today David said: Lala, Yello (Angelo), airpane (airplane), Dan, tash (trash), bu (blue), and marka (marker)

> **Jessica** (four years, five months)
>
> At the bathroom, waits her turn to use toilet, talks with other children.
>
> Toilets independently.
>
> Washes her hands; with no reminding uses soap.
>
> Laughs and hugs teacher.
>
> Goes to snack table.

Jordan: I had to learn not to write a running record and not stress about it. Photos were helpful to add more information to my brief written descriptions.

How Much Detail to Include in Your Observation Notes

Quality documentation can be brief. Good anecdotes include enough facts so that when other adults read them, they can clearly picture the child's actions. If teachers try to write down everything they see children doing, they will not have time to do anything else! Therefore, they need to set goals for their observations and make choices about what and how much to document. The best documentation is often brief, focused, and to the point. It is not necessary to write a running record of everything a child does and says in a set period of time.

Two to four sentences or phrases describing the child's actions, engagement, and interactions can be very informative when teachers make sure they do the following:

- Indicate the purpose of the observation.
- Include the necessary details to meet the proposed purpose.
- Check that the unique characteristics and capabilities of the child being observed shine through in the documentation.

Here are two examples of documented observations to consider. Can you determine the purpose? What details led you to that conclusion? What did you learn about each of the children?

During free choice, Emily organized a group of students to use playdough at the sensory table. She used both signs and her voice as she asked each child. Once all the children were gathered, she divided the playdough and kept reminding them that they must share. The group remained at the sensory table for twenty-five minutes. Their play became interactive, and they had an in-depth conversation about the zoo.

Purpose: To capture Emily's ability to socialize and communicate with others

Details: Descriptions of Emily's actions and the results

Individuality: Shows Emily's initiative and leadership in forming a group of peers

What are some purposes for observations? Generally, teachers focus their observations on what children are showing they can do in various domains. If a teacher is trying to write down how a child uses their fine-motor skills, then they will want to include details about their use of their hands and fingers to manipulate small objects or writing or drawing tools. The teacher will pay attention to the child's hand-eye coordination as they work with materials. If a teacher is trying to show a child's progress in mathematical problem solving, they will want to include a history of what the child has done when figuring out quantities or spatial relationships and then relate that to the current observation. Because of the identified focus, the teacher knows that they do not have to include every single thing the child does or says. Instead, they edit themselves as they write, asking, "What are the essential things to include related to the purpose of this observation?"

Here's an example of an anecdote that is missing some key details.

Tanya (three years, six months)

Tanya did a very good job putting together several puzzles in a row.

In analyzing this observation note, you can see that interpretive language was included in saying "a very good job." Instead of writing such a broad, evaluative statement, it would be better to include specific details to help the reader see what is meant by "a very good job." Such details might include the following:

- the type and difficulty of the puzzles. Were these puzzles with knobs, with clear outlines of where the pieces went, or with no clear delineation of where each piece should go? Was there a picture on a box for her to follow, and did she do so?
- the number of pieces in the puzzles
- the number of puzzles she completed
- how Tanya worked: by herself, with another child, or with an adult helping her
- the amount of time she spent at the task

Here's a rewritten version of the anecdote about Tanya. This note is longer than the first but not excessively so (it is still three sentences). Now readers have a much clearer idea of how Tanya went about working with puzzles.

> **Tanya** (three years, six months)
>
> Tanya goes to the puzzle table and puts together three eight- to ten-piece puzzles with the pieces outlined on the puzzle board. She then takes out a twenty-five-piece floor puzzle and puts it together, looking back at the picture on the box to check where pieces went. "I did it!" she announces when finished.

You do not need to write very lengthy observation notes as long as you include the important details. Length does not equal quality. Keeping that in mind encourages you to be more efficient in your use of language as you write about what you have seen the children do.

• • • • • • •

We recognize that teaching involves being *with* the children, being present and available, being observant and responsive. Documentation should not take away from teaching. Rather, it should contribute to the teaching process by helping teachers gather the information they need to better meet each child where they are and to help them continue to grow and learn.

There are many ways to fit in observation and still have time to interact fully with the children.

Planning and flexibility are the keys to success. The process will be more doable when you try out different times to document, experiment with different recording formats, and figure out what works best for you. In the next chapter, we present ways of using observation and documentation for assessment purposes.

• • • • • • •

Danielle: All of this documentation has made my work easier. Being able to look at and reflect on all of the documentation is really helping to guide instruction. We know what children are interested in—we know what the next steps should be—rather than just pulling it out of the air.

Observation Practice #8:
Running Record

Purpose: To practice writing down everything you can that a child does or says in a set period of time.

What to Do: Watch Video Clip #8 (scan the QR code or go to www.vimeo .com/1022181547) of preschoolers getting their coats on to go outdoors. Focus on three-year-old London, the girl in the short-sleeved blue dress putting on her purple jacket. As you watch, try to write a running record— writing down everything you see London doing.

Guiding Questions: After viewing, consider the ease or difficulty of trying this type of documentation. Could it be done while you were in the middle of running a busy classroom? How practical is such a recording method for your setting? If you are involved in a group discussion, share some of the running records recorded by the group and discuss the previous questions.

Observation Practice #9:
Summative Anecdote

Purpose: To practice writing an observation note that summarizes what you have seen a child do in just two to four sentences.

What to Do: Watch Video Clip #9 (scan the QR code or go to www.vimeo .com/1022181565) of preschoolers playing at the sensory table. We suggest that you focus on the children closest to the camera, three-year-old London on the right and five-year-old Peter on the left. Do not write down your observation while you are watching. Instead, after the clip is over, write down two to four sentences summarizing what you saw the children do. Remember to be factual and descriptive, not interpretive.

Guiding Questions: After viewing, consider the ease or difficulty of trying this type of documentation. Could it be done while you were in the middle of running a busy classroom? How practical is such a recording method for your setting? If you are involved in a group discussion, share some of the summative records recorded by the group and discuss the previous questions.

Observation Practice #10:
Making a List

Purpose: To practice writing an observation note that is a list of what you have seen a child do.

What to Do: Watch Video Clip #10 (scan the QR code or go to www.vimeo .com/1022181585) and focus on Maricella, the four-year-old girl in a long-sleeved, ruffled blue shirt, at the opening group time of the day. Pay close attention to the things she does and says. Either as you watch or afterward, make a list of the things you saw the child do. Do not worry about complete sentences or descriptive phrases. Try to be efficient in your use of words. Still remember to be factual and descriptive, not interpretive.

Guiding Questions: After viewing, consider the ease or difficulty of trying this type of documentation. Could it be done while you were in the middle of running a busy classroom? How practical is such a recording method for your setting? If you are involved in a group discussion, share some of the lists recorded by the group and discuss the previous questions.

Observation Practice #11:
Using the Quick Check Recording Sheet

Purpose: To practice observation and recording by identifying one skill ahead of time and noting the children's accomplishment of that skill quickly on a check sheet.

What to Do: Before you watch Video Clip #11 (scan the QR code or go to www.vimeo.com/1022181605) of preschoolers using writing tools on white-boards, list the children's names (four-year-old Maricella; five-year-old Peter; and four-and-one-half-year-old Mariana) on a Quick Check Recording Sheet (you can copy the form from appendix B in the book or print it out from the Focused Observations product page at www.redleafpress.org). Determine which skill(s) you are observing that can be noted with a brief notation or check mark. Some of the choices that you might focus on include the following:

- right- or left-handedness
- appropriate grasp of the writing tool
- ability to make letterlike shapes or recognizable letters
- writing from left to right

Watch the video clip and record appropriately.

Guiding Questions: After viewing, consider the ease or difficulty of trying this type of documentation. Could it be done while you were in the middle of running a busy classroom? How practical is such a recording method for your setting? If you are involved in a group discussion, share some of the Quick Check Recording Sheets completed by the group and discuss the previous questions.

Observation Practice #12:
Documenting Observations of a Group of Children

Purpose: To practice writing observation information about a group of children.

What to Do: Before watching Video Clip #12 (scan the QR code or go to www.vimeo.com/1022181626) of a group of preschool children listening to a story, determine what specific information you want to record with a brief note about each child (focus on five-year-old Peter in the red shirt, four-year-old Maricella in the ruffled, long-sleeved blue shirt, and three-year-old London in the short-sleeved blue dress) on a Brief Notes Recording Sheet (you can copy the form from appendix B in the book or print it out from the Focused Observations product page at www.redleafpress.org). Here are some of the choices you might focus on:

- pays attention to the story being read
- responds to the teacher's questions
- interacts in the story-reading experience with related ideas and comments

Write the first initial of each child's name on the recording sheet and observe the story time, taking brief notes about each child. Do not worry about complete sentences or descriptive phrases. Try to be efficient in your use of words. Still remember to be factual and descriptive, not interpretive.

Guiding Questions: After viewing, consider the ease or difficulty of this type of documentation. How practical is such a recording method for your setting? If you are involved in a group discussion, share some of the Brief Notes Recording Sheets completed by the group and discuss the previous questions.

Reflection

Purpose: To reflect on which methods of documentation and reflection are effective in your setting.

What to Do: Think about your work setting. Which of the following times will realistically work best for you to fit in observing and writing down what you are seeing? It's likely that you may have more than one time:

- in the moment with the child
- as soon as possible after the event
- when you can step out of the action in teamwork with your colleagues
- in individual reflection or Taking Five with colleagues

Will you combine some? How will you work with your colleagues to figure out what's best for your setting?

Finding Your Observation Style

Purpose: To determine what kind of documentation best fits your observation style.

What to Do: Keep a record in your journal of your experiences and provide examples of how you used each type of documentation we've discussed: memory joggers, Observation Record with Common Preschool Domains, Observation Record with Open Domains, Quick Check Recording Sheet, Brief Notes Recording Sheet, Small-Group Observation Form, running records, summative anecdotes, and lists. Which ones appeal to your own style of teaching, organization, observation, and writing? Why?

CHAPTER 5

How Do You Observe and Document for Assessment?

▲▼▲▼▲

As you learn to focus your observations and become more adept at fitting observation and documentation into your days with the children, you will find that you see children's development in action more clearly and more often. Your written records and your reflection on what you are seeing will help you communicate more effectively to others about the children. You will be able to show how well the children are doing, to identify possible areas of weakness or delay in a child's development, and to demonstrate how you and your colleagues are planning your curriculum to meet children's needs. Families, community members, and policy makers want evidence of the positive impact of early education and care on young children. Using observation and documentation for assessment is an authentic, child-friendly way to provide the evidence for such accountability.

As you assess children through observation, you can connect what they are doing to your state's early learning guidelines. In this way, you are furthering the accountability of your practices because you are linking assessment, curriculum, and desired goals as recommended in the National Association for the Education of Young Children's position statement on developmentally appropriate practice: "Educators can be intentional about helping children to progress when they know where each child is with respect to learning goals" (NAEYC 2020, 19).

As we noted in chapter 2, assessment that is linked to goals is called criterion-based assessment. You are comparing the performance of children (what you see them do and hear them say) to guidelines (Council of Chief State School Officers [CCSSO] 2011). You are not comparing one child to another. You are tracking the progress of each child compared to the guidelines or goals with which you are working. In this way, you learn about each child's capabilities, and you plan curriculum accordingly. Remember that assessing a child does not mean the same thing as testing a

Diana: I have taught preschool for thirty-five years and always done observations. Now I see something happening and I think, "Oh, that belongs in the reading and writing development part," or "Oh, that belongs in the physical development part," or "Oh, it belongs in two or three different areas." And so I am more organized in how I observe.

Anton: Observing helps me see what children enjoy and how they learn best— anything that will help me to help them achieve their individual goals. Without observation, I cannot meet children's needs so they can meet these goals.

child. Specialists in early childhood education define assessment as a three-step process: First you gather information about children through observation, collection of work samples or photographs, family interviews, and tests. Then you document that information. Finally, you reflect on what you have learned and use that information to make judgments about children's characteristics and decisions about appropriate teaching and care for them (NAEYC 2022).

Notice that tests are only one of several ways to gather the information. The problem with relying too heavily on testing is that the younger the child, the less reliable the test information becomes. You probably have recognized that young children do not follow directions consistently well, and they don't complete paper-and-pencil tasks easily. And your experience is verified by others in the field of early education: "Effective assessment of young children is challenging. The complexity of children's development and learning—including the uneven nature of development and the likelihood of children fully demonstrating their knowledge and skills in different contexts—makes accurate and comprehensive assessment difficult" (NAEYC 2020, 19).

Observation of children performing actual tasks gives a truer picture of their capabilities. It is an "authentic measure"—one that reflects children's real-world performance rather than their performance in contrived, adult-determined tasks that may be unfamiliar to them. Having appealing, hands-on activities in a familiar setting helps children feel comfortable and relaxed, and their manipulation of objects, demonstration of concepts, and use of vocabulary will more accurately reflect what they can do. Observing over time provides opportunities for you to witness the frequency of their performance and evaluate whether skills are truly in their repertoire, just emerging, or not there yet.

The word *assess* comes from the Latin verb *assidere,* which means "sit with." In an assessment you "sit with" the learner. When you assess children, you are nearby. Assessment is something you do *with* and *for* the child, not something you do *to* the child. Too often in this present-day world of accountability and high-stakes evaluation in the public schools, standardized tests with quantitative results are used to pass or fail children. The importance of "sitting with" a child and observing what they can do has been lost. Assessment is now typically interpreted as determining whether a child is performing up to a standard or grade level and, if not, blaming the program for failing to educate the child properly.

In the field of early childhood education, professional recommendations have emphasized returning to the original meaning of the word *assessment,* sitting with children to observe them and learn what they can do. Often these

Elizabeth: Observing children and documenting what they do helps me assess developmentally appropriate milestones, determine how the child has progressed, and write IEP goals that are based on present levels of performance.

assessments are called "authentic." Teachers do not have to set up special times or tasks for assessment to occur. Instead, teachers observe children as they go about play, activities, and daily routines. They document some of those observations, and they relate them to reasonable and accepted criteria.

> Educators use a variety of methods—including reflecting on their knowledge of the community; seeking information from the family; observing the child; examining the child's work; and using authentic, valid, and reliable individual child assessments. (NAEYC 2020, 7)
>
> **Assessment focuses on children's progress toward developmental and educational goals.** Such goals should reflect families' input as well as children's background knowledge and experiences. They should be informed by developmental milestones including use of state early learning standards. Goals should be aspirational and achievable and should foster a sense of pride and accomplishment for educators, families, and children. Children, educators, and families should have opportunities to celebrate both small and large achievements, while recognizing that all children need time to build mastery on a current skill before progressing to the next challenge. (NAEYC 2020, 20)

Appendix C has recommended resources for additional information regarding the best ways to assess young children. Appendix D is a glossary of terms related to different types of assessment. We hope that this information will give you a strong foundation of support for using observation as the primary way you collect information to assess children's development.

How Do Young Children Show What They Know and Can Do?

If tests are not the way that young children show their accomplishments, how do they show what they can and can't do? They show their accomplishments

- through their play and exploration,
- by going about their daily routines, and
- by participating in teacher-designed activities.

You can observe the children in these different situations to see how they demonstrate their skills, understand concepts, and are generally developing.

Play and Exploration

Through play and exploration, children are continuously involved in clarifying and extending their understanding of the world, learning new concepts, and rethinking already known concepts. Research in multiple fields supports the importance of play as a vehicle for learning for young children (Ginsburg 2007; Akingbulu et al. 2022; Wenner 2009). And in its position statement on developmentally appropriate practice, NAEYC (2020, 9) states, "Play is essential for all children, birth through age 8."

As infants play with their toes and respond in babbles and squeals as they are bounced on a caregiver's knee, they show beginning awareness of their own bodies and begin to solidify their relationships with familiar adults. Classic games such as peekaboo and patty-cake are ways in which you engage infants in play, helping them to learn about object permanence and fine-motor control. Toddlers stack up a few blocks and knock them down over and over again, experimenting with their ability to manipulate and balance objects. As they play, they are also learning about the consistency of gravity. With activity boards they push buttons and turn knobs to make sounds and feel the competence that comes from bringing about a predictable result. Young preschoolers imitate typical daily life in the house corner, integrating what they know about families and household tasks. Older preschoolers take their experiences into more complex play, planning a camping trip with set roles and use of a variety of materials to represent the needed camping supplies. Play consumes most of the waking hours of children in early childhood and increases in complexity as children grow and develop.

Play themes that are developed by the children help them to sustain play for ever-increasing periods of time, developing their ability to attend to a task. When you watch children playing in ways that are of interest to them, you see more. You get to know children on a deeper level.

Play also reflects the children's cultural and social understanding, enabling you to have a clearer picture of the influences on their activities and behaviors. For example, their representation of family life in house play will reflect the values, traditions, and heritage in which they are being raised.

Daily Routines

The times when preschoolers are washing their hands, preparing for snack, joining in large-group time, and putting on coats to go outside are all opportunities for you to observe children and learn more about them. Observing infants and toddlers as they separate from their parents

Jodi: When you observe children during play, you discover their learning style, what their interests are, and what they are learning. You observe how they manipulate materials in the classroom, what level of understanding they have, and how complex their play is.

at drop-off or watching them at feeding, diapering, and naptimes can contribute information to your assessment process. As children go about their daily routines, you learn much about their capabilities, their growing independence, their sense of self, and their general personalities. Cultural differences and family approaches to routines also become evident as you observe. In their homes, children may be used to eating in different ways than at your program. The ways they are comforted when going to sleep may vary from family to family. Even the way they approach separating from their family members when they arrive will be different for each child and is based in culture too.

Teacher-Designed Activities

Observing children participating in teacher-designed activities will help you learn more about their development and will guide you in planning other activities for them. Designing specific learning activities for the children is an important part of being an early educator. Sometimes you choose certain materials for them. You may give toddlers blocks to build with. Or you may give preschoolers rice and beans to measure for lunch. You may work with a small group of children with a task that is focused on a cognitive skill, such as matching colors or recognizing their names. You may relate the activity to the interest of the children, making a counting game with bird stickers to go along with the children's interest in the bird-house on your playground. When you are observing children in situations you plan, you can observe for their specific developmental accomplishments in the cognitive, physical, social, and emotional areas. You can also watch them to determine which traits of more general cognitive stages or social-emotional competencies they are showing.

Assessing Children's Cognitive Stages

Jean Piaget (1896–1980) is recognized as one of the foremost scholars regarding how children learn to think. His theory is that young children learn by constructing knowledge for themselves in interactions with the physical world and with other children. He identified important cognitive developmental tasks that children are working on during childhood and emphasized that they need ample time to practice and integrate cognitive concepts. For our purposes in early childhood, it's important to know about the first two stages. Infants and toddlers are in the *sensorimotor* developmental stage. Exploration and direct encounter with objects and others are the primary cognitive tasks. The focus of their learning is physical and takes place through their senses. Preschoolers and children in early

Valerie: When I am observing a child, I look at what areas we need to address from her IEP to allow her to be as independent as possible. This includes being able to physically move around the classroom, eating and drinking, toileting and basic dressing skills, being able to make her wants and needs known, and interacting with peers and adults.

Robin J.: A lot of times my coteacher and I plan activities based on a concept that we want to see. And it really does help. So, for example, if we want to see children's cognitive level or skill at matching, we pull out a matching game. We invite the children to come in small groups to play the game with us so we can see where they are as a group and individually. Then we talk about it after the children leave.

elementary grades are in the *preoperational* developmental stage. Dramatic play, representation through language, and creating are the primary cognitive tasks. The focus of learning for preschoolers is problem solving through trial and error and the development of language.

Here are two descriptions of children at play. The first child is a toddler, the second, a preschooler. Read the anecdotes, and decide which Piagetian stage the children are demonstrating. What are their primary cognitive tasks as evidenced in their behavior and interactions?

Jonas (one year, five months)

Jonas pulls several pillows into a pile, flops onto them, rolls around, and laughs. As the pile thins out with his movements, he gets up, stacks them again, and jumps into them, settling in and smiling broadly.

Daniel (four years, ten months)

Daniel chooses to go to the dramatic play area to play post office. He puts on a mail carrier's uniform. Trejo is already dressed up as a mail carrier and has the mailbag. Daniel stands at the counter to give out stamps. He tells two children to be the mom and the dad. They start playing behind the counter with the stamps. Daniel says, "You're supposed to be the mom and the dad. Hey, you're supposed to be the mom and the dad. Hey, Teacher, I'm trying to tell them to be the mom and the dad." He starts pushing Trejo out from behind the counter. Daniel's voice is raised: "Hey, you're not supposed to be the worker. I'm the worker." The teacher starts to intervene as they start to push each other. She asks Daniel, "What's going on?" "He's not the worker, and he's not supposed to be here." She asks, "What is he doing?" "He's trying to get here. He's trying to be the worker." She says, "Did you ask him what he wanted to be, or did you just tell him what to do?" Daniel changes his tone of voice, making it softer, not yelling: "Hey, do you want to be the worker?" Trejo says "No." Daniel says, "Then you pick up the mail. I'm the worker." Trejo takes off the mailbag and says he doesn't want to do that. Daniel picks it up and says, "Okay, I'm going to pick up the mail. You be the worker." They trade positions.

Jonas is very clearly approaching the world through physical knowing, at the sensorimotor stage. He is playing with his environment and experimenting with his own body. Daniel has moved to representational play, improvising and acting out his understanding of postal workers and post offices. Therefore, he is at the preoperational stage.

Watching children and identifying their cognitive stages can help you meet them at their level and plan activities that work well with the important cognitive tasks they are engaged in at that stage. Toddlers—in the sensorimotor stage—are not interested in making drawings or paintings look like something. Instead, they are only interested in the flow of the marker or chalk on the paper or the texture and feel of the paint. They are paying attention to the process and the sensory information. Preschoolers—in the preoperational stage—may be ready to try drawing and painting actual objects and will probably enjoy the process of doing so. Assessing the children's cognitive stage will help you better match activities and expectations so they experience success.

Assessing cognitive stages will also help you figure out how much you can challenge the children to move ahead in their skills. Lev Vygotsky (1896–1934) wrote that children's learning in all developmental areas takes place in a *zone of proximal development* (also called a ZPD)—a zone in which they do not quite have the skills to be completely successful but with support may very well be able to perform. Observing to figure out each child's ZPD will help you be ready to support the child's growth. You will be less likely to overwhelm the child with activities that are too challenging. Instead, you will be providing just the right amount of challenge for each child. ZPD is discussed again in chapter 7.

Assessing Children's Social-Emotional Competencies

A major part of young children's lives is the development of their social and emotional competency. Erik Erikson (1963) identifies sequential stages in this process:

- **Trust** The first important task in infancy is the development of trust and connection to other human beings.
- **Autonomy** As trust is established, toddlers are then able to separate and be autonomous from the all-important base of love and connection that has been formed with their parents or primary caregivers.
- **Initiative** Preschoolers are learning to use their own ideas to think about and understand the world around them. Initiative is important for young children's healthy personality development. When

encouraged and supported by the adults in their lives, children work on developing competence and on mastering their world.

Observing children's behavior in daily routines as well as in play episodes can help you determine their stage of social-emotional competency. Observing for children's sense of trust, autonomy, and initiative gives you more insight into their approach to the world. Children who are untrusting in your setting will not likely try new things or take risks. You may find it hard to learn more about their cognitive capabilities because they hesitate to play with the sorting materials or read a book with you. The first step is building a relationship with these children so they can relax, feel more comfortable in your program, and start showing you what they can do. On the opposite end of the spectrum, children who have lots of initiative may be hard to teach for a different reason. They are likely to be rowdy, with high energy, and confident about their own capabilities. Recognizing that their sense of mastery of their world is strong may help you and your colleagues see them in a new light and figure out ways to channel their energy.

Read the following anecdotes and identify the ways in which the children are working on the development of trust, autonomy, or initiative. What are they learning to master?

Caleb (twenty-four months)

Caleb's parents are out of town, so he got dropped off at school in the morning by his grandparents. As the grandparents were leaving, the teacher held Caleb. Caleb gave her a hug. The grandparents said, "Have a good day." Caleb blew them a kiss goodbye. He cried for a little while and continued to hug the teacher.

Paul (five years, two months)

Today during outside time, Paul is in the sandbox digging with a friend. "See what we're doing, Teacher?" Paul asks me. He continues to dig and says, "We're raking the holes for the prairie dogs. Want to fill it up?" Paul asks his friend. His friend says, "Sure." Paul continues to talk to his friend. "These are very easy holes. We're digging very deep holes." He pats his bucket of sand and says, "There we go." As Paul digs a little more, he says with a great big smile and eyes wide open, "Hey, I can see the bottom of the sandbox!"

Caleb is developing trust and autonomy. He is able to separate from loved ones, although with some tears, and be comforted by his caregivers. Paul is showing initiative and accomplishment. He follows through with his plan to rake, fill up, and dig. His excitement in digging to the bottom is evident.

Sometimes analyzing the types of play, as first defined by Mildred Parten in 1932, will help you learn more about children's social experiences. You may see children engage in any of the following types of play:

- **Solitary play:** Children play on their own, independently of others.
- **Onlooker play:** Children watch others playing, showing an interest but not entering into the play.
- **Parallel play:** Children play alongside other children without really interacting. This is seen in older toddlers as well as preschoolers.
- **Associative play:** During the preschool years, children's play typically becomes more connected to other children. They want to interact and create play episodes with others. You may see children playing with others, but the play is random, not seeming to have an organized plan among the players.
- **Cooperative play:** In this stage, two or more children have a play theme that they are developing. The sense of togetherness is very strong. Children are performing specific roles in the play. This type of play is the precursor to the next stage, organized games with rules, which emerges in middle childhood.

You can observe children's play to identify which of these types you are seeing. Sometimes a toddler may watch other toddlers at a water table before he joins in, thus demonstrating onlooker play. Preschoolers may build with blocks alongside one another, imitating one another's structures and interacting verbally ("Look at mine") but not joining together in a play script or theme. Their play may be seen as parallel or associative play. Read the following anecdote, and decide which type of play these children are engaging in.

> Preschoolers Ellison and Hunter shared space around the table, using several containers filled with warm, sudsy water and several plastic dinosaurs. They spent a short time on their own exploring the sensory elements of the water, dipping the dinosaurs in and out and splashing and moving the water as it spilled over the sides of the bins. Recognizing each other's actions, they joined to play together in many ways, pushing the dinosaurs under the water until they were fully submerged and transformed with dripping, glistening skin. They also worked together to transport the dinosaurs and the water back and forth between the bins, filling and dumping the containers (Rogers 2024, 87–88).

Ellison and Hunter are involved in cooperative play, imitating and engaging together in their dinosaur and water play.

Connecting Observational Assessment to Early Learning Guidelines

When you observe children, you can assess the broader areas of cognitive and social-emotional competencies as we just described. You can relate what children are doing to the 2015 Head Start Child Development and Learning Framework or the *ELOF2GO* mobile app, released in 2020. Or you can relate what children are doing to your state's early learning guidelines. As mentioned in chapter 2, as of 2019, all fifty states and the District of Columbia have developed early learning guidelines documents (National Center on Early Childhood Quality Assurance 2019). These documents can be used as the basis for observational assessment: the criteria by which you consider what children do on a daily basis. Some sets of guidelines include many identified items, and therefore you may find it too cumbersome to try to assess *every* identified guideline. In that case, choosing a smaller set of essential guidelines (or indicators) across domains is recommended. For example, in the State of New Mexico PreK Programs, out of a total of sixty-five indicators, the state requires teachers to assess thirty *essential* indicators.

When you are relating observations to guidelines, you can still observe children in action naturalistically. As stated in the following quote, there are some things to keep in mind when doing so.

Thinking about standards naturalistically requires conscientious attention to what children are doing and familiarity with your early learning standards. It also requires some form of reflection—whether in discussion with your colleagues or in written observations and recording. (Gronlund 2014, 14)

You can also plan your observations and collection of documentation. You can focus on multiple areas of development at the same time or plan to observe specific guidelines or indicators.

Focusing on Multiple Areas of Development

Think back to the observation in chapters 1 and 2 and remember Angel as he went through the everyday routine of snack in his preschool classroom. Almost every major area of development was seen during snack. Children often show their capabilities related to state guidelines as they participate in daily routines and in play and exploration. By being intentional and planning for observation during these times in the day, you will be able to gather important assessment information. In addition, you can design special activities and provide materials so you can observe for guidelines in other ways.

In our review of early learning guidelines, we have noticed that most state documents share similar areas of development or domains. For example, from state to state, preschool guidelines usually address creative arts, math, science, language and literacy, physical development and health, social-emotional competency, social studies, and approaches to learning. Infant/toddler guidelines tend to focus on domains such as knowing ourselves and others, communicating, building concepts, moving and doing, and approaches to learning. Early childhood professionals recognize that within each of these areas children demonstrate their capabilities in different ways.

The following is an example of an observation note about an infant that took place during feeding time. Read the note and determine what you are learning that the child can do. Then look at the developmental areas that can be related to this observation taken from the infant and toddler section of the *New Mexico Early Learning Guidelines: Birth through Kindergarten* (available at www.newmexicokids.org).

Anton: I always have handy a small notepad and clipboard that I can easily carry throughout the classroom and out to the playground. The notes are jotted quickly so that later, when I'm not with the children, I can write them up with more details and categorize them into learning areas.

> ### Elisha (seven months)
>
> During lunch, Elisha is sitting in a chair being fed applesauce when she looks away from the spoon. I call her name, and she turns and babbles and smiles. She grabs the spoon and holds it tightly in her fist. She then continues to babble and look at me. I take her hand and guide the spoon to feed her.

We identified the following indicators that can be learned about Elisha from this observation:

- **Beginning to Know about Ourselves and Others** Expresses feelings; participates in interactions
- **Beginning to Communicate** Responds to verbal communication; coos, babbles; uses sounds in social situations
- **Beginning to Move and Do** Uses hands or feet to make contact with objects or people

The next note was written while observing a preschooler during dramatic play. Read the note and determine what you are learning that the child can do. Then look at the developmental areas that can be related to this observation taken from the *Montana Early Learning Standards* (Montana Early Learning Standards Task Force 2014; available at https://opi.mt.gov/Portals/182/Page%20Files/Early%20Childhood/Docs/14EarlyLearningStandards.pdf).

> ### Gabriella (three years, eight months)
>
> Gabriella is at the cash register, and there is a store set up. Another child comes over and picks up a fire hat. Gabriella says, "The fire hat is 89, 88, 88, 88, and that's all." While she is saying this, she is writing on her tablet. She gives the other child some money from the cash register and says, "This says that will be two moneys." She then writes more and says, "I will write 'Gabriella' right here."

We identified the following indicators that could be learned about Gabriella from this observation:

- **Mathematics and Numeracy** Number Sense and Operations: uses names of a few numbers
- **Communication** Literacy: Print Development/Writing: use print in play; Communication and Language Development: Expressive Communication: initiate and participate in conversations with peers and adults
- **Emotional and Social** Social Development: Interaction with Peers: negotiate play with small groups of children
- **Emotional and Social: Culture, Family, and Community** Community: demonstrate a beginning awareness of the function of money and commerce

Focusing on Specific Developmental Skills

When your goal is to collect information about each child in all of the areas or domains from your guidelines, you can do that through observations that are more general, like the ones you just read. Or you can document with a focus on a specific domain or a set of skills. You may want to capture how the children are using language to communicate with others or how a child shows their growing skills in gross-motor coordination. You and your colleagues choose a focus and plan for your observations (and documentation, of course). The following are two examples of more focused observation notes. For Jesus, his teachers were watching closely for his developing social skills. For Genevieve, the focus was on her problem-solving skills.

> ### Jesus (two years, two months)
>
> During free play, Jesus pushes Angel in a toy car. Jesus pushes the car into another child, and the other child falls on the ground and begins to cry. Jesus runs to the other child, hugs him while still on the floor, then babbles something to him and helps him get up. The other child stops crying, and they each resume their play.

What did we learn about Jesus's developing social skills?

- **Social Development** Plays with another child and shows empathy

Genevieve (three years, four months)

Genevieve is playing with pebbles in the dry water table. She fills up the bucket and then dumps it out a number of times. She fills smaller containers, trying to get more and more pebbles into the container. She then tries pouring pebbles from a tablespoon into a teaspoon and then back and forth. She occasionally puts the pebbles down while trying to get more into the small container.

What did we learn about Genevieve's problem-solving skills?

- **Approaches to Learning** Recognizes and solves problems through observation, active exploration, trial and error, and interactions and discussions with peers and adults

As you collect documentation about domains and specific skills, you will want to keep track of what you collect for each child. This will give you a set of documentation records that provides a full, well-rounded picture of each child's development—you do not want to miss domains or skills. Some teachers find that a record of their collected documentation keeps them on top of the task of observing for all domains. The Collected Documentation Record can be used to note when you document observations on each of the children. At a glance, you can see what information you are missing for which children, and in which domains. See appendix B or the Focused Observations product page at www.redleafpress.org for a form ready to copy and use.

A Caution about Missing Domains or Areas of Development

Sometimes what gets written down about a child shows what the teachers were paying the most attention to or what they were most concerned about for that child. If teachers don't take care to keep track of which developmental areas have been observed, some areas may be missed and others overemphasized. Here is an exercise to do for yourself and with your colleagues. Write down a rank-ordered list of your favorite things to do with the children in your care. For example, if you love to join children in art explorations, you would list that first. Maybe playing outdoors or in gross-motor activities indoors is your second choice, and reading with children your third. Once you've created a list of five or six things, relate your choices to the major domains or areas of development for the age of children with whom you work. So, for the examples above, the domains might be (1) Creative Development, (2) Physical Development (specifically gross motor), (3) Language and Literacy Development. You will analyze your list with the following in mind:

- The areas at the top of your list are most likely the areas that you observe most easily and frequently.
- The areas at the bottom of your list (or those not even listed!) are most likely areas that you may tend not to observe very often or to miss completely.

Share your analysis with your colleagues. Discuss the similarities and differences in your preferences. In this way, you all can plan more intentionally to focus your observations. If your lists are in different rank order, you may want to assign the favorite domains to the appropriate teachers, knowing that will help to get those areas documented. If the lists are very similar, then it is most likely you and your colleagues are missing some of the key domains that are at the bottom of your lists. Then, as a team, you will need to plan for ways to focus on *all* domains or areas of development to make sure none are neglected.

Whether you work in a team or by yourself, to avoid missing a learning domain, occasionally look over the observation notes you have written for each child—you should see notes about all areas of development. For preschoolers, those notes would include observations of their behavior, math and problem-solving skills, language, socialization, early literacy, approaches to learning, creative development, and fine- and gross-motor skills. For infants and toddlers, observations would focus on their separation from their family members, attachment to care providers, capabilities at comforting themselves and getting their emotional and physical needs met, approaches to learning, and skills in exploring their environment. Your collected documentation for assessment purposes should reflect observations in every area so you can give a well-rounded picture of each child's development and progress.

Sometimes children's behavior influences what gets recorded, especially when difficulties arise. Remember our discussion in chapter 3 about considering your own biases and being aware of the lenses through which you view children? Being conscious of these potentially flawed aspects of the observational process is important as you observe for assessment purposes.

The following observation was presented as a focused documentation of the child's math skills. Does it include any information about the child's math skills? You be the judge.

> *Jay* (four years, ten months)
>
> Jay does not sit in his seat at the math table. Instead, he jumps up out of his chair or lies across the table. He does not participate in the counting activity. He stacks the counters in a pile and then knocks it down and laughs.

This anecdote does not include any information about Jay's math skills, does it? Instead, it describes Jay's behavior during a math activity. Certainly his behavior is a concern. And interventions should be tried to help him attend to the task at hand and participate in a counting activity. However, the teacher/observer should also pay special attention to gathering information about Jay's counting capabilities (or other mathematical understandings) in a variety of activities so this important area of his development is not left out of the observation record. Perhaps Jay is keenly aware of who is first and second in line each day. Or maybe he helps count how many children are present and absent each morning. Having Jay help set the table and recording how he goes about matching one cup, one napkin, and one plate to each chair would give evidence of his growing one-to-one correspondence.

Observing and documenting children's behavior is an important part of assessing their social and emotional development. It can be difficult to write a factual description when a child is misbehaving, but it is important to do so. Taking a deep breath and waiting to write until you calm down and have a chance to reflect on what happened will help you stay objective as you describe what the child said and did, and what interventions you and your colleagues provided. In chapter 7 we look more closely at ways to use observation to learn what might be behind children's behavior so you can respond effectively.

Tying Observations to Developmental Checklists or Resources

To determine the age level of a child's capabilities in multiple domains, you can also turn to developmental checklists or resources that specify reasonable expectations for children at different ages. The following chart shows a sample of resources, many of which have been correlated with state preschool and/or infant/toddler guidelines. You can check with their publishers to determine whether this has been done in relation to your state's early learning guidelines.

A Selection of Developmental Checklists or Resources

Infants and Toddlers Only	Birth through age 5	Age 3 to 5	Age 3 to 5th Grade
The Ounce Scale (Meisels et al. 2003)	*ELOF2GO* mobile app (Head Start Early Childhood Learning and Knowledge Center 2020) *Assessment, Evaluation, and Programming System for Infants and Children, Third Edition (AEPS®-3)* (Bricker et al. 2022)	*Early Learning Scale* (Riley-Ayers et al. 2011) *COR Advantage* (HighScope Educational Research Foundation 2013) *Teaching Strategies Gold: Birth through Kindergarten Assessment Toolkit* (Berke, Bickart, and Heroman 2011)	*The Work Sampling System Developmental Guidelines* (Dichtelmiller et al. 2013)

All of these resources give information about age-appropriate expectations in various developmental areas. Some of the resources are more specific than others. Some are formatted along a continuum. Others include a checklist or web-based features. In addition, these resources are designed in such a way as to allow for cultural and socioeconomic differences among children's performance. The goal is to provide developmental information that is not biased toward any one group. All of these checklists and charts can be used to evaluate observations of children in action. You observe the child, write down the observation, and then at some point relate it back to the developmental checklist to determine the level of the child's performance.

Here are some examples of how teachers related their observations to developmental resources in order to identify children's developmental capabilities.

Early Learning Scale

Dionne and Phillip circulated around their Head Start classroom as the children wrote and drew in journals. Both conversed with children, asking open-ended questions, offering to write as the children dictated, and encouraging the children who could to write letters themselves. Both Dionne and Phillip carried clipboards with them with Brief Notes Recording Sheets. The children's names were listed next to spaces where a brief note or two could be jotted. Thinking in terms of their language and literacy strands on their program's assessment tool, *Early Learning Scale*

(Riley-Ayers et al. 2011), both teachers made notes about how the children were demonstrating the following:

- alphabetic awareness (which includes letter identification)
- print knowledge (which includes recognition that print has meaning and beginning print identification)
- composing (which includes writing symbols for a purpose)
- production (which includes making forms that resemble letters and name writing)

They noticed that some children did not identify any letters or recognize that print carried meaning, while others identified some letters and understood that letters formed words. They observed drawing, scribbling, some letter formation, some letter stringing, and name writing. When they compared their notes, they were able to turn back to the indicators in the *Early Learning Scale* to see the level of each child's performance and plan for ways to help each one continue to grow and develop in their writing and print awareness skills.

The Work Sampling System

Pam and Linda, a preschool teaching team, met at the end of one week to plan for the next. As part of the planning discussion, they reflected about what they saw children doing in teacher-led activities as well as child-initiated exploration. Pam noted that many of the children had been participating in block play and combining that play with extensive pretend scripts about pirates and ships and hidden treasure. Children had used the largest wooden blocks to create a pirate ship with a car steering wheel at the helm. Various dress-up clothes and hats were incorporated as children took on different roles within the play. Pam and Linda laughed as they remembered some of the language the children used as they negotiated the actions of the pirates and the enthusiasm they showed as they shouted, "Ahoy, matey!"

Pam and Linda had written down their observations on notepads. As they read through and discussed their documentation, they realized that they were learning much about the children's abilities. They turned to the developmental checklist their program used, *The Work Sampling System Preschool-4 Developmental Guidelines* (Dichtelmiller et al. 2013). As they looked over the checklist, they concluded that they had observational evidence to mark individual children's performance in the following checklist items:

- approach to learning, performance indicator C.3: approaches tasks with flexibility and inventiveness
- interaction with others, performance indicator D.1: interacts easily with one or more children
- speaking, performance indicator B.2: uses expanded vocabulary and language for a variety of purposes
- gross-motor development, performance indicator A.1: moves with balance and control

Pam and Linda thought carefully about the group of children they had observed and marked each child's checklist according to their participation and interactions around the pirate play. The choices for marks on *The Work Sampling System Preschool-4 Developmental Guidelines* include "not yet," "in process," and "proficient." For Mario, who took great leadership in the organization and building of the pirate ship and helped determine the roles and script of the pirate play, they marked "proficient" in all of the indicators identified. For Alicia, who watched the play from afar and then joined in when Mario gave her specific directions but did not verbalize much during the play, they marked "in process" for most of the indicators. Pam and Linda were very careful to think clearly about each child's participation in the dramatic play they witnessed. They decided to focus more closely on dramatic play in the next week so they could collect even more evidence of the children's performance in these areas.

ELOF2GO *Mobile App*

Sarah and Juanita decided to watch the two-year-olds in their class with a focus on their fine-motor skills. They used the *ELOF2GO* mobile app (Head Start Early Childhood Learning and Knowledge Center 2020) to identify reasonable expectations for children's developmental accomplishments. In the Perceptual, Motor, and Physical Development domain, they found the following fine-motor goal: "Child coordinates hand and eye movements to perform actions."

To observe children in action demonstrating this goal, they put out large lacing beads with strings and several knob puzzles, and they sat at the tables with the children with clipboards in hand so they could make note of children's abilities to string the beads and place the puzzle pieces. After the children left for the day, Sarah and Juanita recorded the results of their observations regarding this goal, carefully considering how each child had gone about showing their fine-motor capabilities.

Choosing a Source and Identifying the Documentation Process

The staff and administration of every early childhood program choose a developmental reference that best suits the needs of their setting. Some state or federally funded programs are told which checklist or assessment system to use for accountability purposes. Funding as well as program evaluation may be tied to the results of such assessments. If such mandates are not in place, you and your colleagues should review various checklists and charts to determine which best suits your understanding of child development and correlates with your state's early learning guidelines. It is also important for you to consider the process of documenting and organizing your observations and relating them back to the checklist or chart. Match both the source and the process to the education and experience of your colleagues, to the realities of your day-to-day work with young children, and to the ways in which you want to communicate the information to families. This way you can be sure the chosen observational assessment tool gets used in the most effective manner.

In addition, when choosing your source of developmental information, you have a responsibility to make sure the milestones identified are reflective of the cultural background of the children and families in your program. Again, the resources noted earlier in this chapter have been developed to be valid across cultures, ethnicities, and socioeconomic levels. Here is a story from an early educator who was asked to use an assessment reference tool that was not appropriate for the cultural setting in which she worked.

> I worked for an early intervention agency dealing with children ages birth to three. The agency had an agreement to provide developmental screenings for a western American Indian Nation. As we assessed the children in the Early Head Start Program, we found that, without exception, every child came out with speech and language concerns and a referral for further testing or for speech therapy. Many of the children also showed "cognitive delays," according to the screening. I began to question these results and discovered that many Native people use a lot of gestures to communicate with their children, especially when they are very young. Many of the children were also being raised to be bilingual and communicated in two languages. Another

issue was that children who are not highly verbal often do not do well on developmental screens in the area of cognitive development because they don't respond to the questions. I remember how appalled I was when the psychologist would show a child a picture of a giraffe and ask what it was. If you asked any of the children what an antelope or an elk was, they would surely know. I began to realize that the assessment tool we were using had been developed and normed on white, middle-class children and was not relevant to these children's culture.

In this case, the conclusions drawn about the children based on this child development information were not accurate reflections of their actual performance and capabilities. We suggest that you, your director, or your supervisor borrow or order one copy of each of several observational assessments to review and consider whether it matches the needs of your program, children, families, and staff.

Practice Making Developmental Connections

The following anecdotes show children in action along with portions of developmental checklists and milestones charts from a variety of assessments. First read the anecdote. Then determine how you would mark the child's developmental capabilities based on the developmental information from each source.

Haley (three years, six months)

The gymnastics teacher's son is at gym class today. I notice Haley walking close by him. She then comes up to tell me, "Hey, Laura, I 'hi' to him." She then points up to the ceiling where a ball is stuck between boards and says, "Hey, look. Pink up there."

Using the following developmental resources, how would you rate Haley's language performance?

From *The Early Learning Scale*					
Oral Language	**1**	**2**	**3**	**4**	**5**
Speaking	• Uses gestures to communicate • Unlikely to participate in discussions • May use very short phrases	• Responds using simple sentences • Responds to low-level questions		• Uses complex sentences and strong vocabulary • Participates in discussions by asking questions and making connections	
Story Retelling	• Retells familiar stories using pictures but with little connection to the actual story line	• Retells familiar stories with some main components but may differ from story line		• Retells familiar stories with some accuracy and details	

From The *Early Learning Scale Guidebook* by Shannon Riley-Ayers, Judi Stevenson-Garcia, Ellen Frede, and Kimberly Brenneman. Copyright © 2011 National Institute for Early Education Research. http://www.casadexter.com/source docs/ELS Guide Book.pdf. Reprinted with permission.

From the COR Advantage ©2014 HighScope® Educational Research Foundation							
Child makes verbal sounds such as cooing and babbling.	Child says (or signs) a single word to refer to a person, animal, object, or action.	Child says a two- or three-word phrase to refer to a person, animal, object, or action.	Child talks about real people or objects that are not present.	Child uses the pronouns he, she, him, her, his, and hers correctly.	Child uses a clause that starts with when, if, or since in a complex sentence.	Child uses "what if" or "suppose" talk to spark a conversation about possibilities.	Child participates in a collaborative discussion with another child about specific school-related content.

Anthony (three years, eight months)

Anthony puts a new puzzle on the table and says he is going to make it by himself. He takes one piece at a time and turns and presses until he finds the correct place for the piece. The puzzle has eight small pieces. He does this with no assistance. He turns the last piece and finishes the puzzle.

Use the following developmental resources to assess Anthony's development.

From *The Work Sampling System* Preschool–3 Developmental Guidelines

Personal and Social Development

Self-Concept

2. Starts to show self-direction in action	Rating:	
	not yet	
	in process	
	proficient	

Physical Development

Fine-Motor Development

2. Uses eye-hand coordination to perform tasks	Rating:	
	not yet	
	in process	
	proficient	

Assessment, Evaluation, and Programming System for Infants and Children, Third Edition (AEPS®-3)

Fine Motor

B. Functional Skill Use

Score Key			Note Key
Mastery Performance 2	Emerging performance 1A = Assistance 1I = Incomplete 1AI = Assistance/ Incomplete	No Performance 0	C = Conduct M = Modification Q = Quality R = Report
3. Manipulates object with two hands, each performing different action			
3.1 Assembles toy			
3.2 Aligns objects			
3.3 Fits variety of shapes into corresponding spaces			

Successfully implementing observational assessment that is related to early learning guidelines or developmental checklists takes time, commitment to learning the system, and willingness to experiment with new ideas and change old ways. For many early educators, the learning curve may necessitate one or two years of training, implementation, and ongoing support before they feel comfortable with the new approach. Planning for the time to discuss, share successes and challenges, and seek additional information and ideas about implementation is important. Learning through trial and error brings long-term results. Working closely with colleagues to explore the best and most efficient ways to fit observation and documentation into busy days with children will create a more positive and helpful atmosphere.

Calls for accountability should be examined carefully so all assessment processes are used to the benefit of the children, not to their detriment. Observing children in everyday classroom activities will provide more realistic and truthful evaluations of children's developmental capabilities than evaluations that come from contrived, occasional testing situations. Writing factual, descriptive anecdotes will ground observational assessment in the objective realm, rather than the subjective, judgmental one. Choosing reliable sources of developmental expectations that have been researched across cultures, regions, and economic levels will validate any conclusions drawn about the child's performance and help you make appropriate decisions about how best to support the child's continued growth.

• • • • • • •

The next step in using observation and documentation for assessment purposes is to share the information gained through this process with families. In the next chapter, we show how to build rich and informative portfolios, write narrative reports that summarize documented observations, and conference effectively with families.

• • • • • • •

Observation Practice #13:
Observing for Developmental Capabilities

Purpose: To identify early literacy capabilities.

What to Do: Watch Video Clip #13 (scan the QR code or go to www.vimeo .com/1022181652) of preschoolers acting out a familiar story. The children and teacher are speaking in Spanish. English subtitles are provided. As you watch the children, try to identify what they comprehend about the story. Your observation notes should answer the following questions: Did they understand the basic plot of the story? Did they remember the characters and their actions? Remember to be factual and descriptive, not interpretive.

Guiding Questions: After viewing, look at your notes and consider the capabilities that you identified the children demonstrating. You can relate the identified capabilities to your state's early learning guidelines or to a developmental checklist with which you are familiar. If you are involved in a group discussion, share some of the anecdotes with the group. Look at the similarities and differences in the documentation from the group. Did people identify different capabilities? Why do you think that is?

Observation Practice #14:
Observing for Developmental Capabilities

Purpose: To identify children's problem-solving capabilities and relate them back to a different developmental source of information.

What to Do: Watch Video Clip #14 (scan the QR code or go to www.vimeo .com/1022181685) of four-year-old boys working with ice and various tools at the sensory table. Document what you observe, paying close attention to their problem-solving capabilities. Remember to be factual and descriptive, not interpretive.

Guiding Questions: After viewing, look at a source of information about child development. Were you able to see a variety of problem-solving skills as the boys worked? Where did you place their capabilities on the developmental checklist you used? If you are part of a group discussion, share some of the anecdotes with the group as well as your placement of the boys' capabilities on the developmental checklists. Look at the similarities and differences in the documentation from the group. Did people identify different capabilities? Why do you think that is?

Reflection

Purpose: To reflect on what you know about using developmental resources for assessment purposes.

What to Do: What sources of developmental information are you most familiar with? Identify the advantages and disadvantages of sources of developmental information that you have used or are familiar with. What new ways of documenting children's developmental capabilities would you like to explore?

Finding Your Observation Style

Purpose: To consider which developmental resources work best for your unique observation style.

What to Do: Respond to these questions in your journal:

- Which sources of developmental information best represent your understanding of child development? Why?
- Why do observations of children in action more realistically document their learning and development than giving them an on-demand assessment of a specific skill?
- Why do criterion-based assessments give a better understanding of a child's capabilities and facilitate your planning for the needs of individual children?
- What are some steps that you can take to ensure that you have opportunities to observe children in natural settings for assessment purposes?

How Do You Share Observation, Documentation, and Assessment Information with Families?

▲▼▲▼▲

Early educators have a professional responsibility to communicate with families in supportive and meaningful ways and to ask for their thoughts and opinions regarding their child's care and education. Sharing what has been learned about a child's development through observation and documentation is an essential part of the process. It is through this process that you build a trusting and respectful relationship with families and truly work together for the benefit of the child.

Assessments based on observation provide families with a caring and nonthreatening way to see their child's growth, development, and learning. By sharing descriptions of children in action throughout their days at the program, you are providing much more meaningful information to families than check sheets or report cards. You are giving them a window through which to see their children while in your care.

Once you have chosen a system for recording observations and a resource to interpret those observations and assess the child's developmental capabilities (as described in the earlier chapters), you will want to decide on a format for presenting the information to family members. These decisions are often made by the administrators and staff of a program. This provides consistency among all of the educators in a program and lets families know what kind of assessment information about their child they can expect. In some settings the decision is up to the individual teacher. Again, communicating clearly to families is important.

Communicating with families to share the assessment information you have gathered about their child involves several steps. In this chapter, we address three communication strategies:

Elizabeth: I share documentation with families all the time—when they pick up their child, we talk briefly. I write them notes or may call them on the telephone. I certainly share it at parent-teacher conferences or at an IEP conference when I am presenting the levels of performance their child is demonstrating.

Peggy W.: All of my families are thrilled to hear what I have observed. I feel that because I am willing to share these details with my parents on a daily basis, it builds a stronger trust within our relationship. It confirms that I am observing their children throughout the day and am getting to know each child on a personal level.

1. organizing documentation into meaningful and informative assessment portfolios
2. providing families with a written summary report rather than some sort of assessment checklist or report card
3. meeting face-to-face with family members to share all of this information

Deanna: I am always eager to share the child's portfolio with the family because it shows them that I not only care for the child but I care about her as an individual. Families personally thank me, and some even tear up with joy and pride when they see documentation that shows how their child is learning and growing. Some families laminate their portfolios, scan and email them to a grandparent, or show them off around their workplace.

Organizing Documentation into Meaningful and Informative Assessment Portfolios

Organizing observation notes, photos, and work samples into an assessment portfolio for each child can show a meaningful and informative picture of a child's development. Assessment portfolios are more than a scrapbook or collection of children's work, a photo album, or a checklist. Rather, an assessment portfolio is a representation of what you are learning about each child's performance in selected domains. It becomes part of the assessment process when the collection of observation notes, photographs, and work samples is clearly connected to learning outcomes. And these notes, photos, and work samples are collected at least twice a year (if not three or four times) to document the child's progress. Many assessment tools now have ways for educators to create online assessment portfolios. Check with your leadership to find out what strategies for portfolio collection would work best at your program.

For an assessment portfolio, observation notes are the most important items. Factual, descriptive observation notes or anecdotes create a kind of video that readers can picture in their minds. Photos and work samples add to the richness of that picture but do not stand alone—they must be accompanied by a teacher description or observation to truly be informative. When presented together, these pieces of documentation have the potential to show multiple skills and capabilities across domains. Sharing this kind of documentation becomes a powerful way to communicate with families. As Hilary Seitz (2023b) states, a portfolio "showcases learning experiences by making learning, thinking, and development visible" (12).

Pictured on the left is a work sample from a four-year-old named Jane. Consider how it might be used as documentation in an assessment portfolio.

You can see that she has made either letters or letterlike shapes and lined them up across the page. You may guess that she knows some letters and understands that print has meaning and can be used to communicate. You may also guess that she has strong control of the crayon and good fine-motor skills. You are only guessing, however, because you only have the child's work sample. What you are missing is the teacher's description of what Jane said and did while creating this writing sample. Here is the teacher's anecdote. Read it to see if you learn more about what Jane understands and knows how to do.

> ### Jane (four years)
>
> Today at the writing table, Jane wrote the attached with a crayon, using her right hand in a correct grasp. She brought it to me and said, "I writed a story." When I asked her what it says, she used her index finger to point under each line moving from left to right as she said, "No running in the classroom. Mommy, I love you. I think you are so beautiful. Someday I want to work with you. I love you with all my heart. I like to swing. When I go high, I jump. You are scared. The end."

Do you notice how the teacher's description gives much more information about Jane's capabilities and understandings? Yes, indeed, Jane does understand that print has meaning and can be used to communicate. She does have strong control of the writing tool, is right-handed, and uses a correct grasp. She expresses herself well in long sentences and demonstrates that she understands stories. In addition, it's clear that she loves her Mommy! The combination of work sample and teacher observation gives much more information about who Jane is and what she is a capable of doing.

We recommend using a specific format to share observations of the child along with photographs and work samples with families in a family conference. The second edition of *Focused Portfolios* (Gronlund and Engel 2019) features an approach to conferencing that includes specially designed collection forms. On a form, the teacher writes (or affixes) their observation note, adds photos or work samples, and identifies guidelines or learning goals that are reflected in what the child did and said. For those of you who work with young children with diagnosed disabilities, documentation of children's progress toward an individualized family service plan (IFSP) or individualized education program (IEP) goals can also be done through a portfolio format. In fact, teachers in special education settings report that sharing such documentation with families often has much greater meaning than reporting a score or percentile on a standardized diagnostic measure.

Since they were first published, these forms have been used in a variety of settings with adaptations made to align them with early learning guidelines. Following is a completed example for DeVaughn. See appendix B for a Portfolio Collection Form ready to copy, or download one from the Focused Observations product page at www.redleafpress.org.

Portfolio Collection Form

Child's Name: <u>DeVaughn</u>   Date: <u>4-9</u>   Observer: <u>Phil</u>

Domains(s): <u>Language and Literacy</u>

Learning goal(s) demonstrated in this documentation: <u>Listens to stories read aloud, asks questions, and makes</u>

<u>pertinent comments</u>

_____

Check off whatever applies to the context of this observation:

☐ child-initiated activity   ☐ done independently   ☐ time spent (1 to 5 minutes)

☒ teacher-initiated activity   ☒ done with adult guidance   ☒ time spent (5 to 15 minutes)

☐ new task for this child   ☒ done with peer(s)

☒ familiar task for this child   ☐ time spent (more than 15 minutes)

Anecdotal note: Describe what you saw the child do and/or heard the child say (attach a photo or work sample if appropriate).

DeVaughn listened to the whole *Pancake Story* (a book with no words). He helped Carol tell the story throughout, making many suggestions that made sense to the story. He looked intently at the pictures and made predictions of what might happen.

Robin S.: When I meet with families and share my documentation about their child, the parents can see what is happening and how the work shows what I am talking about. I have had parents ask to keep the documentation because they are so proud of their child. I photocopy it for myself and give them the originals.

After sharing this documentation with DeVaughn's family members, his teachers would continue to document his progress in language and literacy on other portfolio forms so they could compare his performance in language and literacy across time. They would plan to follow his interest in stories and provide many opportunities for him to make predictions, to retell stories, and to create his own stories; they might also see if he is beginning to recognize some print.

Choosing Documentation for an Assessment Portfolio

Some items are more informative for assessment portfolios than others. Checklist documentation should not be part of an assessment portfolio; instead, it can easily be documented (as we showed in chapter 4) on Quick Check Recording Sheets and other types of record keeping. For example, children's gross-motor skills can often be observed and documented through a simple check mark or yes or no on a checklist. Either a four-year-old hops on one foot or does not. Either a baby stands with balance or does not. In contrast, some skills are better assessed through ongoing observation over time. For example, language samples of a child's expressive language—whether it be lists of words for young toddlers or quotes of preschoolers' long, descriptive stories—should be documented as portfolio items. They show the uniqueness in how children are gaining vocabulary, learning to express themselves, and getting their needs met. You are making learning visible, "using documentation to tell the story of the whole child and all their capabilities" (Seitz 2023a, 6).

Planning ahead for the kinds of documentation that will be most informative will make the portfolio process go more smoothly. We suggest you consider the following questions when trying to determine what is best collected in an assessment portfolio:

- Are the skills that you are documenting best demonstrated in a portfolio piece or on a checklist?
- Does the portfolio item (observation note, which may be accompanied by a photo or work sample) show the unique ways the child goes about doing something?
- Does the item show the integration of many skills and capabilities the child has developed?

Checklists are great tools for documenting many skills, and you should refer to your Quick Check Recording Sheets when completing your summary report on a child. But you will not include checklists in the portfolio. If you determine that a skill is noteworthy and should be included in the portfolio, consider including details in your description that go beyond recording only one skill. For example, if you write only "counts to four with one-to-one correspondence" on a portfolio form, you are not showing any other skills (which may come from other domains) that the child might have demonstrated as they went about the task. It's helpful to know what the context was. Did they count at snack, during circle time, or as they played with colored bears? Did they talk about what they were counting with a friend, with an adult, or to themself? Did they also group the items by color or size? Did they use any fine-motor capabilities as they counted? Good portfolio documentation goes beyond a checklist item in that it includes details that show how a child uses multiple skills from multiple domains in integration during work and play. Following is an example of a piece from a child's portfolio that identifies several learning goals across domains.

April: I share documentation with parents when I want them to see where their child started at and how he or she is progressing or not progressing.

Cathy: This really helped me to share more with the families when I met with them for IEP meetings. The photos I included have been so powerful. I describe the activity to the child's family members and tell them what their child was doing. It's hard for them to visualize, so the photos and my written descriptions really help.

Danielle: I found it so helpful that you can use one portfolio sample to discuss and document more than one domain and standard.

Portfolio Collection Form

Child's Name: Thomas   Date: 3/8   Observer: Jarrod

Domain(s): Mathematical Understanding, Social/Emotional, Language, Approaches to Learning

Learning goal(s) demonstrated in this documentation: _____

Geometrical and spatial awareness; mathematical problem-solving; counting with one-to-one correspondence; play cooperatively; communicates with others; persistence

Check off whatever applies to the context of this observation:

- ☑ child-initiated activity
- ☐ teacher-initiated activity
- ☐ new task for this child
- ☑ familiar task for this child

- ☐ done independently
- ☐ done with adult guidance
- ☑ done with peer(s)

- ☐ time spent (1 to 5 minutes)
- ☐ time spent (5 to 15 minutes)
- ☑ time spent (more than 15 minutes)

Anecdotal note: Describe what you saw the child do and/or heard the child say (attach a photo or work sample if appropriate).

Thomas, Dylan, Kylie, and Sam have been working with the Magna-Tiles over the past few days, trying to figure out how high they could build them without them falling down. Thomas has taken the lead with the group and tried to engage them in planning before building. Although he doesn't always get cooperation with that, he helps the group problem-solve strategies for holding on to the structure at various points as it gets taller and taller. If it falls, he shows no frustration. Rather, he says, "Okay, guys, let's do it again!"

See photo.

186

Once you have eliminated the skills you will document through checklist formats, we suggest that you ask yourself these questions: What are the most meaningful portfolio items for the age of children you work with? What is each portfolio item showing about the unique ways the child is developing?

For infants and toddlers, consider building portfolios that contain observational descriptions of their participation in

- daily routines
- interactions with caregivers and other adults
- interactions with other children
- exploration of the environment

Again, you can record these observations on portfolio forms and identify early learning guidelines that reflect what the child is doing or working toward. Accompanying the anecdote with a photograph when possible will give families a window on their child's time with you. Families love photos and appreciate seeing their child in your loving care.

Portfolio Collection Form

Child's Name: Kendall   Date: 14 months

Observer: Deanna   Date: 9/10/08

Domains(s): Interest in others and communication

Learning goal(s) demonstrated in this documentation: Actively shows affection for familiar person and

explores books with interest

Check off whatever applies to the context of this observation:

☒ child-initiated activity	☒ done independently	☒ time spent (1 to 5 minutes)
☐ teacher-initiated activity	☐ done with adult guidance	☐ time spent (5 to 15 minutes)
☐ new task for this child	☐ done with peer(s)	
☐ familiar task for this child		☐ time spent (more than 15 minutes)

Anecdotal note: Describe what you saw the child do and/or heard the child say (attach a photo or work sample if appropriate).

Kendall was looking at the class book when she flipped to a page with a picture of me and Connor. She pointed over and over again at my picture and smiled. I asked her, "Kendall, did you find me?" and she picked up the book, smiled, and kissed the picture of me.

For preschool children, your assessment portfolios should include observation notes, photographs, and work samples. Consider collecting the following portfolio items for this age group:

- language samples
- writing samples
- responses to reading experiences

- mathematical problem solving
- creations that require mathematical understanding (patterning, geometrical creations)
- scientific explorations
- self-reflections
- art/drawing samples

Portfolio Collection Form

Child's Name: _Ethan_   Date: _2/1/12_   Observer: _Davis_

Domains(s): _Science, Fine Motor, Social/Emotional, Approaches to Learning_

Learning goal(s) demonstrated in this documentation: _Uses senses to investigate, grasps small objects, plays_

alongside others, focuses on a task, problem solves

Check off whatever applies to the context of this observation:

☐ child-initiated activity	☒ done independently	☐ time spent (1 to 5 minutes)
☒ teacher-initiated activity	☐ done with adult guidance	☐ time spent (5 to 15 minutes)
☒ new task for this child	☒ done with peer(s)	☒ time spent (more than 15 minutes)
☐ familiar task for this child		

Anecdotal note: Describe what you saw the child do and/or heard the child say (attach a photo or work sample if appropriate).

Ethan (3 yrs. 8 mos.) stayed at the "Potions Table" for one hour, mixing water and sand, oil, glitter, dirt, glue, cornstarch, and baking soda. He did not talk with others as he worked other than to ask the teacher for more water when he needed it.

Whether you are building an assessment portfolio for an infant, toddler, or preschooler, the portfolio items that have been collected as documentation for a group of children should not all look the same. It's important that you plan to have each child's collection of documentation truly represent who the child is and what you have observed them doing over time. This will be the most meaningful for you and for the family. When considering items for your assessment portfolios, you and your colleagues should discuss the following:

- What are the child's interests and delights?
- What engages the child's attention and is worthy of their interest?
- What skills are embedded in this portfolio item?
- How does the child integrate their skills and apply their knowledge?
- What are you learning about the child and their traits as a learner?

As family members review such documentation about their child, they often express that the portfolio is truly a treasure for them. The following are three examples of portfolio items that we feel show the uniqueness of each child.

Portfolio Collection Form

Child's Name: __Ashley__   Date: __4/16/12__ Observer: __Brooke__

Domains(s): __Math, Literacy, Approaches to Learning__

Learning goal(s) demonstrated in this documentation: __Sorts & classifies, converses, vocabulary (color words),__

__responds to stories read, focuses on a task, shows initiative__

Check off whatever applies to the context of this observation:

☒ child-initiated activity	☒ done independently	☐ time spent (1 to 5 minutes)
☐ teacher-initiated activity	☐ done with adult guidance	☒ time spent (5 to 15 minutes)
☒ new task for this child	☐ done with peer(s)	
☐ familiar task for this child		☐ time spent (more than 15 minutes)

Anecdotal note: Describe what you saw the child do and/or heard the child say (attach a photo or work sample if appropriate).

Ashley did this on her own, working for ten minutes or so, then brought it to her teacher and said, "Look. I put all the colors together. There's green, yellow, red, and blue." The class had just read *Chicka, Chicka Boom Boom.* She said, "See. The letters are all falling down."

Lillian: We just had conferences recently, and two mothers specifically stated that they had never had this type of conference for their other children. Using the portfolios helped me make it personal for the families and not so general and impersonal like a report card would be. The parents usually had a small smile after they read their child's comments or saw their pictures in the portfolio.

Portfolio Collection Form

Child's Name: <u>Janelle</u>   Date: <u>11/28/11</u>   Observer: <u>Teresa</u>

Domains(s): <u>Math, Literacy, Approaches to Learning</u>

Learning goal(s) demonstrated in this documentation: <u>Fine Motor, Building Concepts, Approaches to Learning,</u>

<u>Relationships with Others</u>

Check off whatever applies to the context of this observation:

☐ child-initiated activity   ☒ done independently   ☒ time spent (1 to 5 minutes)

☒ teacher-initiated activity   ☒ done with adult guidance   ☐ time spent (5 to 15 minutes)

☒ new task for this child   ☒ done with peer(s)

☐ familiar task for this child   ☐ time spent (more than 15 minutes)

Anecdotal note: Describe what you saw the child do and/or heard the child say (attach a photo or work sample if appropriate).

Janelle tried to get the plastic stars to stick together, turning them and pushing hard with her fingers until they interlocked. Then, she added them to the construction the teacher was helping the group make.

Portfolio Collection Form

Child's Name: __Lucas__   Date: __5/5/12__ Observer: __Margaret__

Domains(s): ___Fine Motor, Literacy, Approaches to Learning___

Learning goal(s) demonstrated in this documentation: __Appropriate grasp, writes recognizable letters,__

__understands print has meaning, converses, vocabulary (schedule), focuses on a task__

_____

Check off whatever applies to the context of this observation:

☒ child-initiated activity   ☒ done independently   ☐ time spent (1 to 5 minutes)

☐ teacher-initiated activity   ☐ done with adult guidance   ☐ time spent (5 to 15 minutes)

☐ new task for this child   ☐ done with peer(s)

☒ familiar task for this child   ☒ time spent (more than 15 minutes)

Anecdotal note: Describe what you saw the child do and/or heard the child say (attach a photo or work sample if appropriate).

Lucas got markers and paper and wrote this by himself, working for almost fifteen minutes. He used his right hand with a correct grasp of the marker. Then he brought it to his teacher and said, "This is a schedule of lower and upper case letters."

Time Management and Portfolio Collection

A caution about collecting portfolio documentation is in order here. Many teachers report that time management is a challenge. They struggle with finding time to fit in documentation and to organize it all. They may procrastinate. Our recommendation is that you do not wait until the end of the collection period to start documenting! Observation and documentation are an ongoing process. The portfolio documentation is not meant to represent where the child is at the end of the collection period. It's more about documenting growth and learning over time. Your portfolios will be far more meaningful and informative to families and to you if you organize your collection strategies across time than if you wait to begin until the week or two before conferences.

> If the process is repeated every month or two and then put together, these pieces will tell a story, and the documentation (authentic assessment) will show how the child is growing and developing. (Seitz 2023a, 7)

The following list identifies some time-efficient methods for collecting portfolio documentation. Anytime you are writing an observation, you can use the many forms of paper and pencil that we have identified in this book or a digital tool or app if that is your preference.

- Have a plan and be prepared with documentation materials (camera, sticky notes, clipboards, and so forth).
- Post your guidelines to remind you of what you're looking for.
- Write a memory jogger or take a photograph if that's all you have time for.
- Remember to Take Five to fill out the details of the documentation and put it on the portfolio forms.

There is nothing wrong with teachers writing one description of an experience or activity and duplicating that description on several children's portfolio forms. This can be a timesaver in some respects. However, the description does not end there. They also add information about how each child went about engaging in the experience or activity. That will be where the differences are evident. Following are examples of portfolio documentation showing how two children participated in the same experience but in unique ways.

Portfolio Collection Form

Child's Name: Zane   Date: 10/29   Observer: Kelly

Domain(s): Cognitive: Math; Social/Emotional; Approaches to Learning

Learning goal(s) demonstrated in this documentation: _____

Describe and compare measurable attributes; work cooperatively with peers;

problem-solve

Check off whatever applies to the context of this observation:

☐ child-initiated activity   ☐ done independently   ☐ time spent (1 to 5 minutes)

☑ teacher-initiated activity   ☑ done with adult guidance   ☑ time spent (5 to 15 minutes)

☑ new task for this child   ☑ done with peer(s)   ☑ time spent (more than 15 minutes)

☐ familiar task for this child

Anecdotal note: Describe what you saw the child do and/or heard the child say (attach a photo or work sample if appropriate).

In small group, I introduced the activity of measuring each other using paper pumpkin cutouts. The children discussed ways to do so and decided that the person being measured would lay down on the floor and the one measuring would line up the pumpkins next to him or her. We practiced in small group and then the materials were made available during Choice Time. Zane and Anton chose to measure each other.

As Anton lay on the floor, Zane placed the pumpkins next to him with varying gaps between the pumpkins. I discussed with both boys about the need for accuracy in measurement. Zane did not make any adjustments to the pumpkins and counted them as they lay—7 pumpkins. We recorded his count. Then, compared it to Anton's measurement of Zane (13). The boys stood back to back and determined they are the same height—but their counted pumpkins were very different. Zane measured Anton a second time, and this time moved the pumpkins right next to each other and got a more accurate measurement of 13.

See photo.

From *Individualized Child-Focused Curriculum: A Differentiated Approach* by Gaye Gronlund © 2016. Published by Redleaf Press. www.redleafpress.org. This page may be reproduced for individual or classroom use only.

Portfolio Collection Form

Child's Name: Anton   Date: 10/29   Observer: Kelly

Domain(s): Cognitive: Math; Social/Emotional; Approaches to Learning

Learning goal(s) demonstrated in this documentation: _____

Describe and compare measurable attributes; work cooperatively with peers;

problem-solve

Check off whatever applies to the context of this observation:

☐ child-initiated activity   ☐ done independently   ☐ time spent (1 to 5 minutes)

☑ teacher-initiated activity   ☑ done with adult guidance   ☑ time spent (5 to 15 minutes)

☑ new task for this child   ☑ done with peer(s)   ☑ time spent (more than 15 minutes)

☐ familiar task for this child

Anecdotal note: Describe what you saw the child do and/or heard the child say (attach a photo or work sample if appropriate).

In small group, I introduced the activity of measuring each other using paper pumpkin cutouts. The children discussed ways to do so and decided that the person being measured would lay down on the floor and the one measuring would line up the pumpkins next to him or her. We practiced in small group and then the materials were made available during Choice Time. Zane and Anton chose to measure each other.

First, Zane measured Anton (with a result of 7 pumpkins). Then Anton measured Zane, carefully placing the pumpkins right next to each other so that the stem touched the bottom of the next pumpkin. His result was 13 (which he counted with 1-1 correspondence). Anton called me over and said, "Ms. Kelly, can you help us see if we're both the same?" I suggested that the boys stand back-to-back and determined they are the same height. Anton told Zane, "You gotta do it again, Zane. Make sure the pumpkins are touching each other so we're the same."

From *Individualized Child-Focused Curriculum: A Differentiated Approach* by Gaye Gronlund © 2016. Published by Redleaf Press. www.redleafpress.org. This page may be reproduced for individual or classroom use only.

Good curriculum planning will also greatly assist with portfolio collection. Make sure you give children ample time for exploration and play so these meaningful samples can be created. Provide materials and activities that are inviting and engaging over time so the children get deeply involved and integrate multiple skills. If you're looking for writing or drawing samples or mathematical representations, you'll need to make sure you are providing the tools and materials that will result in such samples.

Kelly: I have a clear picture of what my portfolio collection should look like. I like this format because I can reflect and really see growth. In the future, I will plan to better identify what my portfolio goals should be and plan more intentionally for them.

A Resource for a Family-Created Learning Journal

For the past several years, I have worked with Make Way for Books, an early literacy agency in Tucson, Arizona. This organization has produced a free app for families of children ages birth to five (available in the Apple or Google Store). The Make Way for Books App includes electronic books, family activities, and a Learning Journal for families to record their interactions with their children around the books and activities. The Learning Journal page appears after a family member reads a book or completes an activity with their child. They can note things their child did or said, list any new words that came up, add a photo of their child engaged in the experience, and see learning goals (taken from the Head Start Early Learning Outcomes Framework and the Arizona Early Learning Guidelines and Standards) that were addressed as they interacted with their child.

You may consider referring the families in your program to this app. It has won a Library of Congress Award, as well as an A+ rating from Common Sense Media. The families involved with Make Way for Books give high praise to the content and to the opportunity to track their children's progress in the Learning Journals. Learn more at www.makewayforbooks.org/app.

Providing Families with a Written Summary Report

The portfolio should provide evidence of what the child can do and may show some developmental skills that are emerging. There will be other developmental areas or skills that are not evident in the portfolio and yet should be reported to the family. Those should be summarized in a brief written report. This report helps family members understand their child's strengths and weaknesses across all domains or areas and gives you a format to address additional skills not included in the portfolio documentation. Setting goals for areas that you and your colleagues, as well as the family members, will work on with the child is also part of the process.

When preparing to write a summary report for families, the beginning step is reflection. Take the time to sit down and go through the documentation to determine the growth and learning that has occurred. This helps you to interpret the child's progress and identify areas of concern. Of course, the process of reflecting has been ongoing for you as the documentation has been collected. But before you write the report, it is time to stop collecting data and focus on what has been collected, making decisions about which information to present. This can lead to new insights about the child.

Before writing a report and scheduling a time for a formal family-teacher conference, teachers need to shift gears from documenting evidence (as in the factual written descriptions of their observations) to evaluating that evidence. Remember, when documenting, the focus is on factual, descriptive, and objective language. When teachers evaluate their documentation, they use their judgment and determine where the child is strong and in what areas they need more support. While teachers may have been doing this all along as they planned curricular activities for the children, when preparing to conference with families, they summarize what they have learned about the child. They can celebrate all the child's accomplishments and use words like "He does a good job at . . ." or "She really knows how to . . ." They can also consider where problems arise for the child and what skills are not as well established. The evaluation process is a time to draw conclusions about how the child is growing, developing, and learning.

To move from documentation to evaluation, teachers need to take the following steps:

1. Stop collecting documentation (evaluating requires a different way of thinking—continuing to gather information may not allow a teacher to shift their viewpoint).
2. Review the documentation for each child domain by domain (examining portfolios, photographs, work samples, quick check, and other formats).
3. Add any nondocumented information from memory about the child's performance in each domain.
4. Relate the information about the child to early learning guidelines or to indicators on assessment tools that are appropriate for the age of the child.
5. Determine where each child has shown growth and progress, what guidelines or indicators they have accomplished, and where they need continued support and assistance.
6. Write summary reports for each child.
7. Schedule and conduct family/teacher conferences to share the portfolios and summaries.

Jordan: Every time I write narratives I discover a thousand things about my children. When you're sitting down at a table reviewing your anecdotal notes, photos, and data from the last six months that you've spent with the child, you reflect and see a whole child. You look back at what they were first doing and see the progress. This is the single most helpful process.

Some published observational assessment systems have reports for you to use when conferencing with families. And some teachers create their own report forms. For example, Diana Lamb at Little Lamb Nursery School in Lebanon, Indiana, uses the *Focused Portfolios* approach for organizing her observations, and she created the following format for reporting to family members.

Little Lamb Nursery School

Child's Name: _____ Date: _____

Developmental Milestones

1. **Gross motor activities**

   Active   Jumping   Hopping

2. **Fine motor activities**

   Scissors   Drawing   Name

   Works Independently

3. **Emotional and Social Competency**

   Type of play

   Relationship with others

   Self-discipline

   Self-image

   Self-help skills

4. **Thinking, Reasoning, and Problem Solving**

   Number readiness

   Attention span

   Curious

   Generates ideas

5. **Language and Communication**

   Understands and follows directions

   Participates in group conversation

   Vocabulary

6. **Creative Development**

   Art

   Music

   Dramatic play

7. **Reading and Writing Development**

   Listens to stories

   Interest in letters, books

Two basic elements should be summarized in a report: the child's growth and accomplishments across all domains and the goals you and your colleagues will continue to work on with the child. In *Planning for Play, Observation, and Learning in Preschool and Kindergarten*, Gronlund (2012) shares a format for teachers to report a child's progress to families. See appendix B for a Family/Teacher Summary Report ready to copy, or download one from the Focused Observations product page at www.redleafpress.org. In the following completed report, you can see that the key elements identified above are included. Notice that the boxes for reporting are small—key aspects of the child's development are to be highlighted so your communication with the family is clear and concise. Remember, you will also be sharing the child's portfolio documentation to round out the discussion. It's important that what is written in the report be aligned with what is contained in the portfolio. The two should be tightly connected. In fact, as you can see in the completed report, you can note "see portfolio item" so you can show the evidence of what you are summarizing.

Family/Teacher Summary Report

Child's Name: Sydney H.   Date: 11/4

Teacher: Peggy   Program: Happy Valley Children's Center

DOMAIN: Mathematics and Numeracy

Growth and accomplishments	Counts objects and refers to the quantity of items (up to 7 consistently with one-to-one correspondence) (see Math Portfolio Item); recognizes and names shapes; experiments with measurement.
We will continue to work on	providing opportunities for Sydney to pursue her interest in number relationships and counting, giving her a variety of items to count and moving toward larger quantities, encouraging more geometric exploration in three dimensions, and offering more measurement experiences.

DOMAIN: Physical Development

Growth and accomplishments	Sydney hops, jumps, and climbs with ease; she grasps writing and drawing tools with a three-finger grasp and uses the small muscles of her hands to manipulate beads, puzzles, and scissors.
We will continue to work on	providing opportunities to use her gross-motor skills in more complex ways, such as doing obstacle courses both inside and out, and to use her fine-motor ones in art and writing experiences and in the manipulatives area of the classroom.

DOMAIN: Language and Literacy

Growth and accomplishments	Writes using conventional words and names (her own name, Mom, Dad, and love) (see Writing Portfolio Item); enjoys books and shows beginning understanding of conventions of print.
We will continue to work on	providing her with different writing tools as well as encouraging her to create her own stories, writing as many of the words as she can on her own; offering many reading opportunities in large and small groups as well as individually.

DOMAIN: Social Studies	
Growth and accomplishments	Sydney demonstrates interest in exploring aspects of home, school, and community both in our planned activities and in her dramatic play (she especially likes to play veterinarian to the stuffed animals!).
We will continue to work on	ensuring that Sydney has opportunities to deepen her understanding of the larger community through field trips and community member visits and will support her acting out of various roles in play.

DOMAIN: Social and Emotional	
Growth and accomplishments	Shows comfort with new people and situations and cooperates in group play and work time; is learning to resolve conflicts as they arise.
We will continue to work on	helping Sydney navigate new and complex social situations and assisting her as needed to express her emotions in productive ways when conflicts arise with other children.

DOMAIN: Science	
Growth and accomplishments	Shows an increased awareness and understanding of changes in materials and cause and effect relationships (see Science Portfolio Item).
We will continue to work on	building on Sydney's natural curiosity about the scientific properties of both living and nonliving things by providing exploratory opportunities, books, field trips, and other resources.

DOMAIN: Creative Arts	
Growth and accomplishments	Explores a variety of expressive media with purpose, often with a product in mind (see Creative Arts Portfolio Item).
We will continue to work on	encouraging Sydney to experiment with various art media and ensuring that she has plenty of time to work on her creations.

Notice the tone of the written comments on the completed report. Growth and accomplishments are celebrated, even though they may involve small steps of progress rather than giant leaps forward. Weaknesses and challenges are addressed when the teacher notes what "we will continue to work on." As you identify goals to be working on with a child, you are addressing areas where you and your colleagues will provide additional support, experiences, skill development, or challenges for that child. In addition, many teachers ask families to join them in goal setting. In the next section of this chapter, we discuss ways to invite more family participation in the family/teacher conference.

Meeting Face-to-Face with Family Members to Share All of This Information

Opening a dialogue with family members about their children can be a wonderfully enriching and meaningful experience. Sharing developmental information with families regarding their children and inviting them to share their joys and concerns helps both parties better understand and meet the needs of the children. Families have a unique perspective on their children, knowing them and understanding them in intimate ways that early educators do not. In addition, children usually function differently in various settings. Families know their baby's home sleeping and eating patterns, and they can share their approach to toilet learning. They can provide information about their preschooler's interests and developmental capabilities that have not been seen during time with you. For all ages of children, families should be invited to share their traditions and unique cultural practices.

This sharing of perspectives can make the process of individualizing curriculum more effective for you and can help family members feel included. For example, a quiet child at preschool may be a very talkative child at home. Learning this information reassures you about the child's language skills and helps you view them in a different light. Children may show more behavioral self-control with you than they do in their home setting. Sharing this information can be reassuring to families who are struggling with tantrums and disruption at home.

Both family members and early educators want children to thrive and be successful. Families also want to know that the program is having a positive impact on their child. They want the early childhood program staff to be accountable for their actions and to know that the goals of the program are reflected in the day-to-day activities with the children. They want to know how their child is doing, what activities their child participates in, and what their child likes to do at school. They want to know what you have observed to be their child's developmental and learning strengths. And they may worry about what you might identify as potential areas of concern. Having a special time to share with family members is another way to give them the message that their child is in good hands, with people who are helping their child grow and learn.

Anton: A lot of the responses I get from families are about what they observe at home. This is particularly true with behaviors. This helps me learn a lot about what is going on at home, which better helps me meet a child's particular needs.

Scheduling Conferences in a Family-Friendly Way

Meetings with family members to share information should be scheduled regularly. Many programs schedule two or three specific times during the course of the year for teachers to meet with family members to discuss

Rosemary: Sometimes I talk to a parent after class at pickup time simply to emphasize what their child has accomplished that day.

Deanna: My favorite part about meeting with families is that it gives me the chance to set goals for the child with the family. Each family has a different culture and different ideas about what is important for their child. Through communicating with the family and building a relationship, I get to know more about the child, the family's interests, and the hopes and dreams they have as their child grows.

their child's development and learning. Most early childhood programs have information in their policies and procedures defining this expectation and alerting families to the time frames involved. Casual meetings with family members, such as at arrival or pickup time, are important times for establishing relationships and for daily communication. But a more formal time for conferencing provides an opportunity for you and the family members to look in depth at the child's accomplishments and struggles and to figure out how to work together as partners in the best interest of the child.

It is imperative that the meeting be scheduled to meet the needs of the family and planned far enough in advance for them to make arrangements to attend. Too often families are not given choices as to where and when to meet. Then the staff feels frustrated when families are not able to attend. Because of the unique needs of families, meeting times and places need to be individualized. Setting up a conference in the evening may be necessary, perhaps even at the family's home. Often breakfast or lunch meetings are successful for family members who are working outside of the home, either meeting in a restaurant or brown-bagging it at a convenient location. Sometimes phone conferencing is the only option. The difficulty with a phone call is that you cannot look at the portfolio items and summary report together. If you can give them to the family members before the telephone conference, then all of you can discuss what has been accomplished by the child with the same point of reference. (You could also consider emailing copies of the documentation or utilizing a webcam or video conferencing application that allows you to show items and see each other.) Finding creative ways to meet with families and share the documentation with them will give them the message that they are cared about and valued. The bottom line is that if families are not showing up for the conferences, it becomes your responsibility to pursue them and find a way to meet successfully.

It is preferable that conferences last from thirty to forty-five minutes. Less time than that makes it difficult to review the portfolio documentation and report in depth. Alternatively, some programs set up conference times so family members first review the documentation without the teacher. Families arrive fifteen minutes before they meet with the teacher and spend those fifteen minutes looking through the observations, photos, and work samples and reading the summary report. Then the time spent conversing with the teacher can be about twenty minutes. Sending out an established agenda with time frames for each part will let family members know what to expect and will keep the conference on task and on time. We suggest that you structure your conversation with families in a way that follows the format of the summary report on pages 119–120: first, address children's growth and accomplishments; then address your goals and concerns, if any. It is much easier for families to hear your concerns when they have first seen examples of their children's progress.

When you meet with families, good listening skills are of critical importance. By listening carefully, you will help family members feel validated and give them the message that their ideas are important and meaningful. It can sometimes be difficult to listen and really hear what family members are saying. Sometimes you are busy thinking about what you want to share regarding the child's growth and development. In that case, you may not hear family members' concerns clearly. For example, your focus may be to talk about the child's development in all areas. But the family may want to talk about the impact on the child of their grandmother's death. In such a situation it can be difficult to truly listen and respond to the family's concerns appropriately, especially within the time constraints of the conference. It might be necessary to schedule another time to get together to further discuss their concerns. The time between these meetings can also provide you with an opportunity to reflect on their issues and be better prepared to discuss them. Being an effective listener does not mean that the family controls the conference or uses all of the time to discuss their issues, ideas, or concerns. It only means that you truly listen and respond to their thoughts in a way that lets them know you appreciate and value their comments.

Keeping in mind the importance of being a good listener, present the child's portfolio to the family members in attendance. Go over the portfolio documentation that has been collected and the summary report prepared for the conference. When presenting both to the family, it is important to be prepared. If you want to talk about a child's growth in the area of math and science exploration, make sure the documentation backs up your thoughts. Have observation notes, and perhaps photos or work samples of the child engaged in math and science activities. If you want to suggest changes in an infant's feeding or sleep schedule, have several daily reports to support what you have been noticing about the child's patterns. Teachers report to us that such documentation helps support their recommendations to families.

After you have shared portfolio documentation and the summary report, you and the family can set goals for the child for both the school and home environments. This is a wonderful way for families to feel a part of the educational process of their child and to know that their contribution is valued by you and reflected in the goals of your program.

The last part of the conference is to let the families know how much you appreciate their coming and how important their input is to you in your planning. It is important to leave them with a convenient way to get in touch with you if they think of something else they want to share. You also

Darlisa: Observation really helps us in responding to parents during conferences. When they say something like "I don't see my child interacting or having a lot of friends," we can look through the social-emotional development observations and say, "This observation note shows your child's verbal skills in talking with other children."

Kelly: I shared the portfolio observations with the families and they were thrilled with them!

Cathy: I did use the portfolios and photos in my IEP meetings, and parents were genuinely excited to see what their child had done.

might want to follow up with a thank-you note for coming to reaffirm your commitment to them and to their children.

The portfolio documentation and a copy of the evaluation reports should be presented to the family for them to keep. Programs do not have the space to keep the portfolios of all of the children enrolled over the years, but they usually do have the capability to keep a copy of the evaluation reports (even storing them electronically). And families treasure the portfolios! They see them as a keepsake, a wonderful way to remember what their child was doing in their time at the early childhood program. It's important for teachers to honor the interest that families have in this documentation and know that their hard work at collecting the items in the portfolio was well worth it.

A successful meeting between teachers and family members can be rewarding for all involved. When you use observational assessments as the format, family members are much more easily engaged and see more clearly just what their child is doing. They are also more aware of what you do with their child and how well you know them. You reach common ground more easily by using an authentic representation of the child's growth and learning.

· · · · · · ·

In the next chapter, we consider how your observations contribute to your curricular planning for each child. Through your discussions with the families in sharing your assessment information, and through your ongoing reflection as you observe each child in action, you can more easily plan for activities and experiences that help each child continue to grow and flourish.

· · · · · · ·

Observation Practice #15:
Using Observation and Documentation Information to Plan a Family Conference

Purpose: To practice preparing for a family conference using observational documentation.

What to Do: Rewatch video clip #7 for toddlers (scan the top QR code or go to www.vimeo.com/1022181531) or #11 for preschoolers (scan the bottom QR code or go to www.vimeo.com/1022181605) and note what a child does and says. Remember to be factual and descriptive, not interpretive.

Guiding Questions: After viewing, look over your documentation and consider how best to present information to family members in a conference or meeting with them. What specifics from the observation would you want to point out to the family? Exactly what would you say? How do you think the child's family members might respond? How will you answer? If you are participating in a group discussion, discuss which anecdotes would be best to share in a family conference. You may even wish to role-play some of these discussions.

Reflection

Purpose: To reflect on what you know about using an informative and meaningful portfolio as a tool for planning an effective family conference.

- Review documentation you have collected about a child. (If you have none of your own documentation, review some of the observation notes you wrote as you watched the various video clips from the *Focused Observations* videos.)
- Identify which documentation pieces are most appropriate to be used as portfolio documentation based on the recommendations in this chapter. Remember to include documentation that reflects the uniqueness of the child.
- Consider ways you would organize this documentation into a portfolio and how you would present it to families.

Finding Your Observation Style

Purpose: To learn from your experiences with family conferences and consider strategies for ensuring the success of future conferences with families.

- Reflect on your own experiences with family conferences. What have you found successful? What has been challenging? How have you overcome some of these challenges?
- Consider a teacher/family conference from the family's perspective. What might be their fears and worries? What strategies can you use to address those fears?
- How can having a meaningful and informative portfolio waylay some of the potential difficult issues for family members *and* help you plan more effectively?

CHAPTER 7

How Do You Use Observation and Documentation for Curriculum Planning?

▲▼▲▼▲

You can use observation and documentation to plan curriculum in two ways: right away, at the time of the observation, or over time, after you have observed multiple times. Sometimes you see a child doing something, and you immediately offer them your assistance. That's curriculum planning! It happens immediately. You make a judgment about what you are seeing, and you act on it.

At other times, you watch the child more than once so you can build a case about their capabilities and determine where they are having trouble. You might be trying to figure out their specific skills so you can plan activities that challenge them at just the right level. You might be noticing that they are particularly interested in something. Or you might be wondering about their general personality and noticing they have some times of the day when they cope more successfully than others. You observe them on different days and document what they do in different situations. That way you can understand them better and decide on a course of action that matches their needs more closely. This is also curriculum planning. It happens over time.

In the preceding instances, you are using observation and documentation to help you plan curriculum for individual children. Your focus on one child helps you learn more about the child's

- developmental skills and capabilities,
- behavior and ways they deal with frustration throughout the day,
- choices and interests,
- expression of their cultural background, and
- learning style.

April: I use observations to learn about what the children are interested in and their individual learning styles, and to incorporate their individual goals into the curriculum. From my observation of each student, I am able to see if she understood the lesson or if a different approach may be needed.

Kelly: In planning, I was more thoughtful. Instead of just planning for the whole group, I was really thinking about how my lessons were going to affect each child.

You can also use observation and documentation to plan for the whole group of children with whom you work. Again, you may act on what you see immediately, or you may document what the group is doing over time before deciding which actions to take. When you are observing the whole group of children, your focus is broader. You may pay attention to the following:

- how the room environment and materials are being used by the children
- the success of activities you have planned
- what topics and activities children are particularly interested in
- how the daily routine is flowing
- where and when behavior problems are arising
- how the cultural backgrounds of the children are being reflected in your activities and environment

Whether you are observing and documenting and acting immediately or doing so over time, the process of planning curriculum based on observation and documentation is cyclical and ongoing. First you observe and document. As you document, you ask yourself questions. If you are watching a specific child, you may ask, "What can I do to help them?" If you are watching the whole group, you may ask, "What is working? What is not?" Then you make and implement a plan in answer to your question. And guess what: you observe and document again to see how well your plan works! The cycle repeats again and again.

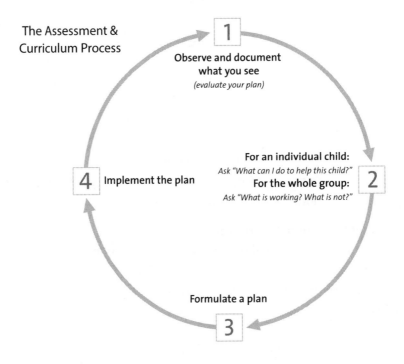

The Assessment &
Curriculum Process

1 Observe and document
what you see
(evaluate your plan)

2 For an individual child:
Ask "What can I do to help this child?"
For the whole group:
Ask "What is working? What is not?"

3 Formulate a plan

4 Implement the plan

What Is Curriculum for Young Children?

It is hard to define curriculum for young children because it can encompass everything that happens throughout the day. Curriculum is about children learning, whether it is alphabet letters, how to trust another person, or how to stack blocks so they don't fall. Good curriculum will build on, sustain, and deepen children's interests in the world around them. And more long-lasting learning will occur when the curriculum is relevant and meaningful to children. To find out what is relevant and meaningful to the children, you have to observe them in action and document what you see them doing!

Teaching looks different when you work with young children than it does when you work with older ones. Teachers of young children provide nurturing and stimulation instead of lecturing or extensive paper-and-pencil tasks. If you work with infants and toddlers, you spend much of your time building a trusting, loving relationship with them; talking and singing with them; providing interesting and safe materials for them; and engaging in the everyday routines of feeding, diapering, and napping. If you work with preschoolers, you carefully arrange the environment so they can explore materials, play with other children, and try out new things safely. You are there to guide and support them more than to tell them what to do.

You watch and interact with children as they play, go about their daily routines, and participate in teacher-designed activities, because these are the ways they show you what they are learning and what they can and can't do. As you do so, you are learning about individual children and drawing conclusions about the whole group. And as you observe, you make decisions about what to do next.

Curriculum for young children is not oriented around textbooks, nor is it centered on teachers imparting knowledge to the children. It is not limited to a theme or letter of the week. Curriculum is based on what works best with the group of children. It is appropriate for the ages of the children and recognizes individual differences as well.

> Children are the focus of the curriculum process. At all times, teachers must keep in mind learning goals in all domains . . . that will support the healthy development of each child: learning goals that are just right for [the age of the child]. These learning goals may come from early learning standards or from assessment tools. Of course, it's ideal for assessment and curricular goals to be the same so teachers don't have to jump back and forth between different sources with differing expectations. (Gronlund 2012, 19)

Jodi: When observing children, I can determine what skills they are obtaining and what they need to work on. Therefore, I have an understanding of what activities need to be planned that will provide children opportunities to work toward the next steps in their development.

Good curriculum reflects the developmental needs and learning styles of young children as identified in recommendations for best practices in early care and education. Developmentally appropriate curricula have the following essential characteristics:

- They foster joyful learning.
- They have explicit goals to meet children's learning and developmental needs.
- They allow for adaptations so each child can engage in full participation.
- Ongoing assessment of progress happens through observation and documentation.
- Opportunities for play are offered to foster development of skills in active and social ways.
- Activities foster development across all domains (social, emotional, physical, linguistic, and cognitive).
- Families' values, beliefs, experiences, cultures, and languages are included.
- Activities follow a predictable schedule that is also flexible to respond to individual children's needs.
- A rich variety of materials are provided to engage children's curiosity and interest. (NAEYC 2022)

And, when implementing developmentally appropriate curricula, teachers pay attention to individual needs and differences as well. Learning goals may differ from child to child, as may teaching strategies. The learning goals for one child may not be at their chronological age. If they have an identified special need, the goals may be different from those for other children their age. If another child is showing advanced capabilities in certain domains, the goals will also have to be adjusted to provide them with the challenges for which they are ready. It's important to learn each child's ways of going about tasks and taking in information so you can provide experiences that are just right for each child.

Many curriculum models and approaches are available to early educators. Some are tied to developmental checklists or criteria (*HighScope; Assessment, Evaluation, and Programming System [AEPS-3]*). Some advocate a more environmentally based approach, in which children explore within a carefully designed and organized set of learning areas and activities (*Creative Curriculum*). Some emphasize following the children's lead so curriculum emerges from the children's interests (emergent curriculum, the Project Approach, Reggio-inspired approaches). Many early childhood

Elizabeth: My documented observations help me modify the activities to meet each child's needs. They help me prepare by being ready with any special equipment I need for an individual student so he can participate in the activity.

programs use a combination of these with adaptations to meet the social and cultural needs of the children and families they serve. Some program staffs write their own curriculum. For example, the Blackfeet Tribe in western Montana wrote a curriculum for its program based on language immersion in its own language. The National Association for the Education of Young Children (NAEYC) does not endorse any one curricular approach, but it does provide frameworks and recommendations for evaluating the appropriateness of a curriculum. *Developmentally Appropriate Practice in Early Childhood Programs Serving Children from Birth through Age 8* (NAEYC 2022) provides guidelines to consult when choosing appropriate curricular strategies.

In *Planning for Play, Observation, and Learning in Preschool and Kinder-garten*, Gronlund (2012) provides planning and reflection frameworks for integrating different curricular approaches. These frameworks include several formal strategies for making individual adjustments to curricular planning and being responsive to children's interests as they develop. Some educators call this individualization or differentiation of curriculum. The goal is to help each child be successful in their own way. Individualizing is not always an easy task, but it is an essential one. Early childhood educators cannot help each child reach their full potential by applying a one-size-fits-all solution. Instead, they must do the following:

- recognize the unique differences of each child
- celebrate those differences
- figure out curricular strategies that build on each child's strengths
- provide support for each child in areas that are challenging

Reflecting Children's Cultural Backgrounds

You can also focus your observations for curriculum planning on children's expression of their cultural backgrounds. This will help you notice if the curriculum is not matching a given child's or group of children's culture or family life. Then you can plan to reflect the child's heritage and family life in your environment, materials, and activities. You can include posters, books, ethnic baby dolls, and dramatic play items that represent cultures and peoples from around the world.

You will be providing a window onto the cultures of the world and a mirror for the child's life experience that will make them feel welcome and validated, as the following story demonstrates.

Consider the following if you are seeking further resources for making your learning environment culturally responsive

Susan Friedman and Alissa Mwenelupembe, eds. 2020. *Each and Every Child: Teaching Preschool with an Equity Lens.* Washington, DC: NAEYC.

Angèle Sancho Passe. 2020. *Creating Diversity-Rich Environments for Young Children.* St. Paul, MN: Redleaf Press.

Toni Sturdivant. 2023. *I Like Myself: Fostering Positive Racial Identity in Young Black Children.* St. Paul, MN: Redleaf Press.

Visiting

Lucy, who was three years old, and her mother visited a new program to consider enrolling her. This program had posters of young children from around the world displayed at children's eye level, and it also had a variety of multicultural materials available to the children. As Lucy and her mother were led on a tour of the facility, Lucy noticed a contemporary picture of another American Indian child. She ran to the poster, pointed to the girl in the photograph, and with a big smile on her face said, "Oh, Mommy, look! She looks just like me." Lucy's mother later reported that this experience was a critical factor in her decision to enroll her child.

This story illustrates how important it is to make sure environments reflect all cultures. Early childhood programs throughout the United States need to reflect the diversity of our population. Children and families with differing experiences, religions, languages, and values should feel welcome to join together and form an accepting community, whether in the child care setting or in the neighborhood. You can play an important role in helping integrate cultural differences while celebrating the unique characteristics of each family and individual. It's critical to move beyond artifacts, holidays, food preparation, and dress as reflections of culture. You need to incorporate values and beliefs that deeply affect children's everyday lives. It's only by doing so that you can provide culturally appropriate care for all children. And educators have their own cultural backgrounds.

The fourth edition of *Developmentally Appropriate Practice* (NAEYC 2022, 51) places emphasis on the impact of educator context: "Educators bring their own experiences and contexts to their decision making. . . . that should be taken into consideration. . . . educators [must be] aware of, and [counter], their own unconscious and larger societal biases that may undermine a child's positive development and well-being." Working to develop awareness of how your life experiences impact your work with children is an ongoing task for early childhood professionals.

Sometimes you see expression of a family's culture in the way a child goes about daily routines.

Sleeping

A southeast Asian immigrant family enrolled their baby in an infant center program. The baby had never slept by himself before, and when he was put into a crib off in a quiet, darkened room, he got very upset. It wasn't just the ordinary upset of a child who was resisting going to sleep even though tired; it was a panic reaction of a child who was very fearful of the situation. No matter what the staff tried to do to help this child sleep alone, nothing worked. He would sleep only near someone in the midst of the activity of the playroom. Being by himself to sleep was a fearful and foreign situation for him. (Gonzalez-Mena 1993, 30)

Views and values related to attachment and separation vary according to cultural expectations, beliefs, and life experiences. Some cultures stress autonomy and separateness, while others emphasize connection and dependence on others. Each family's behavior regarding separation and attachment looks very different based on the family's value system.

Avi (three years)

Avi and his family had recently moved to the United States from Israel. Right away we noticed that Avi's mother was reluctant to leave him. She stayed for the entire three hours each day. As we thought about reasons for her reluctance, we imagined that a part of her hesitance was the fact that they had left a strife-torn country. We guessed that safety was probably an issue for this family. We wanted to give her and her son plenty of time to feel safe and to learn to trust us. So we just let her stay for the first three weeks of school. Then we asked her if she would be willing to go for a short walk each day. She reluctantly agreed and would always peek in the window before she would go for her walk to ensure that Avi was fine. Slowly, she began to leave for longer and longer periods of time. After about the first two months of school, she felt comfortable leaving for the entire morning. Avi's mom became one of the most devoted parents we had and could always be depended on to help out in any way we needed. I often wonder how different this scenario might have been if we were not sensitive to the family's unique attachment and separation needs.

Some families believe in holding their child more than you may have experienced with other families. The child may therefore expect more physical contact and holding from you. Being sensitive to these issues and asking the families about their beliefs, values, and life experiences will help you be more in tune with their children.

Planning for Individual Children

If you are focusing on an individual child, you may decide to take a more passive role and let the child take the initiative. It's as if you and the child are dance partners and you are following the child's lead in the dance steps. At other times, you may take the lead, recognizing that you need to be more proactive to help the child. Sometimes it's best to stand back, watch, and encourage. At other times, it's more helpful to support the child with your assistance, to provide a scaffold that helps them do things they cannot quite do on their own. And sometimes it's necessary for you to direct or demonstrate for the child so they know exactly how to go about something. You move back and forth between being more and less involved with the child.

Here is a continuum that provides a way of looking at the choices you have as you consider which strategy works most effectively in various situations. You will notice in the following graphic that the child's engagement changes as the teaching strategy moves back and forth.

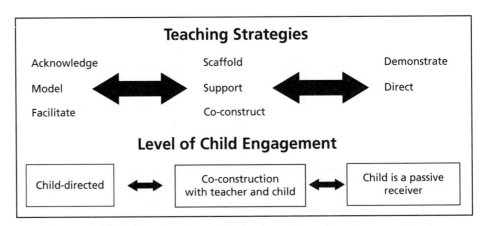

For young children, it's important that teaching strategies and curricular experiences are most frequently to the left and middle of the continuum in the graphic. Why is that? Because young children learn best through active engagement. When teachers acknowledge, model, or facilitate what children are doing, they are allowing the children to take the lead and direct the activity. This would be done only when the children's engagement is safe and productive. When teachers scaffold, support, or co-construct with children, they join in the children's direction of the activity as a co-player or helpmate. Again, the children have an active role in leading what they are doing. Notice when the teacher is demonstrating or directing that the child is in a more passive role. Hopefully, these moments are few, as this is not the most effective curricular approach for young children. Children benefit most when they are active participants in the learning process. Of course, in those moments when safety concerns arise, a teacher does need to direct their actions.

Your job becomes one of figuring out the level of teaching and intervention that is most appropriate in each situation throughout the day. You engage in continual decision-making, asking yourself, "What is the most effective strategy to use with each child in each situation?" If you work with young children with disabilities, neurodivergence, or developmental delays, you will consider each child's capabilities and try to provide them with the support they need and any special equipment or assistance necessary. For typically developing children, you do much the same as you figure out how extensive your involvement will be. When thinking about individual children, you have several choices of what to do:

- observe and encourage the child to continue what they are doing
- select different materials or change the environment in some way
- plan for specific teacher guidance and intervention
- use peer interactions
- design special activities
- bring in additional resources

Lillian: When I notice that a child is low in a specific area, I try to include activities in the center they go to most often. I plan activities that all the children can participate in also. I have found that children are more likely to join in an activity if someone else is doing it or they can do it with their friends.

The only way to judge the success of your planning is to try it out and observe to see what happens. Certain choices may be more effective when you are focusing on a child's developmental skills or behavior. Others may be more appropriate for building on a child's interests or responding to their expression of their cultural background. Keep in mind that you can apply your plan anytime of the day: while the child is playing, engaged in daily routines, or joining in an activity that you have designed especially for them.

There are times when children need nothing more than your acknowledgment and encouragement. Laughing along with a joyous child, sitting next to a child busy at work in the art area, quietly watching a child building with blocks, or verbally describing a child's problem solving with the waterwheel at the sensorimotor table are all ways of encouraging children. Through your behavior, you are saying, "I like what you are doing. Keep it up!" And through comments like "You are working hard on that painting,"

"I think you used every block in the bin," and "You can do it," you are expressing your acceptance of what the children are doing and your expectations that they should continue in the direction they are going.

And there are times when you don't need to do anything at all. In the following situation, Kaylee's teachers observed and saw no need to intervene in any way.

Kaylee (four years, five months)

After waking up from a nap, Kaylee walks to Riley and says, "Hey, Riley, come over here. I'm the teacher. You sit there and pay attention!" Then Riley says, "No, I don't want to play. I'm busy right now, okay?" Then Kaylee says, "Come on, Riley. Please. I'll play with you later. But you got to say the colors in English and Spanish. Come on. It won't take long. Okay, please?" So Riley says, "Okay. Red, yellow, orange, purple, white." Then Kaylee says, "Now, say it in Spanish!" Then Riley says, "White, blanco."

They continue to play until it is time for snack.

Kaylee used language to engage Riley in play and was successful in negotiating with him to stay involved with her until snacktime. Her teachers noted her high level of verbal interaction, interest in Spanish words, pretend play abilities, and social skills.

Determining Next Steps for Individual Children

Kaylee's teachers also considered what next steps they might plan in their curriculum for Kaylee and Riley. It was clear that both were interested in Spanish words. The teachers decided to provide more Spanish books, teach the children Spanish songs and poems, and encourage more dramatic play around being teachers and students. They also watched closely to make sure Riley was a willing participant each time Kaylee asked him to play. They assured him that he could tell Kaylee if he wanted to play someplace else in the classroom or if he wanted to have a turn being the teacher sometimes.

Determining next steps for individual children based on your observations is an important part of curriculum planning. Look at the following example about Robert as he shows what he can do to solve the problem of getting a toy he wants. As you read this anecdote, think about what experiences you might plan next for Robert based on what he is showing he can do.

Robert (ten months)

Robert crawls over to the shelf where the musical toys are kept. He pulls himself up to stand in front of the shelf holding the toy drum. He stands for a minute looking at the drum. Then he reaches for the drumstick attached to the drum. Using the drumstick, he pulls the drum toward him until he pulls the drum off the shelf. He sits down on the floor and begins playing with the drum.

It's clear that Robert is balancing and getting ready to walk. He acts with purpose and problem solves to get the drum off the shelf. And he shows interest in musical instruments. If you were his teacher, you may plan next steps such as these:

- Give him many opportunities to stand, balance, and take steps with your support.
- Provide him with stacking rings and other toys that require problem solving.
- Bring out other musical instruments, such as a xylophone and striker and shakers, that make different sounds.

At other times when children are involved in an activity, you recognize that they could take this activity a bit further if they had some different materials. Your goal may be to lengthen their attention span and engagement. Or you may recognize that the skills they are demonstrating are easy for them. Therefore, you want to extend the activity so they can use more complex approaches to the task or deepen their understanding of the concepts involved. You also may be building on an interest a child is showing in using particular materials. You want to provide additional opportunities for them to follow up on that interest. The following anecdote describes one such situation. Read it and identify other materials you might provide for Hudson to continue and extend his interest in sorting and patterning.

Hudson (three years)

One day Hudson went over to the block area and spent approximately ten minutes sorting through all of the unit block shapes. Then he made a tower with five cylinder-shaped blocks. "Look what I did!" he called out to me. My coteacher and I recognized that he was grouping objects and decided to provide Hudson with additional materials for sorting and grouping. We set out colored plastic teddy bears in a large red basket, and over the next few days, he got several small boxes off the shelf and sorted the bears by color so that the red bears were together, yellow bears were together, and so on. He put both blue and purple into the same small box. On another day, he took small colored pegs and lined them up across the floor in a recurring pattern.

Sometimes you see a child take the same actions again and again with poor results. Dealing with difficult behaviors can be a challenging part of your work with children. You may feel that you need to be on constant alert as to a particular child's whereabouts. You may have to take steps to protect other children and remove a child from a certain area of the classroom. You may get to the point where you have to admit that you just don't understand the meaning of a child's behavior. As you read the following anecdote, think about how taking the time to observe the situation helped the teacher see Jeremy's behavior more clearly and allowed her to offer assistance to him so he could more successfully join in play.

Jeremy (four years, three months)

I observed Jeremy closely over several days in the block area. Each day he would watch the children for a few minutes, especially two boys building complex block structures. Then, with no warning, he would wander over to where they were and knock down their structure.

After observing and documenting this for a few days, Jeremy's teacher began to realize that Jeremy lacked the social skills to enter into play with others. So she asked him if he wanted her to play with him. He immediately responded with an emphatic yes. From that point on, the teacher worked with him to help him learn appropriate ways to enter into play. As they played, the other boys came and joined them. The teacher modeled appropriate ways for Jeremy to play with them. After a few days, she was able to sit close by but not be very involved. After a couple of weeks, Jeremy and the other boys were playing cooperatively without any help from the teacher. A month or so later, he routinely asked other children if he could play with them or asked an adult for help. The teacher said, "If I hadn't taken the time to watch and wonder, and document what I saw, I would have assumed that Jeremy was misbehaving once again. If I had acted too soon, I imagine the outcome would have been very different for Jeremy."

Jeremy's teacher offered him the support he needed to help him move to the next level in his social skills. This process is called *scaffolding* and is based on the theories of Lev Vygotsky. As we discussed in chapter 5, it involves providing just the right amount of challenge. You'll know it's just right because the child will be successful and begin to take responsibility for the task as their skill increases. This place where children do not quite have independent skills but where they can be successful with adult or peer support is called the zone of proximal development, or ZPD. When a task is within a child's ZPD, the child can become more and more independent in completing it.

> According to Vygotsky, the role of education is to provide children with experiences that are in their ZPDs—activities that challenge children but that can be accomplished with sensitive adult guidance. Consequently, adults carry much responsibility for making sure that children's learning is maximized by actively leading them along the developmental pathway. The teacher's role, rather than instructing children in what they are ready for or giving them tasks for which they have already acquired the necessary mental operations, is to keep tasks in children's ZPDs, or slightly above their level of independent functioning. (Berk and Winsler 1995, 26)

The following is a description of a situation in which the adults determined that the best curricular strategy was to provide a challenge for the child but also to offer adult help or scaffolding so he could be successful and overcome his fear.

Kyle (two years, two months)

Lately, when we go outdoors, Kyle spends time watching the other children climbing up and sliding down on the toddler-sized slide. We ask him if he wants to go up. He shakes his head no and continues to stand nearby each day, watching the others. Even though he is saying no, we think he is capable of climbing and sliding. Today I said to him, "Even though I hear you saying no, I think you really want to go up the stairs and down the slide. How about if I hold your hand and help you walk up and help you slide down?" He looked at me wide-eyed, took my hand, and off we went. After holding my hand tightly two times, he climbed up by himself with me standing close by.

Here's a graphic that illustrates the zone of proximal development.

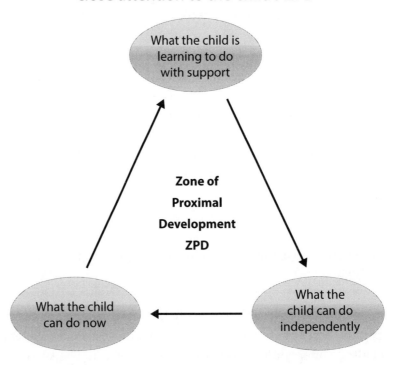

For individual children, teachers pay close attention to the child's ZPD

Scaffolding occurs along the left-hand arrow in the graphic as a teacher recognizes what the child can do now and what they could do with teacher support. The goal is to initially provide that support and then to slowly step back so that at a later time the child will be able to complete similar tasks on their own. It's a matter of observing what the child can and cannot do and assessing the child's potential response when encountering problems.

> Teachers who use effective scaffolding also know to wait patiently as they figure out how much support to give a child. In the waiting process, they can
>
> - take in the situation and observe closely,
> - see if the child will relish the challenge or not,
> - ask the child if he wants assistance, or
> - consider small amounts of assistance so the child will stay engaged. (Gronlund and Rendon 2017, 31)

Sometimes the best way to bring about successful results with a child is to use peer interactions. This can be an effective curricular strategy that can distract an angry child or bring out a quieter one. In the following example, the adults had observed Olivia over time, noticing her social isolation. They decided to use peer interactions as the way to move Olivia into more conversation and socialization.

Olivia (four years, ten months)

Usually Olivia plays and works all by herself. She does not seek out other children. If others sit down next to her, she will continue to work on her own without much interaction. We have wanted to see if we could help Olivia start engaging in more conversation and social interaction. So today, when she chose to go to the playdough table where dinosaur figures were also available, we suggested to Lydia that she join Olivia. Lydia is a very verbal and interactive child. We thought maybe the pairing of the two might bring Olivia out a little more. As they worked with the playdough and dinosaurs, both girls talked to each other about what the dinosaurs could do and eat. They then sat next to each other at snacktime and talked as well! Our strategy was a success!

Sometimes your plan involves designing special activities or bringing in additional resources. Here is an example in which the adults recognized they needed to have more resources in a child's first language to reflect his culture in the program and develop his communication skills.

Yuta (twenty-four months)

When Yuta began our program, he communicated through gesture only. We asked his mom to teach us some Japanese words, and we got a book with Japanese words in it. We also purchased a CD with Japanese music on it. Now Yuta responds to us in Japanese and does understand some English. He chooses the book frequently, bringing it to us to read to him.

And here is an example in which the adult provided additional materials, resources, and activities in response to a child's interest.

Taneisha (five years, two months)

After a heavy rainfall, the sidewalk to the classroom was covered with earthworms. I took a cafeteria tray, went outside, collected several worms on the tray, and brought it inside for the children to study. All of the children were interested, but Taneisha more than anyone else. She spent fifteen to twenty minutes sitting quietly, watching the worms wriggle about on the tray. I asked Taneisha if she wanted to make worms out of playdough. Her eyes lit up. She played with the playdough near the tray of worms and made many different versions of her own earthworms. The next day I brought in books about earthworms. Taneisha spent much time looking at them and studying the pictures. I read several to her and invited her to make her own earthworm book. She dictated to me, "Some worms are long. They don't like the wet grass. They don't look like they have any eyes." Even though we put the worms back outside at the end of that rainy day, Taneisha stayed interested in the topic for several days afterward.

Planning for a Group of Children

As you observe the group of children, you may find that certain times of the day go more smoothly than others. Focusing on how children negotiate time within the daily schedule helps you determine if there is an appropriate balance among activities, routines, and transitions throughout the day, varying passive and more active opportunities for children. It's likely that you evaluate the flow of the routine intuitively each day. You probably recognize when children need a change in the pace of activities. Even so, observation can help you notice if one part of the routine is always problematic. Paying attention to that often troublesome time of the day for a week or so can give you insight into the cause of the problem so you can address it in a thoughtful way. Making a change so children are happily engaged is a smart decision.

You can also use observation to plan for the whole group of children with whom you work. When you do this, you are still watching individual children and noting what you are learning about them. But you are compiling this knowledge to use for different purposes. You are answering the questions, "What is working for this group of children? What is not working?" Then, based on the answers you are gaining to these questions, you may do some or all of the following:

- Rearrange the room and change materials as needed, paying attention to children's choices and where behavior problems arise.
- Plan activities that will better engage the children.
- Plan based on children's interests and issues.
- Stay flexible within the daily schedule based on the needs of the children.
- Reflect children's cultural backgrounds and become more sensitive to their families' approaches to child rearing.

When you think broadly about curriculum for all of the children, your observations can enhance your understanding of the children and help you make adaptations and changes so you and the children feel successful.

> Each group of children looks and acts differently depending on their prior knowledge and their families' experiences and expectations. When the teacher looks at these elements holistically and builds opportunities based on the group's assets, the community of learners comes together and is culturally relevant to the children and their families. (Seitz 2023a, 7–8)

Rosemary: Observing my students is probably how I learn the most about them—their personalities, how they get along with friends, when and how they are most comfortable (playing with friends or by themselves), their ability to focus or persist on tasks, their language and vocabulary, and their math and numeracy skills beyond just counting. This helps me know how best to lesson plan for my students as individuals and as a group.

Room Environment and Materials

You already observe intuitively every day to determine whether the physical environment of your program is meeting the needs of the children. When you see poor behavior, misuse of materials, and high levels of frustration on the part of the children, you know that you are seeing warning signs that something is amiss. Loud noisy play rather than a pleasant hum of activity can be a sign that an area is not working well. Sometimes children totally avoid an area or set of materials. Sometimes too many children want to engage with a few specific items or gather in a space that is too small to accommodate them.

Many early childhood classrooms are organized into interest areas or learning centers. Older toddlers and preschoolers are given at least one fairly long block of time each day during which they can move from center to center, choosing from the variety of activities available and interacting with different children and adults. Most programs include the following interest areas:

- art
- blocks
- dramatic play
- manipulatives
- science and math
- movement and music
- library
- sensory table
- writing center

Monitoring the children's choices in these areas and their levels of engagement and interactions can be a useful way to approach evaluating your environment. When observing children, you can use a Choice Record as shown on the next page as a quick way to jot down information about their engagement in the areas of your room. As you watch the children, you note the areas they visit during a set time period. If one child is being observed, a tally mark in various areas may be all you record. You can also include the amount of time they stay engaged with the materials in that area. If you are observing several children, you can write their names in the areas they visit that day. We have provided two Choice Record formats in appendix B and linked on the Focused Observations product page at www.redleafpress.org—one for preschoolers and one for toddlers.

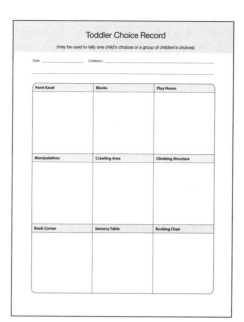

You can learn a lot about children by observing the choices they make of activities and the areas of the room they choose to spend time in. Often children choose to do something again and again. Their choices may look repetitive to you, yet there may be a very good reason why they are involved in the same activity or choosing the same materials. Here are some things to consider when observing children who repeat activities:

- They may feel comfortable with the activity because it is familiar to them. They may have done it at home.
- They may be afraid to try something new.
- They may feel successful if they are able to do it easily. It's something they have accomplished.
- They have almost mastered it and are practicing it again and again to get better at it. It may require them to use a skill they are working on.

When children choose areas of the room to return to again and again, they are showing us their personalities and their strengths. An artistic child may choose to paint and draw every day. At daily outdoor time, a very physical toddler may climb up to the top of the climber as they use their big muscles to their fullest. A very verbal child may love to get other children to join in pretending with dress-up clothes and dolls. They take the lead,

Robin J.: I am in a classroom with three-year-olds. Observing with more focus forces me to set the environment up in a way that's more process oriented so that it allows me the time to concentrate on the children and to observe them and be able to write down the things that I need to write down.

Mark: I have noticed that so many children are interested in building structures in the block area. I realize that I need to provide more tools (such as plastic hammers, saws, and screwdrivers) and more picture books with different block constructions and buildings. I think I'll add writing materials too and see what they do with those. I'll encourage them to make signs for their buildings or plans before they build. It ought to be interesting.

providing the script ideas and assigning roles because of their ability to use language effectively. In contrast to choosing favorites based on their strengths, children may avoid activities and play experiences in which they have to use skills that are not as strong. Children with strong gross-motor skills may avoid fine-motor activities that are more challenging for them. Children who have not developed social skills or the language to communicate effectively with others may avoid dramatic play experiences. They may not feel confident negotiating roles in pretend play. They may play alone or off to the side of groups who are actively interacting, using materials, and taking on various pretend roles.

Choice Records not only help you identify children's choices and interests but also can help you determine how effectively the environment is being used by the children. If you have lots of marks in one area and very few in another, you may want to make changes in the less popular one. Here are two examples of Choice Records—the first for a preschool child, including time tallies, and the second for a group of toddlers.

Preschool Choice Record

(may be used to tally one child's choices or a group of children's choices)

Date __Feb. 10__   Child(ren) __Miguel, 3 yrs. 8 mos.__

Art	Blocks	Dramatic Play
10 min.	0	5 min.
Manipulatives	**Science/Math**	**Music/Movement**
9 min.	0	0
Library	**Sensory Table**	**Writing Center**
0	15 min.	0

Toddler Choice Record

(may be used to tally one child's choices or a group of children's choices)

Date __April 15__   Child(ren) __Makenra 1 yr. 6 mos.; Jesse 1 yr. 10 mos.;__
__Hurriell 24 mos.__

Paint Easel	Blocks	Play House
H	M, J	M, H
Manipulatives	**Crawling Area**	**Climbing Structure**
J	H, M	J
Book Corner	**Sensory Table**	**Rocking Chair**
	M, J, H	M

As teachers observe for children's engagement and record their choices of play areas and activities on the Choice Record, they continue to act as play facilitators. They are ready to step in and out of play experiences, offering support and assistance, engaging in problem solving with the children, providing different materials or ideas, and helping them engage in high-level play with all of its benefits.

You can decide how best to record information about children's choices. You can write children's full names or just their initials in the appropriate boxes for the areas where they get engaged productively. You can also include the amount of time each child stays working in that area or at that activity. The time does not need to be determined to the second or the minute—no stopwatch is needed! However, it should be a good approximation of the time the child was involved.

You can also pay attention to children's behavior and try to figure out where in the room you see problems develop. Keeping a record of where you see tears or hear angry words will help you rethink the arrangement of furniture, shelves, and materials. Making changes to the arrangement of furniture, the organization and availability of materials, or the use of space based on those observations can often create dramatic and positive changes in children's behavior.

When analyzing the environment to identify where inappropriate behaviors are arising, the first step is to document where they occur. Some teachers use small sticky notes and post them on the wall above the areas (out of reach of the children) where problems are seen. Doing this over a few days or a week's time will help identify the areas that need to be addressed. You may notice that traffic patterns are the source of problems; for example, children are crossing through the block area to get to dramatic play and accidentally, but routinely, knocking down others' block structures. A simple rearrangement of the block shelves to protect the building area and reroute the traffic flow is all that may be needed. It may help to get down on your knees so you can look at the environment from a child's viewpoint (sitting on a child-sized chair can give you a similar vantage point). Looking from this perspective can help you evaluate safety issues: Are the corners on the cupboards showing signs of splintering? Is there enough space to get around the legs of the art easel? It can also provide insight into how clearly defined and inviting areas of the classroom appear to the children. If children are avoiding an area, it may be because they cannot easily see the materials available there or because the area is not clearly defined by the arrangement of shelves and tables.

Sara: I feel this is at the heart of teaching—looking at the individual children, looking at their interests and what they can do. It feels really good to me. It's the basis for good teaching.

Evaluating the Success of Activities

How do you know whether an activity you planned for the children is successful? What are the signs? Evaluating the success of your planning is something you do spontaneously, at the time you are involved with the children, and in reflection, as you think about it at a later time. You know an activity is successful when you notice signs like these:

- The children's eyes are bright; they smile and show enthusiasm as they participate in the activity.
- The children stay for a long period of time (anywhere from ten to thirty minutes depending on their age).
- They tell you that they like what they are doing, saying things like "This is fun!" or "I like playdough."
- They ask to do it again or talk about it at a later time.
- You see very few behavior problems as children engage in the activity.
- The children take the activity to more complex and deeper levels than you had originally planned, adding their own ideas, bringing new materials, or using the materials in different ways.

In contrast, how do you know when an activity is not working, when it is not successful? Sometimes you see difficulties arise right on the spot, and trying to keep the group on task can become nearly impossible, as in this example:

Colored Bears

Three four-year-old boys are invited by their teacher, Gina, to sort colored bears into round sorting trays with multiple compartments. As long as she is there with them, the boys cooperate in the sorting activity, talking about the colors of the bears as they sort them. As she moves on after five or six minutes to help in another area of the classroom, their interaction with the bears changes. "Hey, I know," says Alec. "Let's see who can throw them into the tray!" The boys move the trays to the opposite end of the table and begin to throw the bears. Their initial throws involve aiming at the small compartments. As bears fly across the table and land in the compartments, some of them bounce out again onto the table from the force of the throw. The boys laugh hysterically and continue to throw the bears harder and harder. Their laughter grows louder by the minute. Soon bears are flying across the table and onto the floor. The boys' laughter is high-pitched. They pound on and lie across the table as each bear lands. (Gronlund and James 2008, 50)

Although this small-group activity was of interest to the children when the teacher stayed closely involved, it was not one this group of boys could sustain on their own. Through their behavior, they demonstrated some of the following ways that communicate to an observant teacher that an activity is not successful:

- The children look away or get distracted or their eyes glaze over.
- They wiggle or get more physical than the activity calls for, so that they may lose control of their bodies, getting silly or being rougher in their actions.
- If they are monitoring their own involvement, they stay involved for a very short time and quickly move on to something of more interest.
- Their general behavior deteriorates.
- They act unenthusiastic (no bright eyes, no excitement) and ask questions such as "Do I have to?" or "When can I leave?"
- They tell you, "This is boring," or "I already know how to do this."

When you see these behaviors, you need to make a change in what you are doing, and the sooner the better! For the preceding example, here is how the teacher intervened to reengage the boys in more productive interaction with materials.

Colored Bears (continued)

Gina moves across the room and says to the boys, "It's gotten very loud over here. And I see that you're throwing the bears instead of sorting them." The boys stop throwing but still giggle. She continues, "It looks to me like you wanted to do something different with the bears. That's okay. But throwing them into these small compartments probably isn't safe. What are some other things you might do with the bears?" The boys look at her blankly, and Noah says, "I don't know." Gina says, "I wonder if you might like to practice throwing with something else, like beanbags and soft balls. We could set up a hoop as the target over there across the room. You could try throwing from different distances and see how many times you can get the beanbags and balls inside the hoop. What do you think?" Noah and his friends yell out, "Yeah! Let's do that." Gina suggests that they clean up the bears first, then help her get out the throwing items and hoop. She then supervises as they play the throwing game. (Gronlund 2010, 83–84)

Sometimes you design activities like Gina did that address specific skills. You may plan to work with a small group of children and will document what you see them doing so you can assess their progress on these skills. For example, you want the three-year-olds to work with you on matching colors. You design a matching game using wallpaper samples cut into squares. At playtime you invite a few three-year-olds to join you in this activity. And as they do so, you document their matching capabilities on your clipboard. Some children may come readily; others may choose not to. Some may enthusiastically play the matching game; some may only stay for a minute. You will know how successful the activity is when you look over the responses of all the children and ask yourself these questions:

- Were the children interested and engaged? How did I know that?
- How many children participated?
- Did the children seem to enjoy the activity?
- Did I learn what I needed to learn about their skills? (Loomis and Wagner 2005)

Implementing teacher-designed activities may be more successful if you think of a variety of ways you can meet your goal of learning about the children's particular skills. Considering again the example of wanting to observe children's color-matching skills, in addition to the wallpaper matching game, you could also provide small colored blocks and colored bowls or trays, strings and colored beads, markers, and colored paper. You could offer a selection of matching activities to the children to give them a choice of materials that better suit their interests. This selection may keep them engaged for a longer period of time and give you more information about how well they are recognizing similarities and differences across varying materials. This helps you avoid mistaking boredom for a lack of skill or understanding.

Children's Interests

Building on children's interests makes your curriculum more relevant to them. Sometimes a group of children become absolutely fascinated with a topic such as dinosaurs or trains. They relate much of their play to this topic. They ask lots of questions and show excitement when you respond by providing materials and resources related to their interest. They engage more readily in activities and sometimes take their own level of exploration and knowledge deeper than you might have thought was possible. Think of how many young children have an extensive vocabulary of dinosaur names and traits and understand the basic definition of extinction.

Planning curricular activities based on children's interests is a "win-win" approach—good for the children and good for the teachers. Here are some examples of children expressing their interests and favorite activities.

> "I love playdough. It's my favorite!" Lupita smiles broadly as she mushes the playdough between her hands. Her teacher, Mary, has noticed that Lupita chooses playdough almost every time it is available.

> Josiah often plays in the pretend kitchen in his toddler classroom. "I cook," he says as he bangs a wooden spoon inside a metal pot. "Me make soup." He stirs and bangs and offers the "soup" to his teachers and to other children. The other children mimic their teachers, blowing on and sipping from Josiah's outstretched spoon as he grins broadly.

> "When can we build the marble run again, Mr. Mark?" Mallory and Todd ask this question almost daily. Todd touches Mallory's arm gently as he says to his friend, "We wanna make the marbles go really fast, huh, Mallory?" Mallory nods her head and smiles. Mr. Mark has noticed that these two will play for up to forty minutes at a time when the marble run is available.

Young children who are given the opportunity to choose from among a variety of play areas and activities will demonstrate interests and choose favorites. As teachers observe these choices and identify trends in the children's engagement, they can learn a lot about each child. Children tend to choose activities that engage them. And, usually, they are more fully engaged by activities and play experiences in which they can use their developmental strengths.

Listening carefully to the questions children ask and paying attention to the play themes they are acting out can help you identify their deep interests and passions. You will also understand more about the knowledge they are constructing. You can ask open-ended questions to learn more about their thinking. One group of four- and five-year-olds showed interest in the pipes under the bathroom sink. A child asked, "Where does the water go?" The teacher responded, "Where do you think it goes?" This started

Peggy S.: When I ask, "Is there something more you would like to learn about?" children usually produce a wealth of questions. For example, as part of our study of farms, children asked questions such as, "Why is the milk always white even if the cows are different colors?" "Where do puppies come from, because my friend's dog had puppies?" and "I want to know about big fat pigs!" So one of our plans is to visit a farm and specifically try to learn more about their interests.

an investigation for the group. They visited other bathroom and sink areas in the center. The teacher took notes on the number and size of the pipes. They flushed toilets and checked outdoor faucets and hypothesized about where the water went. The teacher brought in plastic pipes for building and tubes for using at the water table. She found books showing plumbing systems and underground sewer systems. She continually responded to the children's queries by asking for their thinking and by providing information and opportunities for them to figure things out for themselves.

Sometimes you see behavior that is silly and inappropriate because the children do not have information to explain what is happening. The fascination with each other's bodies and the sounds they make can easily turn into giggles or embarrassment and lead to misbehavior. You can provide books about human bodies and how the digestive system works to turn the silliness into understanding. Sometimes children behave in ways you do not understand. You see them acting out situations in your house corner that concern you. Or you see obsessive attention to play based on the latest movies and television shows. This play often deteriorates to the point where a child is hurt or angry. The following is a description of just such an incident:

The Doll Corner

The four girls in the doll corner have announced who they are: Mother, Sister, Baby, Maid. . . . Charlotte is the mother because, she tells the others, she is wearing the silver shoes. . . .

Karen: I'm hungry. Wa-a-ah!

Charlotte: Lie down, baby.

Karen: I'm a baby that sits up.

Charlotte: First you lie down and sister covers you and then I make your cereal and then you sit up.

Karen: Okay.

Teddy watches the scene as he fills up the number board for the second time. Charlotte returns his stare and says, "You can be the father." He inserts the last two tiles and enters the doll corner.

"Are you the father?" Charlotte asks.

"Yes."

"Put on the red tie."

She doesn't know Teddy's name yet, but she can tell him what to wear because she is the mother.

The girls look pleased. "I'll get it for you, honey," Janie says in a falsetto voice. She is the maid. "Now, don't that baby look pretty? This is your daddy, baby." Teddy begins to set the table, matching cups and saucers as deliberately as he did the tiles on the number board.

Abruptly, the mood changes. Andrew, Jonathan, Jeremy, and Paul rush in, fingers shooting. "We're robbers. Do you got any gold?"

"No," Charlotte says, stirring an empty pot.

Jeremy climbs on the refrigerator and knocks over several cartons of plastic food. "Put up your hands. You're going to jail!"

"We're telling!" The girls stomp out. . . . (Paley 1984, 1–2)

Play that is influenced by the media can be very troublesome in early childhood programs. Problems arise because such play is imitative and is not as rewarding to children as is play they have created from their own imaginations. Much intervention on your part may be necessary to protect children's safety and encourage more positive interactions. It may be hard for you to want to build on the children's interest in this kind of play. Yet the underlying themes of feeling powerful and keeping safe are important and universal ones for children. "The sense of power and competence that is experienced in war play—as children pretend to be superheroes with super powers, for instance—can help children feel like strong and separate people who can take care of themselves" (Carlsson-Paige and Levin 1987, 27).

When observing children involved in play scripts that imitate Spider-Man movies or superhero television shows, you can recognize the important developmental issues that children are exploring. If you only intervene and attempt to stop or forbid the play, you are missing the strong need that children have to feel powerful in a sometimes scary and violent world. You can recognize the play theme as an important one for children to explore and then intervene in ways to help the play move beyond mere imitation and develop instead into more complex and rewarding play. In this way, you will tame the inappropriate behaviors that arise and help children to take control of their play so they feel empowered or gain a sense of resolution (Carlsson-Paige and Levin 1987).

Many early educators find that one way to encourage children to move beyond media-influenced play is to explore the same developmental themes of power, safety, and conflict resolution through children's literature about fairy tales, monsters, outer space creatures, dinosaurs, and scary things. In fact, much of children's fascination with dinosaurs probably comes from their deep, internal need for safety. They see dinosaurs as safe monsters because they are extinct.

In describing her attempts at working with children in their superhero play, Gronlund (1992, 23–24) wrote the following about her results:

> The aggressiveness of the play lessened. As I watched more closely, I saw that most of the kicking and karate chopping was indeed an attempt at "fake fighting." . . .
>
> If play became overwhelming for a child, or if actions were leading toward out-of-control behaviors, I engaged the children again using the lingo of their play. . . .
>
> I began to realize that fairy tales provided an outlet for children to explore the very same themes that Ninja Turtles did. . . . Dinosaur parades; building the Troll's bridge for the staging of The Three Billy Goats Gruff; making monster masks; and doing many readings of [favorite monster books] . . . all became regular events in our classroom.
>
> My acceptance of the children's favorite shows allowed everyone to express their feelings more openly. . . .
>
> I, as a teacher, needed to recognize the ways boys and girls work through the issues of power, aggression, and violence as different, but interrelated, and help the children see that connectedness.

For more information on working with children in regard to issues of superhero and fantasy play in early childhood classrooms, see Eric Hoffman's book *Magic Capes, Amazing Powers: Transforming Superhero Play in the Classroom*, Diane Levin's book *Teaching Young Children in Violent Times: Building a Peaceable Classroom*, and Donna King's *Pursuing Bad Guys: Joining Children's Quest for Clarity, Courage and Community*.

The next two examples show children playing out themes of power. As you read these, think about how you might interact with these boys in a way that respects the importance of the issues they are exploring and helps them keep the play productive and rewarding for them.

Wyatt (three years, six months) and
Salimu (three years, eight months)

Salimu and Wyatt are playing at the sand table. They're putting sand into a container together.

WYATT: Let's make a cake.

SALIMU: Yeah, a bad cake.

WYATT: Yeah, because we're bad guys.

WYATT: Bad guys making a bad cake.

SALIMU: Yeah, with people on top. They got stuck in my mouth.

WYATT: Bad guy people are on top of the cake.

SALIMU: Real! We're gonna eat them.

Waylon (four years, eight months)

Waylon is in the loft with four other boys playing firefighters. He is in the front of the two other boys and says, "Let's go. There's a fire!" One boy moves forward, and Waylon tells him, "Get back, guys. Get back. You're supposed to be in the back. You're in the driver's seat." Then he yells, "Let's go! There's another fire!" He goes to the *atelier* (art studio) and pretends to spray the fire with a hose and yells again, "There's another fire!" They run back up into the loft, and again Waylon looks to the front and tells one of the boys, "No, there's the driver's spot." Another boy tells him he is a Ninja Turtle, and Waylon says, "Ninja Turtles are not firefighters. This is a firefighter truck. Go find a Ninja Turtle truck."

• • • • • • •

In the next chapter, we examine ways to collect a set of documented observations that will help you build a well-rounded and informative case about a child. We look at several such sets and consider each child's developmental capabilities and how to plan next steps for each one.

• • • • • • •

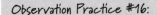

Observation Practice #16:
Determining the Best Curricular Approaches for a Child

Purpose: To identify the best ways to support a child.

What to Do: Watch Video Clip #16 (scan the QR code or go to www.vimeo .com/1022181710) of a toddler working with a puzzle with the support of her teacher. As you watch, write down what the child does and says. Remember to be factual and descriptive, not interpretive.

Guiding Questions: After viewing, identify in your notes when the child was most successfully engaged. How did the teacher's support help the child with the activity? Identify ways you might try to help the child be successful in future interactions. If you are participating in a group discussion, discuss some of the anecdotes written by group members and consider how the teacher's involvement helped the child's behavior.

Observation Practice #17:
Encouraging and Extending a Child's Interests

Purpose: To determine ways to use materials to set up the environment and interact with children to build on their interests.

What to Do: Watch Video Clip #17 (scan the QR code or go to www.vimeo .com/1022181719) of three-year-old children as they work with a variety of materials to make "potions." Pay close attention to all of the things the children are interested in and are able to do. Focus on how the environment is set up with materials that interest them and what the teachers do to encourage their interest and learning.

Guiding Questions: In what ways does the physical environment capture the children's interests? What might be some additional strategies to extend their interests and discoveries? If you are participating in a group discussion, discuss some of the anecdotes written by group members and plan additional strategies to capture the children's interest or expand them.

Reflection

Purpose: To reflect on how observation can assist curriculum planning.

What to Do: Think of examples of when you have created a zone of proximal development (ZPD) for a child. What was the specific activity? How did you scaffold, or provide support, for the child to be successful? What were the results?

Next, use these questions to plan individualized curriculum for children in your class: How do you ensure that children's interests are integrated into the curriculum? And, how do you know that a curricular approach is culturally appropriate? What will you see as far as the environment, materials, and interactions?

Finding Your Observation Style

Purpose: To determine how your observation style relates to your planning of curriculum.

What to Do: In your journal, respond to these questions:

- What ways of planning for children do you tend to choose most often?

  - through their play
  - as they go about their daily routines
  - in teacher-designed activities

- Which of the above do you find engage the children most fully? Why do you think that is?
- How do you incorporate your documentation in your curriculum planning?
- What are some new things you can commit to trying in your planning?

CHAPTER 8

How Do You Build a Case about a Child?

▲▼▲▼▲

This chapter gives you the opportunity to pull together information about children in order to assess their development and plan curriculum that will best meet their needs. We share several observation notes about pre- schoolers and toddlers so you can practice evaluating children's strengths and weaknesses and planning activities and teaching strategies for them. This is the all-important task of an early educator: reflecting on what you are learning about a child, figuring out what you are going to plan for them, implementing that plan, and observing them again.

When reviewing observation information, ask yourself these questions:

- What can and does this child do? What are their interests, and how do they show them? What specific skills do they have?
- What would the next steps be for this child in their development? What are they not doing yet?
- What would you plan to do with this child to help them build on their strengths and interests or to work on what they are not doing yet? What materials, activities, teacher support, peer support, and special resources would you use?

We recognize that the observation notes in this chapter provide limited information. You do not have the in-depth knowledge of these children that their teachers have. You do not know these children or work with them closely. We feel strongly, however, that practice is important in becoming a better observer and documenter and in using the information gained through observation. We hope you find the experience helpful in your learning process.

Claudia, a Four-Year-Old

The observation notes that follow document Claudia's development across several areas. All of these observations occurred over three months in the fall. Read through these notes about Claudia and the reflection we wrote in answer to the questions posed at the beginning of the chapter.

Claudia's Fall Language Observation

(four years, one month)

Claudia announces, "I'm going to Tucson with my family—my mom and dad and my sister. And we are going to stay in a hotel with a swimming pool." She then carefully selects red, yellow, blue, and green markers and makes a rainbow. She draws four people. She says, "Look. It's my family in a rainbow."

Claudia's Fall Writing Observation

(four years, one month)

Claudia often asks for the *Sleeping Beauty* story tape to act out the story. Today she gets lined story paper and says, "I'm writing the *Sleeping Beauty* story." She then draws a picture with a black pen and paints it with watercolors. "This is the picture of her sleeping on the bed" (see sample).

Claudia's Fall Problem-Solving Observation
(four years, two months)

It is afternoon discovery time after naptime. The large pattern blocks are out on a table. The children have been exploring them for the past two weeks. Claudia is at the table by herself. She takes a large yellow hexagon and adds six triangles. Then she starts to layer the shapes. She plays there for some time. Her dad arrives to take her home. "Dada, come see what I'm doing," she says. She undoes her work and redoes it exactly the way it was.

Claudia's Fall Social-Emotional Observation
(four years, two months)

Claudia has become more comfortable separating from her parents at drop-off time. Today she comforts Emilia, who cries after her mom leaves. Claudia says, "It's okay. Mommy's coming back." She looks at me and says, "Mommy always comes back, right, Michele?" I smile and nod yes. Claudia gently puts her arm around Emilia and says, "I miss my mom. But see. I'm not crying." At pickup time Claudia tells Emilia's mom, "Emilia was crying for you, but I told her you would come back."

Claudia's Fall Gross-Motor Observation
(four years, two months)

Claudia plays on the climbing equipment with Quinn and Fernando. All three of them are growling and roaring. Claudia climbs easily up the ladder to the platform. Quinn says, "Okay, I'm a baby jaguar." He paws the air in front of Claudia. She responds by saying, "Now there are two baby jaguars!" She moves quickly around the platform, jumps on the slide, and slides down. Then she runs around and climbs back up again.

What Does Claudia Do?

Here are the questions to consider: What can and does this child do? What are her interests, and how does she show them? What specific skills does she have? Try to answer them for yourself before reading the next paragraph.

Claudia uses language to talk about her family and life experiences and to communicate with others. She showed great complexity in her design with the blocks, was proud to show her dad what she could do, and re-created the design exactly. She shows interest in pretend play and in writing. She makes letterlike shapes in her writing and is not yet making all letters correctly. She uses her body with balance and agility as she runs and climbs. She has an awareness of her emotions and the emotions of others and can respond with empathy.

Next Steps for Claudia

What would the next steps be for Claudia in her development? What is she not doing yet?

Next steps will involve building on Claudia's successes by helping her to continue to use language effectively, providing opportunities for her to use her large muscles, supporting her to solve even more difficult problems, and building on her interest in writing.

Planning for Claudia

What would you plan to do with Claudia to help her build on her strengths and interests and to work on what she is not doing yet? What materials, activities, teacher support, peer support, and special resources would you use?

One strategy might be just to continue to encourage her conversational language usage, modeling back to her more complex language. Providing more materials for her to use for creating and representing her ideas would build on her problem-solving capabilities. Perhaps she would enjoy working with a set of gears or a marble run that requires planning in order to be successful. You could follow up on her interest in jaguars and other animals and bring in nonfiction books about them. Providing some cards with familiar words for her to copy, such as "I love you," might provide a scaffold to take her to the next level of writing skills. She could choose some of the words and phrases that she would like to have as models on the cards. You could also encourage her to continue to show empathy to other children and ask her to be Emilia's special helper at arrival time.

What other strategies do you think would work well to help Claudia continue to grow and develop in these areas?

Corey, a Toddler

The observation notes that follow document Corey's development in the fall and in the spring. These notes are paired together specifically to track his progress in several developmental areas. Read through these notes about Corey. Then add your own thoughts to the answers we give to the reflection questions listed earlier.

Corey's Fall Language Observation
(one year, two months)

Corey is sitting in the block center playing with a bucket of blocks. The other teacher in our class walks in, and Corey looks up at her and says, "Hi." I've also heard him say, "Mama," "Dada," "kitty," "dat" (for "that"), and "ball."

Corey's Spring Language Observation
(one year, six months)

Corey chooses a book called *Can You Hop?* from the library center. He takes the book over to Ms. Dorothy, who is sitting in a rocking chair. He turns around so she can pick him up and says, "Up, pease." This is the first time we have heard him combine words. He also often points at things and asks, "Dat?" and sometimes repeats what he hears us tell him.

Corey's Fall Problem-Solving Observation
(one year, two months)

Corey sees another child playing with the stacking rings. He crawls toward the child, reaching for the rings. I get another set for him. He removes the rings one at a time. He replaces them on the post in random order. He plays for maybe three minutes longer. Then he crawls across the room toward the bookshelf, where he pulls down a board book and sits and looks at it, turning the pages himself.

Corey's Spring Problem-Solving Observation

(one year, seven months)

Today Corey picks up the whole set of stacking rings and turns it upside down. All the rings come off. He then starts replacing them one by one in random order using his right hand. He picks up the spindly and dumps all of the rings off again. He starts to put the rings back on with his right hand. Then he picks up a toy snake in that hand. Holding it, he finishes by putting the last ring on with his left hand. He is successful, but he does not have the rings stacked in any particular order.

Corey's Fall Social-Emotional Observation

(one year, one month)

When Corey arrives in the morning and sees me, he smiles broadly and laughs. Then he reaches for me to hold him. He pats me on the back and gives me kisses on my face.

Corey's Spring Social-Emotional Observation

(one year, five months)

I hold one of the children on my lap. She is not feeling well. Corey comes over and pats the child on her leg. Then he gives her a toy he has in his hand.

Corey's Fall Fine-Motor Observation

(one year, three months)

Corey comes to the table where he sees other kids coloring. He chooses a purple marker. He holds the marker in his right hand with his fingers. He makes a few random marks up and down and side to side (see first sample).

Corey's Spring Fine-Motor Observation

(one year, eight months)

In the fall, Corey used markers with little control. Now he shows more control making horizontal marks. Today he chooses a blue marker and holds it in his right hand, full fisted, and makes a few marks back and forth. He then switches to his left hand, which he holds full fisted for a few more strokes. He goes back to his right hand, and this time holds it in his fingers like a pencil and makes a few more horizontal strokes. He also pounds on his paper to make some dots and shows signs of attempting to make circles (see second sample).

Corey's Fall Gross-Motor Observation

(one year, two months)

Corey is just beginning to walk without holding on to something or someone. He falls occasionally but not often. Although his balance is steady, he still will crawl very fast much of the time. Today he walks away from the snack table toward the aquarium. He falls on his bottom and quickly crawls the rest of the way.

> ## Corey's Spring Gross-Motor Observation
> (one year, seven months)
>
> Corey hardly crawls at all anymore. He walks easily and even runs without falling. Today, outdoors, he is fascinated with the wood chips. He runs to the climber area, squats down, and picks up several wood chips in his hands. Then he throws them up in the air and laughs as they land all around him.

What Does Corey Do?

Try to answer these questions about Corey before reading further: What can and does this child do? What are his interests, and how does he show them? What specific skills does he have?

Corey is labeling objects in his environment and asking his teacher to name things for him. He is able to combine two words, and by getting a book and saying, "Up pease," ask his teacher to read to him. Corey is developing an understanding of cause and effect, taking the rings off and putting them back on. While he is not yet putting them back on in any discernible pattern or sequence, he does understand the concept of stacking the rings and puts all of the rings back on. Corey has formed a trusting and comfortable attachment with his teacher and separates easily from his family members. He is also aware of the feelings of others; you could see this as he tried to comfort another child with the toy. Corey is using markers as he experiments with art. He has moved from making random marks on his paper to experimenting with a variety of marks, even trying to make circles. He is able to run and throw small objects.

What's Next for Corey?

Now answer these questions, again before you read further. What would the next steps be for Corey in his development? What is he not doing yet?

The next steps might be to continue to support his growth and development by ensuring that he has ample opportunities to use language, to problem solve, to use fine- and gross-motor skills, and to interact with the adults and the children in the environment.

Planning for Corey

Finally, use the information in the preceding observations to think about planning for Corey. What would you plan to do with him to build on his strengths and interests and to work on what he is not doing yet? What materials, activities, teacher support, peer support, and special resources would you use?

One strategy might be to make sure there are new books with pictures of things he can label and to continue to read to him and converse with him using short, simple sentences, encouraging his growth in sentence length. Another strategy might be to provide him with different cause-and-effect toys such as simple shape sorters. You could also give him containers of things that can be dumped out and put back in, such as a basket full of balls of various sizes. Something else to do might be to encourage his awareness of others by talking about how other children are feeling, labeling his feelings and the feelings of others as they occur. As Corey's interest in drawing continues to grow, it will be important to provide him ample opportunities to use a variety of writing and art tools. Continuing to offer him opportunities to walk, run, balance, climb, and throw will build on his growing gross-motor skills.

What other strategies do you think would work well to help Corey continue to develop in these areas?

Glenda, a Two-Year-Old

This set of observation records is from a home-visiting program where the teacher spent time with the child in her home and at a playgroup. It contains spring observation notes only. As you read them, answer the questions about Glenda. How does having only one set of information affect your ability to understand her?

Glenda's Spring Gross-Motor Observation
(two years, six months)

At the home visit today, Glenda and I go out in her backyard and play on the swing set. Glenda sits on the swing and asks me to push her. I do so, and she starts yelling, "No, not so high!" and begins to cry. I stop the swing and help her get off. Then I ask her if she wants to go on the slide. "No, I'm scared," she says. "I'll help you," I offer. "No, let's just swing a little bit." So she climbs back on the swing, and I push her very gently so that the swing moves only a little bit. She asks to go back inside after five minutes outdoors.

Glenda's Spring Problem-Solving Observation
(two years, seven months)

Glenda plays with blocks and says, "I make a chair for my baby." First she lines the blocks in a row. Then she stacks some on top of each other. They fall, and she picks them up and builds again. Finally, she tells her mom, "Look at the table and chair I make for my baby." She then takes the doll and sets her on the chair she made out of blocks.

Glenda's Spring Language Observation
(two years, seven months)

During playgroup Glenda and I play with Mr. Potato Head. Glenda's friend comes into the room, and Glenda says, "Come and play," and "Come sit down." She also says, "Where does this go?"

Glenda's Spring Fine-Motor Observation
(two years, seven months)

During this home visit, I offer Glenda pencils, colored markers, and a dry-erase marker. She chooses the dry-erase marker and board. She holds the marker with a three-fingered grasp. She draws several small circles with a line coming down and tells me she has made balloons.

Glenda's Spring Social-Emotional Observation
(two years, eight months)

During playgroup another child begins to cry for his mom, who is in the other room at the parent meeting. Glenda sees him crying and goes to the shelf. She gets a tissue from the tissue box and gives it to him. He grabs the tissue and wipes his tears. Glenda smiles and pats him on the back.

Now practice pulling the information together and building a case about Glenda. Do you wish you had observations that show progress—or lack thereof—over time? Reflect on the observations you just read and answer the following questions. Also, consider any other possibilities for ways to assess Glenda's development and plan appropriate curriculum for her.

- What can and does this child do? What are her interests, and how does she show them? What specific skills does she have?
- What would be the next steps for her in her development? What is she not doing yet?
- What would you plan to do with her to help her build on her strengths and interests or to work on what she is not doing yet? What materials, activities, teacher support, peer support, and special resources would you offer?

Niko, A Four-Year-Old

This set of observation records about Niko includes both fall and spring observations so you can note his progress across time.

Niko's Fall Language Observation
(four years, six months)

Niko is playing with some small toy people outside of the dollhouse. I ask, "Can you open the house, put the baby in her bed, and then put the little boy on the potty?" He follows all of the instructions correctly, looks at me, and asks, "Now what?" We do another set of three directions, and he follows all of them correctly too. He says, "This is easy, Ms. Kathy! I can do this."

Niko's Spring Language Sample
(four years, eleven months)

Mateo and Niko build an "island" with the hollow blocks. Then, using a clipboard with paper and pencil, they take turns drawing the "map" to show where the island is located. Mateo tells Niko to jump off the island and go into the water.

NIKO: Are there any fishes in here?

MATEO: You're a mommy, now.

NIKO: No, I'm not. I'm a captain.

As other children join in the play, Mateo: We're pirates.

NIKO: Aye, aye, matey.

The play ends up involving treasure (dress-up necklaces), food, and a measuring tape.

Niko's Fall Problem-Solving Observation
(four years, seven months)

When Niko is playing with small manipulative figures, I encourage him to find all of the creatures that are the same shape. At first he focuses on the color. After I model finding different shapes, he sorts them by shape. Then he again sorts by color. Donald points it out, and Niko moves his creatures to the correct shape bin.

Niko's Spring Problem-Solving Observation
(four years, eleven months)

Niko chooses games from the game center two or three times a week. His favorite is Candy Land. Niko will often play by himself, moving the pieces randomly around the board or matching the color cards with spaces on the board. At the suggestion of a teacher, he will invite a friend to play with him and will play for five to ten minutes.

Niko's Fall Writing Observation

(four years, eight months)

Niko chooses to go to the art area today. He takes a blue marker and paper to use. He sits at the art table looking at what other children are drawing on their papers. He traces his left hand and makes some letterlike shapes at the top of his paper. "That's my name," he says. He uses his right hand throughout, holding the marker with his thumb, pointer, and middle fingers (see first sample).

Niko's Spring Writing Observation

(five years, one month)

Niko often goes to the writing center now and writes on lined and unlined paper. Today he writes chains of letters in a spiral notebook. When I ask him about his writing, he tells me, "I wrote my mom's name, my aunt's name, my dad's name, and my brother's name." I label each as he points them out to me. He uses his right hand, holding the marker correctly (see second sample).

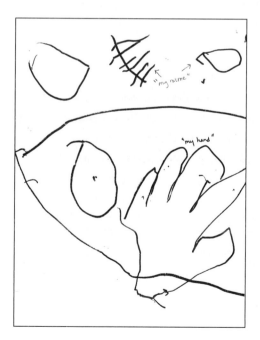

Niko's Fall Social-Emotional Observation

(four years, seven months)

One of the activities that Niko often chooses outside is riding bikes. Today when he gets off his bike to go play somewhere else, another child jumps on his bike. When Niko returns and sees the child, he says, "Hey, that's my bike."

The other child says, "No, it's mine."

Niko walks over to him and pulls the handlebars on the bike, saying, "Get off. It's mine."

I walk over and ask, "What's going on?"

Niko says, "This is my bike."

The other child says, "No, it's mine."

I ask, "What do you think we should do?"

Niko says, "I'm mad because he took my bike."

"Where were you when he took your bike?" I ask.

"Over there," he says, pointing to the sandbox. By this time, the other child has lost interest in the bike, and Niko jumps back onto it and rides away.

Niko's Spring Social-Emotional Observation

(five years)

Today during outside play, Niko and another child are playing at the water table with small cars. Another child attempts to join in the play, bringing a car that is muddy. Niko says, "Don't bring that big car in here, because it's dirty." The other child ignores him. Niko then grabs at the car and says, "You are making the water all dirty. Look." They pull the car back and forth for a few seconds, and then Niko lets go. He grabs another small car that is in the water and hands it to the child, saying, "Do you want to play with this one? It's clean." The child takes the clean car and puts the dirty one down to the side of the table. They continue to play together for another ten minutes.

Niko's Fall Gross-Motor Observation

(four years, eight months)

It is Niko's turn to crawl like an alligator during a large-group activity. He keeps his tummy on the ground and pulls himself around the classroom with his arms. He has a big smile on his face.

Niko's Spring Gross-Motor Observation

(five years)

I observe Niko walking around the swing area, balancing on the wooden planks that surround our playground. He concentrates on each step and does not fall once as he goes around the whole area!

Now practice pulling the information together and building a case about Niko. Are you noticing that you learn more when you have at least two observations that track a child's progress across time? Reflect on the observations you just read and answer the following questions. Also, consider any other possibilities for ways to assess Niko's development and plan appropriate curriculum for him.

- What can and does this child do? What are his interests, and how does he show them? What specific skills does he have?
- What would the next steps be for him in his development? What is he not doing yet?
- What would you plan to do with him to build on his strengths and interests and to work on what he is not doing yet? What materials, activities, teacher support, peer support, and special resources would you use?

· · · · · · ·

As we conclude this book in the next chapter, we focus on ways for you to continue to grow as an observer and documenter. We recognize that there are differences in your work settings and in your experience with children and make suggestions to help you be successful as you implement observation and documentation fully.

· · · · · · ·

www.vimeo.com/1022181739

www.vimeo.com/1022181760

www.vimeo.com/1022181787

www.vimeo.com/1022181812

www.vimeo.com/1022181834

www.vimeo.com/1022181863

www.vimeo.com/1022181886

Observation Practice #18:
Building a Case about a Child

Purpose: To practice pulling together information about a child to assess their development and plan curriculum that will best meet their needs.

What to Do: Watch Video Clips #18a through #18g (available by scanning the QR codes or going to the web addresses under the QR codes). Some of these clips have been viewed before and we have grouped and renumbered them to show how the three children (three-year-old London, four-year-old Maricella, and five-year-old Peter) participate in multiple activities across their day in preschool. Observe the children doing the activities, and take notes about the things they do and say. If you wish, you can choose to focus on one child, or you can write about all three. Remember to be factual and descriptive, not interpretive.

Guiding Questions: After viewing, use your observation notes to answer the following questions for any or all of the three children:

- What can and does this child do? What are their interests, and how do they show them? What specific skills do they have?
- What would the next steps be for them in their development? What are they not doing yet?
- What would you plan to do with them to build on their strengths and interests and to work on what they are not doing yet? What materials, activities, teacher support, peer support, and special resources would you use?

Reflect on your ideas about the child's accomplishments, interests, and needs, and about the next steps you planned for them. If you are participating in a group discussion, share your ideas about the child's accomplishments, interests, and needs. Compare the next steps you planned.

Reflection

Purpose: To reflect on the benefits of looking at children's growth and development over time.

What to Do: Think about the value of reviewing your documentation of a child over time.

- How does reviewing documentation in specific domains twice a year help you to plan effectively for each child's developmental and learning needs?

- How does this type of documentation help you review each child's strengths and weaknesses?
- How can building a case about a child over time enable you to plan more effectively?

Finding Your Observation Style

Purpose: To think about ways to build a case about a child.

What to Do: Reflect on and write about your experiences with this type of documentation and how it is helpful to you as you plan for children. If you are not currently doing this, what might be some ways you could build this into your practice, and how specifically would you use the documentation?

CHAPTER 9

How Do You Continue to Grow as an Observer?

▲▼▲▼▲

Throughout this book we have presented many ways for you to use observation and documentation to get to know children better. We hope that you will use what you learn by observing children to create opportunities for them that maximize their development.

We have encouraged you to take into account your personal observation style and consider the setting in which you work with young children. Doing so will help you become a more effective observer. Being prepared and ready for children to show you what they can do will allow you to see much more. Trying out clipboards, sticky notes, Quick Check Recording Sheets, and electronic devices will help you figure out your own documentation style. Having writing tools handy and several clipboards or documentation sheets available will assist you in capturing documentation of children in action in a busy classroom. Recognizing your own ability to remember what happened so you can write a clear description will determine when you write it down. If you tend to forget, you will want to write down observations as you see them or as quickly as you can afterward. If your memory is good, you may be able to wait until a quieter moment in the day, such as naptime, to write down what you saw and heard.

Keeping in mind the purposes for your observations will help you focus clearly on what needs to be documented and what you are going to do with the information:

- Are you observing an individual child to assess their development?
- Or are you observing to see how the group of children is using the room arrangement and materials to their fullest?
- Are you trying to find out if your curriculum plans match the needs of particular children?
- Or are you just trying to get more acquainted with the interests of the children in your program so you can build on those interests?

What you learn through observation can be used for both assessment and curriculum planning.

Developing your own ability to be open and ready to see children's growth and learning as they play and interact is an ongoing process. If you are new to the field of early education, you may not see children's capabilities as clearly as a more experienced teacher. Give yourself time to watch children and to learn to see development in action. Think of yourself as a researcher in the field of child development. Ask yourself, "What are the children showing me? What can each one do?" Writing only the facts, with no interpretations, will provide you with evidence for your research. Relating that evidence to early learning guidelines, developmental checklists, or resources will educate you in reasonable expectations for children at different ages.

Even experienced early educators can grow and learn as observers and documenters. Developing more awareness of the filters through which you see the world is an important first step in the process of growth. Sometimes such steps are difficult. Self-reflection and willingness to discuss issues of bias and prejudice with colleagues can improve your ability to record observations that are grounded in truth rather than in preconceived notions or skewed views of children.

Adapting to Each Early Childhood Setting

Each early childhood setting is unique. You may work in a large child care center or a small preschool program. You may run your own family child care business or work in a Head Start program. You may make home visits regularly or be housed in a public school setting. No matter your setting, you will need to figure out how to make observation and documentation work for you by creating a sustainable system.

If you work in teams, it's helpful to divide the tasks up among the members of your team to ensure that all children will be observed and that documentation will include all areas of development. This requires communication among all of the staff involved. Setting aside time to discuss who will observe and when the observation will be written down is necessary. Having regular team meetings, even for five to ten minutes (remember our suggestion for Take Five team meetings), will help everyone be on the same track and provide an opportunity to share what has been observed and what the next steps will be. This reflection and sharing are essential to curriculum planning.

If you work in family child care or other settings where you are alone with children, planning ways to fit in observation and documentation will be necessary. Recognizing that your primary role is to take good care of children will help prioritize your efforts. Always having writing tools available to write down what you see the children doing will ensure that you are prepared for documentation. And setting aside reflection time for your-self will provide you with the opportunity to plan activities and strategies that are more in tune with the children in your care.

Whether you are just starting out or you have been using observation and documentation already, the following suggestions will help you create and maintain a system that will be successful:

- Give yourself many opportunities to practice both observing and documenting.
- Be easy on yourself—learning something new takes time.
- Try out different methods of documentation to find the ones that work best for you.
- Talk with your colleagues about their successes as they observe and document.
- Enjoy what you are learning about the children as you observe and document.
- Share what you are learning with families, colleagues, and the children themselves.

Throughout this book we have asked you to keep a journal in response to the activities and questions at the end of each chapter. Our goal was for you to find your unique style as an observer. We encourage you to continue to use your journal as you reflect on your observations and documentations. This ongoing reflection will aid in your efforts to integrate observation into your daily routine. Journaling will enable you to think about the highs and lows of your implementation process and to brainstorm ideas and tech-niques for success. Change comes only with practice. And the best learning comes from solving the problems that arise from your trials and errors.

Being in the Moment with Children

Children honor adults by allowing us to witness their ability to be truly who they are as they negotiate their environment and use their bodies and minds to learn about the world and the people in it. We know firsthand that early educators are very fortunate to be able to watch this process. To fully appreciate and enjoy the growth and learning of the children in your care, you need to reflect on what you see children doing and remember that at the heart of the matter is learning to be in the moment with each child.

Curtis and Carter (2011, 301–4) suggest several useful dispositions for early educators to acquire as part of their personal and professional develop-ment. These dispositions apply to professional development in observation as well:

- Be curious about children's learning and development.
- Value children's play.
- Expect continuous change and challenge.
- Be willing to take risks and make mistakes.
- Make time for regular reflection and self-examination.
- Seek collaboration, mentoring, and peer support.
- Be a professional watchdog and a whistle-blower.

The last disposition listed above has particular significance because the effective use of observation provides you with an opportunity to grow as an advocate for children and as a professional in the field of early childhood education. As we have demonstrated in this book, professional recommendations from throughout the field of education advocate for observational assessment rather than testing of young children. Early childhood professionals must take a stand on behalf of children and inform others of appropriate ways to assess young children's development. Together we can demonstrate the effectiveness of observational assessment that is grounded in objective documentation and tied to accepted and culturally sensitive developmental guidelines. By being knowledgeable and joining together with colleagues to speak up and share what you know about assessment, you can make a difference in children's lives.

In some settings you may not be able to choose your assessment tool or methodology. Many state and federally funded programs are mandated to use specific assessment systems. If you find yourself in such a situation, you can still work to do what is best for the children. Even though the mandated system may not be observational in nature, you can make observation and documentation an integral part of your practice. Keep watching the children. Keep taking anecdotal records. You know that you are gaining important information about the children and their development.

Using Observation and Documentation to Advocate for the Importance of Play

Not only can you be an advocate for authentic assessment practices, but you can also use such practices to inform others about the importance of play in young children's lives. We are highly aware of the ways in which child-directed, open-ended play experiences are threatened in programs for young children. (For a deep dive into the subject, see Gronlund and Rendon's [2017] *Saving Play: Addressing Standards through Play-Based Learning in Preschool and Kindergarten.*) When you observe children at play, document those observations, and relate them to early learning guidelines or other developmental resources, you are showing the value and the embedded learning in that play experience. And when you share those observations with the child's family members, with your colleagues and administrators, and with decision-makers at even higher levels, you are providing evidence to support the benefits of play for children.

> We also believe that teachers and administrators' use of appropriate assessment for young learners, especially when integrated with standards, can actually make children's play even more beneficial. Through observation and reflection, teachers can determine the success of play experiences related to learning. They can make changes in approaches, materials, activities, and teacher support. And they can observe and document how each child is showing progress in multiple domains as she plays. (Gronlund and Rendon 2017, 183–184)

By sharing the ways you link play and learning goals, you are combining some of the dispositions listed above and continuing to do what is right for young children.

Delighting in Children's Growth and Development

Imagine a three-year-old girl running freely on a playground on a lovely spring day. She moves from a climber and slide to a balance beam to a set of swings. Throughout, she has a broad grin on her face, a sense of joy in her movements, and confidence in her own physical abilities. We hope you remember that at times the most important task in observing children is to enjoy them. Children do not always need intervention or specific curricular planning. Yes, this girl's physical capabilities could be assessed as a result of observing her actions. However, she is deriving so much pleasure from her running, climbing, swinging, and balancing that doing a formal assessment of capabilities seems beside the point. Instead, delighting in her actions is most appropriate.

This is a perfect opportunity to return to the meaning of the word *assess*. In chapter 5, we noted that this word comes from the Latin verb *assidere*, which means "to sit with." Enjoying children, being in the moment with them, and observing their actions for multiple purposes can truly be a form of sitting with them. Being the assessor, the one who sits beside, has the alternative meaning of "the one who shares another's rank or dignity" (Wiggins 1993 in Marzano and Kendall 1996, 123). When enjoying children in action, each of us should take the opportunity to silently thank them for honoring us by sharing a small part of their lives with us. Sit back. Smile. Rejoice with the children in your care, as they rejoice in their very being.

Celebrate childhood. Be in the moment with children. And reflect on how you are learning and growing because you can observe children and learn from them.

· · · · · · ·

Purpose: To learn to enjoy children's exuberance and zest for life.

What to Do: Watch Video Clip #19 (scan the QR code or go to www.vimeo .com/1022181911), which contains a montage of video clips of children in action. Do not worry about observing for assessment or curricular planning. Do not take notes or document in any way. Instead, let yourself be with each child as they openly share their enthusiasm and energy. Appreciate them as they enjoy the pleasures of being a child. Celebrate and enjoy what they do.

Guiding Questions: If you are participating in a group discussion, share your feelings as you watched the children. Talk about the importance of being in the moment with children and having an appreciation for being a part of their enthusiasm and zest for life.

Reflection

Purpose: To reflect on your own growth and learning.

What to Do: Continue to use your journal to reflect on your own growth and learning as you observe the children in your care. What you have written becomes a means of remembering the importance of observation for assessment and curriculum planning as well as for enjoying children and being in the moment with them. Continue to value how young children honor us by sharing their openness and honesty.

Finding Your Observation Style

Purpose: Finding a balance as you observe children.

What to Do: Think about and respond to the following in your journal:

- What are some things you can do to ensure that you are finding time to enjoy children to the fullest in the course of your busy day?
- What are some of the ways you can work toward finding a balance between observing and documenting to plan for development and learning and being in the moment to discover and enjoy the unique nature of each child?
- Is there one issue that you want to work on more? What is it?

Observation Notes to Review

The following observation notes can be reviewed for many purposes. You might do any of the following:

- Read through them as examples of quality documentation about children of different ages.
- Identify what early learning guidelines might be seen in the child's actions.
- Relate the description to a developmental assessment tool with which you are familiar.
- Consider what next steps you might plan for the child based on this observation note about what they can do.
- Think about ways you would use the observation note to communicate with the child's family members so that, together, you are learning more about the child's capabilities and setting goals for them.

Infant/Toddler Observation Notes

Laila (fourteen weeks)

Laila was lying on her back. She turned to her side and almost rolled over. I commented on her attempt, and she looked at me and smiled.

Max (two years, ten months)

Today when the toddlers were outside, Paulina fell on the grass and started to cry. Max ran inside and brought her teddy to her and said, "You hurt; here is teddy to help you feel better." He took her teddy to her and patted her on the head and said, "You are better now, right?"

Marcus (ten months)

Marcus crawled up our small, carpeted ramp and then crawled down the three small, carpeted stairs. He repeated this five or six times with a big smile on his face.

Adriana (two years, six months)

One morning Adriana was repeating "Cane here? Cane here?" When I asked her, "Are you wanting Cane to come to school today?" she nodded her head up and down and started smiling. Fifteen minutes later when Cane came into the room with his dad, Adriana ran over and wrapped her arms around him, saying, "Cane here!"

Juliana (seventeen months)

Juliana toddled over to her teacher with a doll in one hand and a blanket in another. She handed her teacher the doll and the blanket, saying, "Wrap baby." The teacher handed the wrapped baby back to her, and she snuggled with it and rocked it in her arms.

Allen (twenty months)

Allen was looking out the door window onto the play yard. He squealed, stomped his feet up and down, and started pointing his finger outside. I asked, "Allen, what do you see out there?" He ran over to me, grabbed my hand, and led me to the door. He pointed out the window again, saying, "Doggie! Doggie!" I responded, "Wow! That's a big dog!" Allen said, "Niii . . . doggie. Niiii doggie!" I responded, "Oh yeah, your dad always says, 'Nice doggy!'"

Wren (eight months)

Wren was lying on her back on the floor with a soft block in her hand. I saw Wren's brother Haden standing at our door and asked him if he wanted to come in. He told me he was here to visit his baby sister. When he opened the door and shouted, "Wren!" she quickly turned her head in his direction, dropped the block, and started kicking her legs. He came down and kissed her several times on her face and neck, and she giggled.

Chin (fourteen months)

Today we put out the light table for the first time. Chin toddled over and started moving the colored shapes around the tabletop. He spent more than five minutes. He was smiling and babbling to himself the entire time.

Katsu (twenty-four months)

All week Katsu has asked me, "Me help?" when I go into the hallway to gather everyone's coats before we go outside. One by one, we get the coats off their hooks and stack them into a pile outside of our door. Today I held up a purple coat and asked, "Do you remember whose coat this is?" and he said "Ava!" I held up a blue coat and asked him the same question. He said, "Keiko!" I held up a third coat, and he quickly shouted, *"Mine!"*

Ben (six months)

Ben was lying on his back when Weston crawled over with a rattle in his mouth. Ben looked up at Weston and reached his left hand across his chest. He splayed his fingers out and reached farther toward the rattle, turning onto his right side. Then he reached farther, grasped the rattle with his left hand, and pulled it from Weston's mouth. He returned to his back and started shaking the rattle by moving his arm up and down.

Danni (twenty months)

One morning in the yard, Danni and her six-year-old sister, Erica, were playing with a soccer ball. Erica asked, "Danni! Can you kick it? Here, watch me first!" Erica kicked the ball and Danni ran after the ball, stopped right in front of it, swung her right leg back, and kicked it forward at the ball. She watched the ball roll and stop about three feet in front of her. She ran up, stopped, swung her right leg back, and kicked it again. She repeated this another five times. Erica shouted, "Yay! Now you can play soccer like me!"

Infant/Toddler Observation Notes and Possible Domains from Early Learning Guidelines

We have identified that the following domains or areas of learning are being demonstrated by the children in the above observation notes. For the infants and toddlers, we used the *Montana Early Learning Standards* (Montana Early Learning Standards Task Force 2014). We encourage you to use your own state's guidelines or the developmental information on the assessment tool your program is using.

Laila (fourteen weeks)

Physical Large Muscle: rolling to side; **Emotional Sense of Self:** responds to others' attention; **Language Receptive:** smiles when spoken to

Max (two years, ten months)
Social: offers comfort by giving a favorite toy or blanket; **Language Expressive:** uses words or sign language to convey events

Marcus (ten months)
Physical Large Muscle: crawls; **Thinking Skills and Cognition:** problem solving

Adriana (two years, six months)
Social Peer Interaction: favors playing with one or two peers; **Language Expressive:** uses words or sign language to convey events

Juliana (seventeen months)
Social: asks for help verbally or with gestures when needed; **Cognitive Problem Solving:** demonstrates how familiar objects are used in combination

Allen (twenty months)
Language Expressive: speaks clearly enough for familiar listeners to understand; **Social:** maintains interactions with a familiar adult using conversation

Wren (eight months)
Language Receptive: reacts to name, perhaps turning head toward speaker; **Social:** responds to others' attention

Chin (fourteen months)
Cognitive Problem Solving: experiments with objects or tasks to achieve a result; **Physical Large Muscle:** moves toward interesting sights in the environment; **Emotional:** shows likes and dislikes

Katsu (twenty-four months)
Cognitive: classifies when sorting toys and other objects; **Language Expressive:** responds to questions or simple requests with a nonverbal or verbal answer

Ben (six months)
Physical Fine Motor: reaches or grasps a toy, object or person; **Social:** responds to the attention of others

Danni (twenty months)
Physical Large Muscle: walks and eventually runs; **Social:** demonstrates enthusiasm in the company of other children; **Language Receptive:** responds to action words by performing the action

Preschool Observation Notes

Lydia (three years, two months)

Lydia uses colored markers to draw: she switches back and forth from hand to hand, gripping the markers in her fist and pounding them on her paper. "Look, I making dots!" When her teacher shows her how she is smashing in the tip of the marker, she makes dots more gently. On another day, she draws with markers again. This time she holds the markers in her right fist only. She says, "Look, teacher. I being gentle," as she makes tiny circles on her paper. Some of the circles are closed in. Others are not.

Tomas (four years, four months)

Today in blocks, Tomas built two symmetrical towers with Juan. "You gotta put them up so they don't fall, huh, Juan?" He carefully placed each block. Then at cleanup both boys placed the blocks on the shelves, matching the size and shapes of the labels on the shelves.

Eun Joo (four years, eight months)

Eun Joo often chooses the art area, where she will work for ten to fifteen minutes. She paints detailed pictures with many colors at the easel, holding the paintbrush in her left hand. She also spends time at the listening center and listens to several stories in a row. When she has a problem, she sometimes tries to solve it herself and at other times asks for adult help. Today she needed help with the earphones and tape recorder and called to a teacher to help her, saying, "I can't get this to work, Ms. Ellen. Can you help me?"

Jennifer (three years, one month)

Jennifer lines up the colored bears, cars, and dinosaur figures in front of her (in no particular order), then covers them with a blanket. "They sleeping," she says. As she pulls the blanket off, she announces, "Wake up! Wake up!" She continues this game three more times before she moves on to another activity. Lester sat next to Jennifer, watching as she lined up her items. Then he lined up his own small items, including shells, buttons, and colored blocks. When Jennifer covered hers with a blanket and said, "They're sleeping," Lester said, "Me too!" and covered his collection with a basket. When she said, "Wake up, wake up," he imitated her, removing his basket and saying, "Wake up," as well. And when she left the table, he left too.

Spencer (four years, six months)

Today Spencer took the bin of small cars to the block area. "I'm making a road," he said. He placed several small blocks on the floor and tried to "drive" the cars on them by pushing them and seeing how far they would go. They stopped after a few inches. "I know," he said. He built up one end of the road with two smaller blocks and placed a long block on them so that he had a ramp. He then sent cars down the ramp. "Hurray! Now they go fast!" he said. Marcus (four years, ten months) joined him and said, "Let's make a big bridge." Spencer agreed, and the two worked together for a long time, talking about what they needed for their bridge. "We gotta make it tall," Spencer said. "Okay, let's build two tall towers," said Marcus.

Cole (five years, two months)

As Cole and three other children were pretending to go on an airplane, Cole announced, "We need tickets." He went to the art area; found colored paper, scissors, and markers; and returned to the area where children had set up chairs to be the airplane. Using his right hand, he cut the paper in strips and wrote numbers on each one. "Here, you're number one, you're number sixteen, and you're number four" (the numbers were correctly written). He then directed children to their "seats" and collected the tickets.

Peter (three years, three months)

Today Peter ran to the window and pointed to the snowflakes that had begun to fall. He smiled and clapped his hands as he jumped up and down. Last week I asked him to check on the sand in the sensory table to see if it was still wet. He went to the table and looked but did not touch. When he plays with wet sand, he uses tools to move it around but does not use his hands.

Mario (four years, eleven months)

Mario often has new ideas for ways to do things in the classroom. The other day as we read a story at large group, some children complained that they couldn't see. Mario said, "How about those in the back get on their knees? Then they can see." Today he suggested that we make a pattern of boys and girls at the snack table. The other children agreed, and Mario directed everyone so that the children were seated boy, girl, boy, girl. The last child made it girl, girl, and Mario said, "That's okay. We'll do it different another day."

Corey (three years)

Corey often plays by himself or watches other children as they play. Today he stood next to the water table and watched as other children poured water through tubes, into cups, and through the water wheel. When I asked him if he wanted to play with the water, he shook his head no. I suggested that he and I draw, and we sat at the art table drawing side by side. Corey held the crayon in his left hand, alternating between a fisted grasp and wrapping the tips of his fingers around the crayon, making marks all over his paper. I asked if he was writing something, and he nodded his head yes.

Joelle (four years, three months)

Almost every day when she arrives at school, Joelle seeks out her best friend, Mariah. "Want to play house, Mariah?" she'll ask. Most days Mariah agrees. The two pretend to cook and take care of the babies. Joelle directs the play scenario, while Mariah follows along. Today Joelle said, "Okay, sister, it's time to make them pancakes. We gotta give these babies some breakfast, huh?" Mariah looked through the food items in the play refrigerator and found the pancakes. Joelle put plates on the table and placed a pancake on each one. "We got four, one, two, three, four, pancakes, huh?"

Lynnae (three years, two months)

Lynnae was playing with the xylophone in the music area when Suzanna joined her and began playing on it with another stick. "No!" Lynnae shouted. "Mine! Teacher!" I came over and talked with both of the girls about taking turns. Lynnae again said, "No, it's my turn" and pushed Suzanna away. Suzanna began to cry, and as I comforted her, I talked with Lynnae about hurting Suzanna's feelings. I asked her to show Suzanna that she was her friend, and Lynnae reached over and patted Suzanna's arm and said, "I'm sorry." Then I showed the girls how one could play the high notes and the other the low ones, and they played the xylophone together for a few minutes.

Andre (four years)

Andre arrived at school as the muffins for breakfast finished baking in the oven. "Something sure smells good," he said. "I smell blueberries! Yum, yum." He joined friends at the table and held the warm muffin to his nose. "It's warm like the sun," he said.

Rose (four years, five months)

Rose asked to play with playdough and came with me to the cupboard to get out the materials. She carried the big bowl of playdough to a table where other children had spread out puzzles and manipulatives. "There's no room here," she told me as I brought the tub of cookie cutters and rollers. "Can you ask the other children if you can use part of the table?" I asked. She said, "Hey, guys, can I play playdough here?" The other children moved their materials over. As she began to play with the dough and cutters, they joined her and ended up putting away all of the manipulatives and puzzles and playing with the playdough. Rose rolled out flat pieces and used cookie cutters to make shapes.

Preschooler Observation Notes and Possible Indicators from Early Learning Guidelines

We have identified that the following domains or areas of learning are being demonstrated by the children in the above observation notes. For the preschoolers, we used the *New Mexico Early Learning Guidelines* (New Mexico Kids 2014). We encourage you to use your own state's guidelines or the developmental information on the assessment tool your program is using.

Lydia (three years, two months)
oral language, listening skills, following directions, fine-motor, writing/drawing

Tomas (four years, four months)
oral language, playing cooperatively, fine-motor, sorting and categorizing, classroom responsibility

Eun Joo (four years, eight months)
focuses on a task, creativity, fine-motor, interest in books, problem solving, asking for adult help, oral language

Jennifer (three years, one month)
purposeful play, oral language, fine-motor, imitation

Spencer (four years, six months)
oral language, cooperative play, problem solving, creativity, focus, scientific experimentation

Cole (five years, two months)
role plays, initiative, oral language, fine-motor, mathematical representation, cooperative play, focus

Peter (three years, three months)
observation of scientific phenomena, listening skills, following directions, problem solving

Mario (four years, eleven months)
problem solving, creativity, oral language, patterning, initiative

Corey (three years)
solitary play, communicates, listening, fine-motor, writing

Joelle (four years, three months)
identifies friends, associative play, oral language, role plays, sorting, counting quantities with one-to-one correspondence

Lynnae (three years, two months)
oral language, conflict resolution, showing empathy, plays with others

Andre (four years)
oral language, scientific exploration, comparisons

Rose (four years, five months)
initiative, seeking adult help, oral language, problem solving, fine-motor, cooperative play

APPENDIX B

Forms and Formats

▲▼▲▼▲

1. Words and Phrases to Avoid and to Use
2. Facts/Interpretation Form
3. Observation Record with Common Preschool Domains
4. Observation Record with Open Domains
5. Quick Check Recording Sheet
6. Brief Notes Recording Sheet
7. Small-Group Observation Form
8. Collected Documentation Record
9. Portfolio Collection Form
10. Family/Teacher Summary Report
11. Preschool Choice Record
12. Toddler Choice Record

The forms can all be downloaded from the Focused Observations product page at www.redleaf.org.

Words and Phrases to Avoid	Words and Phrases to Use
The child loves . . .	He often chooses . . .
The child likes . . .	I saw him . . .
He enjoys . . .	I heard her say . . .
She spends a long time at . . .	He spends five minutes doing . . .
It seems like . . .	She said . . .
It appears . . .	Almost every day, he . . .
I thought . . .	Once or twice a month, she . . .
I felt . . .	Each time, he . . .
I wonder . . .	She consistently . . .
He does . . . very well . . .	We observed a pattern of . . .
She is bad at . . .	He tried three times to . . .
This is difficult for . . .	

Facts/Interpretation Form

Date _____   Child's Name _____

Facts	Interpretation

Observation Record with Common Preschool Domains

Child's Name _____

Language	Social-Emotional

Physical (gross and fine motor)	Creative

Cognitive (math, problem-solving)	Early Literacy (reading and writing)

Observation Record with Open Domains

Child's Name _____

Quick Check Recording Sheet

Children's Names	Date and Activity	Date and Activity	Date and Activity	Date and Activity
....				
....				
....				
....				
....				
....				
....				
....				
....				
....				
....				
....				
....				
....				
....				
....				
....				
....				
....				
....				

Brief Notes Recording Sheet

Children's Names	Date and Activity

Small-Group Observation Form

Date _____   Activity: _____

Goal(s): _____

Child's Name:	Child's Name:	Child's Name:
Child's Name:	Child's Name:	Child's Name:
Child's Name:	Child's Name:	Child's Name:
Child's Name:	Child's Name:	Child's Name:

Collected Documentation Record

Teacher: _____   Collection Period: _____

Child's Name	Domain: Dates Collected	Domain: Dates Collected	Domain: Dates Collected	Domain: Dates Collected	Domain: Dates Collected	Domain: Dates Collected	Domain: Dates Collected

Portfolio Collection Form

Child's Name: _____   Date: _____   Observer: _____

Domains(s): _____

Learning goal(s) demonstrated in this documentation: _____

_____

_____

Check off whatever applies to the context of this observation:

☐ child-initiated activity   ☐ done independently   ☐ time spent (1 to 5 minutes)

☐ teacher-initiated activity   ☐ done with adult guidance   ☐ time spent (5 to 15 minutes)

☐ new task for this child   ☐ done with peer(s)

☐ familiar task for this child   ☐ time spent (more than 15 minutes)

Anecdotal note: Describe what you saw the child do and/or heard the child say (attach a photo or work sample if appropriate).

Family/Teacher Summary Report

Child's Name: _____ Date: _____

Teacher: _____ Program: _____

DOMAIN:

Growth and accomplishments	
We will continue to work on	

DOMAIN:

Growth and accomplishments	
We will continue to work on	

DOMAIN:

Growth and accomplishments	
We will continue to work on	

(continued on next page)

(continued from previous page)

DOMAIN:

Growth and accomplishments	
We will continue to work on	

DOMAIN:

Growth and accomplishments	
We will continue to work on	

DOMAIN:

Growth and accomplishments	
We will continue to work on	

DOMAIN:

Growth and accomplishments	
We will continue to work on	

Preschool Choice Record

(may be used to tally one child's choices or a group of children's choices)

Date _____ Child(ren) _____

_____

Art	Blocks	Dramatic Play
Manipulatives	**Science/Math**	**Music/Movement**
Library	**Sensory Table**	**Writing Center**

Toddler Choice Record

(may be used to tally one child's choices or a group of children's choices)

Date _____   Child(ren) _____

_____

Paint Easel	Blocks	Play House

Manipulatives	Crawling Area	Climbing Structure

Book Corner	Sensory Table	Rocking Chair

Additional Resources on Assessment in Early Childhood

▲▼▲▼▲

CCSSO (Council of Chief State School Officers). 2011. "Moving Forward with Kindergarten Readiness Assessment Efforts: A Position Paper of the Early Childhood Education State Collaborative on Assessment and Student Standards." Position paper. Washington, DC: CCSSO. https://files.eric .ed.gov/fulltext/ED543310.pdf.

NAEYC (National Association for the Education of Young Children) and NAECS/SDE (National Association of Early Childhood Specialists in State Departments of Education). In 2003 NAEYC and NAECS/SDE adopted a position statement titled "Early Childhood Curriculum, Assessment, and Program Evaluation: Building an Effective, Accountable System in Programs for Children Birth through Age 8," which identifies the indicators of effectiveness regarding assessment in the early childhood years. www.naeyc.org/positionstatements.

NAEYC (National Association for the Education of Young Children) www.naeyc.org

NAEYC is the largest professional organization for early educators and has long supported "developmentally appropriate" assessment of young children. In its fourth edition of *Developmentally Appropriate Practice in Early Childhood Programs Serving Children from Birth through Age 8* (2022), the significant publication of the basic tenets of this organization, the authors describe sound assessment.

Snow, Kyle P. 2011. *Developing Kindergarten Readiness and Other Large Scale Assessment Systems: Necessary Considerations in the Assessment of Young Children.* Washington, DC: NAEYC.

Using the Right Assessment Process for the Right Purpose

The Early Childhood Education State Assessment Collaborative of the CCSSO designed the following table, which identifies what kind of assessment process should be used for what purpose. This information is helpful to early childhood educators when they are asked to be accountable for children's learning. Notice that observational assessment is a criterion-referenced and formative assessment process—it does not fit the requirements of the other assessment purposes or measurement types. Being clear on why you observe and document, what your goals are, and how you are going to use the information you gain about children are important parts of being an early childhood education professional.

Appropriate Purposes of Kindergarten Assessments, Measurement Types, and Goals

Assessment Purpose	Measurement Types	Goals
To identify groups of students who may have developmental or health needs	**Screening**	• Collect information with large number of students • Identify need for additional diagnostics
To identify children in need of specialized services or interventions	**Diagnostic**	• Determine developmental or medical needs • Determine specific intervention needs • Establish student eligibility for services
To track students across programs, schools, districts, and states for comparisons and social benchmarking	**Norm-referenced**	• Provide point-in-time snapshot of a student's knowledge compared with other students • Compare students from different programs, schools, and communities against a norm • Provide student-level performance in comparison with a population norm or other students of the same age/situation
To determine whether students meet specified academic standards or defined performance levels	**Criterion-referenced**	• Provide a point-in-time snapshot of a student's knowledge compared with defined standards or specified criteria • Track student's progress against specified standards over time
To guide program-, classroom-, or student-level instruction	**Formative**	• Document individual student learning and knowledge, probing student understanding and competencies • Identify student strengths and weaknesses • Monitor individual student learning progress over time
To evaluate programs	**Summative** **Norm-referenced** **Criterion-referenced** **Descriptive**	• Collect information on a sample of students • Determine and explain the impact of a program or service on defined outcomes • Address questions about programmatic investments • Get information about structural and process characteristics of children, families, teachers, programs, and other learning environment variables

Glossary of Assessment Terms and Phrases

▲▼▲▼▲

This glossary of assessment terms and phrases is from the position paper by NAEYC and NAECS/SDE (2003, 27–28). We include these terms here to support your efforts in following their recommendations and hope knowledge of the terms will contribute to your learning to use observation for assessment purposes.

assessment: The process of obtaining information about a child in order to make judgments about their characteristics and decisions about appropriate teaching and care.

child development: The social, emotional, physical, and cognitive changes in children stimulated by biological maturation interacting with experience.

criterion- or performance-oriented assessment: Assessment in which the person's performance (that is, score) is interpreted by comparing it with a prespecified standard or specific content and/or skills.

developmentally appropriate: Practices that result from the process of professionals making decisions about the well-being and education of children based on at least three important kinds of information or knowledge: what is known about child development and learning . . . ; what is known about the strengths, interests, and needs of each individual child in the group . . . ; and knowledge of the social and cultural contexts in which children live.

documentation: The process of keeping track of and preserving children's work as evidence of their progress.

early learning standards: Statements that describe expectations for the learning and development of young children.

norm-referenced: A standardized testing instrument by which the person's performance is interpreted in relation to the performance of a group of peers who have previously taken the same test—a "norming" group.

observational assessment: Assessment based on teachers' systematic recordings and analysis of children's behavior in real-life situations.

reliability: The consistency of an assessment tool; important for generalizing about children's learning and development.

screening: The use of a brief procedure or instrument designed to identify, from within a large population of children, those children who may need further assessment to verify developmental and/or health risks.

standardized: An assessment with clearly specified administration and scoring procedures and normative data.

validity: The extent to which a measure or assessment tool measures what it was designed to measure

Terms adapted from "The Words We Use: A Glossary of Terms for Early Childhood Education Standards and Assessments" by Council of Chief State School Officers. Copyright 2003 Council of Chief State School Officers. www.ccsso.org. Reprinted with permission.

Guidelines for Instructors or Staff Development Leaders for Using *Focused Observations*

▲▽▲▽▲

We have written this book as a practical explanation of observation and documentation in all of their facets. We recognize that the professional recommendations from the field of early childhood education strongly support using observation and documentation for assessment and curriculum planning. And we know that early educators throughout the world are attempting to do so in a variety of early childhood settings. As they do so, they face challenges, time constraints, and other barriers to effective implementation. We believe that when teachers have opportunities to apply what they have read, try out new ideas and strategies, analyze what worked and didn't work, and reflect on what was learned through the observation and documentation experience, they have a greater understanding of children and will increase their own professionalism in the process. Therefore, we designed the book and the accompanying videos and documentation formats to go hand in hand so that information is coupled with practice and implementation. Such practice can be done with the video clips provided or in the learners' own life settings. It's the practice that is the most important! We kept all of this in mind as we wrote the book and put the additional resources together. In addition, we have designed PowerPoint slides for you to use in your work. These slides contain the key points of each chapter. You can order the PowerPoint slides from www.redleafpress.org.

We want you, as an instructor or staff development leader, to be able to easily use these tools to teach observation and documentation skills. At the end of every chapter, we suggest video clips to observe and provide activities to do that illustrate the points of the chapter. The book can also be used without the videos: the activities can be adapted so that teachers practice observation in their own work or family settings. All of the activities can be used in college coursework, staff development sessions, in-service workshops, and staff meetings.

In this appendix, we give you guidelines for how to use the following:

- the video clips and documentation formats with your students or participants
- the activities at the end of each chapter of the book
- the observation notes throughout the book and in appendix A

We hope these guidelines will help you support early educators as they learn to watch children in action and document what is seen for assessment and curriculum planning purposes.

How to Use the Video Clips

In our experiences as consultants and college educators, we have seen that early educators benefit from practicing observation and documentation in order to do it better. That is why each copy of the third edition of this book now comes with online access to a dedicated set of video clips. Each reader can practice observation and documentation on their own, or if they are enrolled in coursework or participating in staff development sessions or staff meetings, they can share their experiences with others in those settings.

Over and over, we have seen the value of practicing observation and documentation with video clips. We have learned that sharing multiple ways of documenting observations answers questions about time constraints. We have seen that it takes time to try methods out, to watch children in action, and to learn more about specific assessment tools. Before many early educators are ready to apply what they are learning to curriculum planning, they need to learn to focus as they observe and practice organizing observational documentation.

We suggest that the instructor or staff development leader view the set of video clips in its entirety first. In that way, you can determine how best to make use of this set. When you do this, please note that we do not suggest your participants watch all of the clips in one sitting. Instead, we suggest that one clip at a time be viewed by the individual or a group in a staff development session or a college class. Then each clip can be discussed in depth, and key points related to the chapter content can be reinforced.

The set of video clips includes the following features to make it easier for users to be prepared and focused for each observation:

- Each video clip is numbered and correlated to an Observation Practice in each of the chapters. There are a total of nineteen Observation Practices in the book.

- Some video clips are suggested to be viewed again for a different purpose. Sometimes, the numbering remains the same. And sometimes, it is changed to correlate to their placement in the Observation Practices in the chapters.
- Clear directions are given in each Observation Practice to help viewers focus their observations and try out different documentation strategies. It's important that viewers refer to those directions before, during, and after viewing. Guiding Questions for individual reflection and group discussion are given to make the observation practice most beneficial.
- Viewers can access the video clips by scanning the QR code or entering the URL in their web browser.

In addition, in appendix F, we provide a list of the contents of the video clips and resources. This list includes the focus we identified for each Observation Practice, the age(s) of the children involved, the activity in which they are engaged, and the running time of the video clip. Remember, you are always welcome to use the video clips for other purposes as well.

How to Use the Activities at the End of Each Chapter of the Book

We suggest that participants read the chapter before doing any of the activities at the end of it. In this way, they come to the practice exercises with basic knowledge, terminology, and suggestions to apply to the viewing. There are three kinds of activities at the end of each chapter:

- Observation Practice
- Reflection
- Finding Your Observation Style

For the Observation Practices, we have identified a purpose related to the content in the chapter. We suggest video clips to observe. Viewers can access the video clips by scanning the QR code or entering the URL in their web browser. We describe the process for watching the child and documenting what is seen and give guiding questions to consider as the observation takes place. We also offer a focus for group discussion.

You can use each practice observation in many ways. Feel free to use them in any way that is most beneficial to your group. You may want to encourage your participants to view each video clip more than once. Sometimes multiple viewings increase understanding of how much can be learned through observation and give more in-depth knowledge of ways to interpret what is seen. While we recognize that realistically teachers do not see a child do *exactly* the same thing more than one time, we have discovered from our experiences that multiple viewings of the same clip can lead to more in-depth discussion among the viewing group. Multiple viewings can also increase teachers' ability to focus their observations, to use documentation strategies more effectively, to recognize that observations often encompass multiple domains, and to consider a variety of ways they can use the observation to better plan for the child.

For chapter 8, you will notice that most of the video clips are ones that were viewed for earlier chapters. We felt it important to offer a series of video clips that follows a group of children throughout their day in preschool. In this way, viewers can practice building a case about one or more children, as recommended in chapter 8.

In addition to the video activities, two other types of activities are included at the end of each chapter: Reflection and Finding Your Observation Style (a journaling activity). The reflection activities are designed to help the participants think about the content of the chapter, analyzing and applying that content to their experiences with observing young children. The questions can be answered in writing as a formal assignment or can be used for discussion starters. The second set of activities, Finding Your Observation Style, is designed to be used in an ongoing journal format. We have learned that there are many right ways of using observation to take in information about children's growth and development. Each person implementing observation will bring to the task their own personal style, organizational and management tendencies, and understanding of child development. We hope the questions we ask and the personal journaling in response to those questions will help each individual recognize their own strengths and weaknesses in learning to implement this important task.

How to Use the Observation Notes throughout the Book and in Appendix A

Observation notes describing children in action appear throughout the book. And we have included additional ones in appendix A. We encourage you to make use of the observation notes in whatever ways help your students or participants to recognize good documentation based on focused observations. Here are some suggestions for ways to use the observation notes:

- Read through them as examples of quality documentation about children of different ages.
- Identify which early learning guidelines might be seen in the child's actions.

- Relate the description to a developmental assessment tool with which you are familiar.
- Consider what next steps you might plan for the child based on this observation note about what they can do.
- Think about ways that you would use the observation note to communicate with the child's family members so that, together, you are learning more about the child's capabilities and working to set goals for them.

Our hope is that by the end of their experience with this book and online video clips and resources, early childhood educators will have learned new techniques and determined more successful ways to implement observational assessment in the setting in which they work with children. We hope that what they learn through observational assessment will help them plan rich and meaningful curriculum based on the needs of individual children as well as the needs of the group of children. Finally, we hope we have provided you with a helpful tool to plan for professional development or coursework about observation and documentation.

Online Content

▲▽▲▽▲

The forms that appear in appendix B are also available to print in typable PDF format online at www.redleafpress.org. The following is a list of the video observation practices by chapter, which are accessible via QR code or URL.

Chapter 1

Observation Practice #1: What Can You Learn by Observing a Child?

Running Time: 47 seconds

Purpose: To identify what can be learned by observing a child for a brief period of time.

What to Do: Watch Video Clip #1 (scan the QR code or go to www.vimeo .com/1022181405). As you watch this very brief clip, consider what you are learning about this four-and-one-half-year-old girl. Since the video clip is so brief, we suggest that you watch it more than once to make sure you capture as many details as possible in your observation.

Guiding Questions: After viewing, generate a list of the child's capabilities, skills, social interactions, personality traits, and behaviors that you observed her demonstrating. In addition, consider these questions:

- Were you surprised at how much you learned in a short observation?
- If you had a history with this child, do you think that you would have seen things differently? In what ways?
- What curriculum plans might you make based on what you learned?

Be prepared to share with others the list you made about the girl as well as your thoughts about the questions above.

Observation Practice #2: What Can You Learn by Observing a Child?

Running Time: 2 mins. 51 secs.

Purpose: To identify what can be learned by observing a child engaged in a longer play experience.

What to Do: Watch Video Clip #2 (scan the QR code or go to www.vimeo .com/1022181412) of a two-year-old boy, a three-and-one-half-year-old girl, and a teacher engaged in dramatic play. Focus on the two-year-old boy.

Guiding Questions: After viewing, generate a list of the child's capabilities, skills, social interactions, personality traits, and behaviors you observed him demonstrating. In addition, consider these questions:

- Were you surprised at how much you learned in a longer observation?
- If you had a history with either of these children, do you think that you would have seen things differently? In what ways?
- What curriculum plans might you make based on what you learned?

Be prepared to share with others the list you made about this boy as well as your thoughts about the questions above.

Chapter 2

Observation Practice #3: Relating Infant/Toddler Guidelines to Observation and Documentation

Running Time: 2 mins. 29 secs.

Purpose: To see the connection between what toddlers do and say and early learning guidelines.

What to Do: Watch Video Clip #3 (scan the QR code or go to www.vimeo .com/1022181431) of young toddlers playing in the sand with their teacher.

Guiding Questions: After viewing, use your state's infant/toddler guidelines (you should be able to access them easily online) to find specific indicators that match what you observed the children doing and saying. Do not hesitate to look in multiple domains or areas of development. In addition, consider these questions:

- Were you able to relate what you observed back to the infant/toddler guidelines?

- Could you relate your documentation across multiple domains or areas of development? What domains were you able to identify?

Be prepared to share with others the list of infant/toddler guidelines you identified and your thoughts about the questions above.

Observation Practice #4: Relating Preschool Early Learning Guidelines to Observation and Documentation

Running Time: 3 mins. 42 secs.

Purpose: To see the connection between what preschoolers do and say and early learning guidelines.

What to Do: Watch Video Clip #4 (can the QR code or go to www.vimeo.com /1022181458) of a preschooler reading a familiar story. He reads in Spanish. English subtitles are provided for you if you are not a Spanish speaker.

Guiding Questions: After viewing, use your state's preschool early learning guidelines (you should be able to access them easily online) and find specific indicators that match what you observed the child doing and saying. Do not hesitate to look in multiple domains or areas of development. In addition, consider these questions:

- Were you able to relate what you observed back to the preschool early learning guidelines?
- Could you relate your documentation across multiple domains or areas of development? What domains were you able to identify?

Be prepared to share with others the list of preschool guidelines you identified and your thoughts about the questions above.

Chapter 3

Observation Practice #5: Factual versus Interpretive Anecdotes

Running Time: 4 mins. 25 secs.

Purpose: To learn to document what is actually seen and record what is taking place rather than writing anecdotes that are influenced by value judgments and interpretation.

What to Do: Watch Video Clip #5 (scan the QR code or go to www.vimeo .com/1022181480) of preschool girls and their teacher involved in dramatic play. Take notes about what you observe. As you write, think about the difference between factual and interpretive anecdotes. One of the girls is a Spanish speaker. English subtitles are provided.

Guiding Questions: After viewing, look over your notes. Decide which comments are factual and which are interpretive, referring back to the chart of words and phrases to use and to avoid on page 44 (you will also find the chart in appendix B and linked on the Focused Observations product page at www.redleafpress.org). Were you surprised by what you discovered about your use of words? Be prepared to discuss your own thinking about factual and interpretive words and phrases with others.

Observation Practice #6: Considering the Lenses through Which We View Children

Running Time: 5 mins. 31 secs.

Purpose: To learn another way to distinguish between fact and interpretation when writing anecdotes.

What to Do: Before you view Video Clip #6 (scan the QR code or go to www.vimeo.com/1022181502), consider the lenses that we shared for a negative versus a competent view of a child on page 40. As you do your observation, think in terms of these two lenses and take notes that would reflect each one.

Guiding Questions: After viewing the video clip, consider how your observations were different depending on the lens through which you were looking. Did you find that it was easier to view the child's actions through one lens or the other? Be prepared to discuss with others why you think that might be so.

Observation Practice #7: Using the Facts/Interpretation Form

Running Time: 2 mins. 51 secs.

Purpose: To learn another way to distinguish between fact and interpretation when writing anecdotes.

What to Do: For this observation, you will watch Video Clip #7 (which is a repeat of #2) (scan the QR code or go to www.vimeo.com/1022181531). Before viewing, be prepared to use the Facts/Interpretation Form to record your observation (you can copy the form from appendix B in the book or print it out from the Focused Observations product page at www.redleafpress.org). You may focus on one of the children or attempt to document what you see each of them doing. As you document, edit your notes to separate your factual description of what they are doing from your interpretation of their actions.

Guiding Questions: Consider how you separated the facts from your interpretations. Did the use of the form help you in this process? Why or why not? Be prepared to discuss with others.

Chapter 4

Observation Practice #8: Running Record

Running Time: 2 mins. 34 secs.

Purpose: To practice writing down everything you can that a child does or says in a set period of time.

What to Do: Watch Video Clip #8 (scan the QR code or go to www.vimeo .com/1022181547) of preschoolers getting their coats on to go outdoors. Focus on three-year-old London, the girl in the short-sleeved blue dress, putting on her purple jacket. As you watch, try to write a running record— writing down everything you see London doing.

Guiding Questions: After viewing, consider the ease or difficulty of trying this type of documentation. Could it be done while you were in the middle of running a busy classroom? How practical is such a recording method for your setting? If you are involved in a group discussion, share some of the running records recorded by the group and discuss the previous questions.

Observation Practice #9: Summative Anecdote

Running Time: 3 mins. 8 secs.

Purpose: To practice writing an observation note that summarizes what you have seen a child do in just two to four sentences.

What to Do: Watch Video Clip #9 (scan the QR code or go to www.vimeo .com/1022181565) of preschoolers playing at the sensory table. We suggest that you focus on the children closest to the camera, three-year-old London on the right and five-year-old Peter on the left. Do not write down your observation while you are watching. Instead, after the clip is over, write down two to four sentences summarizing what you saw the children do. Remember to be factual and descriptive, not interpretive.

Guiding Questions: After viewing, consider the ease or difficulty of trying this type of documentation. Could it be done while you were in the middle of running a busy classroom? How practical is such a recording method for your setting? If you are involved in a group discussion, share some of the summative records recorded by the group and discuss the previous questions.

Observation Practice #10: Making a List

Running Time: 1 min. 31 secs.

Purpose: To practice writing an observation note that is a list of what you have seen a child do.

What to Do: Watch Video Clip #10 (scan the QR code or go to www.vimeo .com/1022181585) and focus on Maricella, the four-year-old girl in a long-sleeved, ruffled blue shirt at the opening group time of the day. Pay close attention to the things she does and says. Either as you watch or afterward, make a list of the things you saw the child do. Do not worry about complete sentences or descriptive phrases. Try to be efficient in your use of words. Still remember to be factual and descriptive, not interpretive.

Guiding Questions: After viewing, consider the ease or difficulty of trying this type of documentation. Could it be done while you were in the middle of running a busy classroom? How practical is such a recording method for your setting? If you are involved in a group discussion, share some of the lists recorded by the group and discuss the previous questions.

Observation Practice #11: Using the Quick Check Recording Sheet

Running Time: 4 mins. 34 secs.

Purpose: To practice observation and recording by identifying one skill ahead of time and noting the children's accomplishment of that skill quickly on a check sheet.

What to Do: Before you watch Video Clip #11 (scan the QR code or go to www.vimeo.com/1022181605) of preschoolers using writing tools on white-boards, list the children's names (four-year-old Maricella; five-year-old Peter; and four-and-one-half-year-old Mariana) on a Quick Check Recording Sheet (you can copy the form from appendix B in the book or print it out from the Focused Observations product page at www.redleafpress.org). Determine which skill(s) you are observing that can be noted with a brief notation or check mark. Some of the choices that you might focus on include the following:

- right- or left-handedness
- appropriate grasp of the writing tool
- ability to make letterlike shapes or recognizable letters
- writing from left to right

Watch the video clip and record appropriately.

Guiding Questions: After viewing, consider the ease or difficulty of trying this type of documentation. Could it be done while you were in the middle of running a busy classroom? How practical is such a recording method for your setting? If you are involved in a group discussion, share some of the Quick Check Recording Sheets completed by the group and discuss the previous questions.

Observation Practice #12: Documenting Observations of a Group of Children

Running Time: 5 mins. 15 secs.

Purpose: To practice writing observation information about a group of children.

What to Do: Before watching Video Clip #12 (scan the QR code or go to www.vimeo.com/1022181626) of a group of preschool children listening to a story, determine what specific information you want to record with a brief note about each child (focus on five-year-old Peter in the red shirt, four-year-old Maricella in the ruffled, long-sleeved blue shirt, and three-year-old London in the short-sleeved blue dress) on a Brief Notes Recording Sheet (you can copy the form from appendix B in the book or print it out from the Focused Observations product page at www.redleafpress.org). Some of the choices you might focus on include the following:

- pays attention to the story being read
- responds to the teacher's questions
- interacts in the story-reading experience with related ideas and comments

Write the first initial of each child's name and observe the story time, taking brief notes about each child. Do not worry about complete sentences or descriptive phrases. Try to be efficient in your use of words. Still remember to be factual and descriptive, not interpretive.

Guiding Questions: After viewing, consider the ease or difficulty of this type of documentation. How practical is such a recording method for your setting? If you are involved in a group discussion, share some of the Brief Notes Recording Sheets completed by the group and discuss the previous questions.

Chapter 5

Observation Practice #13: Observing for Developmental Capabilities

Purpose: To identify early literacy capabilities.

Running Time: 4 mins. 43 secs.

What to Do: Watch Video Clip #13 (scan the QR code or go to www.vimeo .com/1022181652) of preschoolers acting out a familiar story. The children and teacher are speaking in Spanish. English subtitles are provided. As you watch the children, try to identify what they understand and comprehend about the story. Your observation notes should answer the following questions: Did they understand the basic plot of the story? Did they remember the characters and their actions? Remember to be factual and descriptive, not interpretive.

Guiding Questions: After viewing, look at your notes and consider the capabilities that you identified the children demonstrating. You can relate the identified capabilities to your state's early learning guidelines or to a developmental checklist with which you are familiar. If you are involved in a group discussion, share some of the anecdotes with the group. Look at the similarities and differences in the documentation from the group. Did people identify different capabilities? Why do you think that is?

Observation Practice #14: Observing for Developmental Capabilities

Running Time: 3 mins. 55 secs.

Purpose: To identify children's problem-solving capabilities and relate them back to a different developmental source of information.

What to Do: Watch Video Clip #14 (scan the QR code or go to www.vimeo .com/1022181685) of four-year-old boys working with ice and various tools at the sensory table. Document what you observe, paying close attention to their problem-solving capabilities. Remember to be factual and descriptive, not interpretive.

Guiding Questions: After viewing, look at a source of information about child development. Were you able to see a variety of problem-solving skills as the boys worked? Where did you place their capabilities on the developmental checklist you used? If you are part of a group discussion, share some of the anecdotes with the group as well as your placement of the boys' capabilities on the developmental checklists. Look at the similarities and differences in the documentation from the group. Did people identify different capabilities? Why do you think that is?

Chapter 6

Observation Practice #15: Using Observation and Documentation Information to Plan a Family Conference

Purpose: To practice preparing for a family conference using observational documentation.

What to Do: Rewatch video clip #7 for toddlers (scan the top QR code or go to www.vimeo.com/1022181531) or #11 for preschoolers (scan the bottom QR code or go to www.vimeo.com/1022181605) and note what a child does and says. Remember to be factual and descriptive, not interpretive.

Guiding Questions: After viewing, look over your documentation and consider how best to present information to family members in a conference or meeting with them. What specifics from the observation would you want to point out to the family? Exactly what would you say? What do you anticipate the possible response of the child's family members might be? How will you answer? If you are participating in a group discussion, discuss which anecdotes would be best to share in a family conference. You may even wish to role-play some of these discussions.

Chapter 7

Observation Practice #16: Determining the Best Curricular Approaches for a Child

Running Time: 2 mins. 32 secs.

Purpose: To identify the best ways to support a child.

What to Do: Watch Video Clip #16 (scan the QR code or go to www.vimeo .com/1022181710) of a toddler working with a puzzle with the support of her teacher. As you watch, write down what the child does and says. Remember to be factual and descriptive, not interpretive.

Guiding Questions: After viewing, identify in your notes when the child was most successfully engaged. How did the teacher's support help the child with the activity? Identify ways you might try to help the child be successful in future interactions. If you are participating in a group discussion, discuss some of the anecdotes written by group members and how the teacher's involvement helped the child's behavior.

Observation Practice #17: Encouraging and Extending a Child's Interests

Running Time: 3 mins. 15 secs.

Purpose: To determine ways to use materials to set up the environment and interact with children to build on their interests.

What to Do: Watch Video Clip #17 (scan the QR code or go to www.vimeo .com/1022181719) of three-year-old children as they work with a variety of materials to make "potions." Pay close attention to all of the things the children are interested in and are able to do. Focus on how the environment is set up with materials that interest them and what the teachers do to encourage their interest and learning.

Guiding Questions: In what ways does the physical environment capture the children's interests? What might be some additional strategies to extend their interests and discoveries? If you are participating in a group discussion, discuss some of the anecdotes written by group members and how you might plan additional strategies to capture the children's interest or expand them.

Chapter 8

Observation Practice #18: Building a Case about a Child

www.vimeo.com/1022181739

www.vimeo.com/1022181760

www.vimeo.com/1022181787

www.vimeo.com/1022181812

Running Times:
18a. The Day Begins 1 min. 31 secs.
18b. Story Time 5 mins. 15 secs.
18c. Dramatic Play 4 mins. 25 secs.
18d. Sensory Table 3 mins. 8 secs.
18e. Writing 4 mins. 34 secs.
18f. Putting on Jackets 2 mins. 34 secs.
18g. Playing Outdoors 1 min. 58 secs.

Purpose: To practice pulling together information about a child to assess their development and plan curriculum that will best meet their needs.

What to Do: Watch Video Clips #18a through #18g (available by scanning the QR codes or going to the web addresses under the QR codes). Some of these clips have been viewed before and we have grouped and renumbered them to show how the three children (three-year-old London, four-year-old Maricella, and five-year-old Peter) participate in multiple activities across their day in preschool. Observe the children doing the activities and take notes about the things they do and say. If you wish, you can choose to focus on one child, or you can write about all three. Remember to be factual and descriptive, not interpretive.

Guiding Questions: After viewing, use your observation notes to answer the following questions for any or all of the three children:

- What can and does this child do? What are their interests, and how do they show them? What specific skills do they have?
- What would the next steps be for them in their development? What are they not doing yet?
- What would you plan to do with them to build on their strengths and interests and to work on what they are not doing yet? What materials, activities, teacher support, peer support, and special resources would you use?

Reflect on your ideas about the child's accomplishments, interests, and needs, and about the next steps you planned for them. If you are participating in a group discussion, share your ideas about the child's accomplishments, interests, and needs. Compare the next steps you planned for them.

www.vimeo.com/1022181834

www.vimeo.com/1022181863

www.vimeo.com/1022181886

Chapter 9

Observation Practice #19: Celebrating Children and Being in the Moment

Running Time: 2 mins. 30 secs.

Purpose: To learn to enjoy children's exuberance and zest for life.

What to Do: Watch Video Clip #19 (scan the QR code or go to www.vimeo .com/1022181911), which contains a montage of video clips of children in action. Do not worry about observing for assessment or curricular planning. Do not take notes or document in any way. Instead, let yourself be with each child as they openly share their enthusiasm and energy. Appreciate them as they enjoy the pleasures of being a child. Celebrate and enjoy what they do.

Guiding Questions: If you are participating in a group discussion, share your feelings as you watched the children. Talk about the importance of being in the moment with children and having an appreciation for being a part of their enthusiasm and zest for life.

References

▲▼▲▼▲

Akingbulu, Oluwatosin, Boniface Kakhobwe, Aaron Lee Morris, Radhika Mitter, Benjamin Perks, and Euan Wilmshurst. 2022. "Towards a World of Play and Connection, for Every Child: Why Play Is So Important and How to Enable Every Child to Benefit." UNICEF and the Lego Foundation. https://www.unicef.org/blog/towards-world-play-and -connection-every-child.

Berk, Laura E., and Adam Winsler. 1995. *Scaffolding Children's Learning: Vygotsky and Early Childhood Education.* Washington, DC: NAEYC.

Berke, Kai-lee, Toni S. Bickart, and Cate Heroman. 2011. *Teaching Strategies Gold: Birth through Kindergarten Assessment Toolkit.* Washington, DC: Teaching Strategies.

Bricker, Diane, Carmen Dionne, Jennifer Grisham, JoAnn (JJ) Johnson, Marisa Macy, Kristine Slentz, and Misti Waddell. 2021. *Assessment, Evaluation, and Programming System (AEPS-3) for Infants and Children.* Baltimore, MD: Brookes Publishing.

Carlsson-Paige, Nancy, and Diane Levin. 1987. *The War Play Dilemma: Balancing Needs and Values in the Early Childhood Classroom.* New York: Teachers College Press.

CCSSO (Council of Chief State School Officers). 2011. "Moving Forward with Kindergarten Readiness Assessment Efforts: A Position Paper of the Early Childhood Education State Collaborative on Assessment and Student Standards." Position paper. Washington, DC: CCSSO. www .ccsso.org/Documents/CCSSO_K-Assessment_Final_7-12-11.pdf.

Curtis, Deb, and Margie Carter. 2011. *Reflecting Children's Lives: A Handbook for Planning Your Child-Centered Curriculum.* 2nd ed. St. Paul, MN: Redleaf Press.

Derman-Sparks, Louise, and Julie Olsen Edwards. 2010. *Anti-Bias Education for Young Children and Ourselves.* Washington, DC: NAEYC.

Dichtelmiller, Margo L., Judy R. Jablon, Dorothea B. Marsden, and Samuel J. Meisels. 2013. *The Work Sampling System Preschool-4 Developmental Guidelines.* 5th ed. Minneapolis: Pearson.

Epstein, Ann S. 2014. *The Intentional Teacher: Choosing the Best Strategies for Young Children's Learning.* Rev. ed. Washington, DC: NAEYC; Ypsilanti, MI: HighScope Press.

Erikson, Erik. 1963. *Childhood and Society.* 2nd ed. New York: Norton.

Ginsburg, Kenneth R. 2007. "The Importance of Play in Promoting Healthy Child Development and Maintaining Strong Parent-Child Bonds." *Pediatrics* 119 (1): 182–91.

Gonzalez-Mena, Janet. 1993. *Multicultural Issues in Child Care.* Mountain View, CA: Mayfield.

Gronlund, Gaye. 1992. "Coping with Ninja Turtle Play in My Kindergarten Classroom." *Young Children* (48) 1: 21–25.

———. 2010. *Developmentally Appropriate Play: Guiding Young Children to a Higher Level.* St. Paul, MN: Redleaf Press.

———. 2012. *Planning for Play, Observation, and Learning in Preschool and Kindergarten.* St. Paul, MN: Redleaf Press.

———. 2014. *Make Early Learning Standards Come Alive: Connecting Your Practice and Curriculum to State Guidelines.* 2nd ed. St. Paul, MN: Redleaf Press.

Gronlund, Gaye, with Bev Engel. 2019. *Focused Portfolios: A Complete Assessment for the Young Child.* 2nd ed. St. Paul, MN: Redleaf Press.

Gronlund, Gaye, and Marlyn James. 2008. *Early Learning Standards and Staff Development: Best Practices in the Face of Change.* St. Paul, MN: Redleaf Press.

Gronlund, Gaye, and Thomas Rendon. 2017. *Saving Play: Addressing Standards through Play-Based Learning in Preschool and Kindergarten.* St. Paul, MN: Redleaf Press.

Head Start Early Childhood Learning and Knowledge Center. 2020. *ELOF2GO.* Mobile app. Washington, DC: Office of Head Start.

Head Start Early Childhood Learning and Knowledge Center. 2024. "Identifying the Lenses through Which Staff and Families Observe Children." Accessed July 22.
https://eclkc.ohs.acf.hhs.gov/child-screening-assessment/child -observation-heart-individualizing-responsive-care-infants-toddlers /identifying-lenses-through-which-staff-families.

HighScope Educational Research Foundation. 2013. *COR Advantage.* Ypsilanti, MI: HighScope Press.

Jones, Natacha Ndabahagamye, Amber T. Fowler, and Jennifer Keys Adair. "Assessing Agency in Learning Contexts: A First, Critical Step to Assessing Children." *Young Children* 78 (1): 16–23.

Loomis, Catherine, and Jane Wagner, 2005. "A Different Look at Challenging Behavior." *Young Children* 60 (2): 94–99.

Marzano, Robert J., and John S. Kendall. 1996. *A Comprehensive Guide to Designing Standards-Based Districts, Schools, and Classrooms.* Alexandria, VA: Association for Supervision and Curriculum Development.

Meisels, Samuel J., Dorothea B. Marsden, Amy Laura Dombro, Donna R. Weston, and Abigail M. Jewkes. 2003. *The Ounce Scale: Standards for the Developmental Profiles.* Minneapolis: Pearson.

Montana Early Learning Standards Task Force. *Montana Early Learning Standards.* 2014. https://opi.mt.gov/Portals/182/Page%20Files/Early%20 Childhood/Docs/14EarlyLearningStandards.pdf.

NAEYC (National Association for the Education of Young Children). 2020. *Developmentally Appropriate Practice in Early Childhood Programs Serving Children from Birth through Age 8.* Position statement. Washington, DC: National Association for the Education of Young Children.

———. 2022. *Developmentally Appropriate Practice in Early Childhood Programs Serving Children from Birth through Age 8.* 4th ed. Washington, DC: NAEYC.

NAEYC (National Association for the Education of Young Children) and NAECS/SDE (National Association of Early Childhood Specialists in State Departments of Education). 2003. "Early Childhood Curriculum, Assessment, and Program Evaluation: Building an Effective, Accountable System in Programs for Children Birth through Age 8." Position statement. www.naeyc.org/files/naeyc/file/positions/CAPEexpand.pdf.

National Center on Early Childhood Quality Assurance. 2019. *Early Learning and Development Guidelines.* https://childcareta.acf.hhs.gov/sites /default/files/new-occ/resource/files/075_1907_state_eldgs_web_ final508.pdf

New Mexico Kids. 2014. *New Mexico Early Learning Guidelines: Birth through Kindergarten.* www.newmexicoprek.org/wpfd_file/new-mexico-early -learning-guidelines-birth-to-kindergarten-black-and-white-pdf.

Paley, Vivian Gussin. 1984. *Boys and Girls: Superheroes in the Doll Corner.* Chicago: University of Chicago Press.

Petitpas, Dawn, and Teresa K. Buchanan. 2022. "Using Observation to Guide Your Teaching." *Teaching Young Children* 16 (1). www.naeyc.org /resources/pubs/tyc/fall2022/observation-guides-teaching.

Riley-Ayers, Shannon, Judi Stevenson-Garcia, Ellen Frede, and Kimberly Brenneman. 2011. *Early Learning Scale.* New Brunswick, NJ: National Institute for Early Education Research.

Rogers, Rukia M. 2024. *The Many Stories of Our Beloved Community: Honoring Young Children's Kinship and Connections with the World.* St. Paul: Redleaf Press.

Seitz, Hilary. 2023a. "Authentic Assessment: A Strengths-Based Approach to Making Thinking, Learning, and Development Visible." *Young Children* 78 (1): 6–11.

———. 2023b. "Making Thinking, Learning, and Development Visible through ePortfolios." *Young Children* 78 (1): 12–13.

Snow, Kyle P. 2011. *Developing Kindergarten Readiness and Other Large-Scale Assessment Systems: Necessary Considerations in the Assessment of Young Children.* Washington, DC: NAEYC.

Wenner, Melinda. 2009. "The Serious Need for Play." *Scientific American Mind,* February. www.scientificamerican.com/article/the-serious-need-for-play.

Wiggins, Grant P. 1993. "Assessment, Authenticity, Context, and Validity." *Phi Delta Kappan* 75 (3): 200–214.

Index

▲▼▲▼▲